BESTSELLING BOOK SERIES

Home Decorating For Dummies, 2nd Edition

P9-DIA-685

Cheat Sheet

Decorator's Bag of Tricks

Decorating magic to go! Pack a portable carry-all filled with all the must-haves of a professional decorator:

- **Glue gun:** Use this for a variety of decorating and crafts projects.
- **Hammer:** Choose one that lets you hammer in nails and pry them up, too. Pick a size that fits comfortably in your hand.
- **Magic Hem:** Iron-on Magic Hem creates seams without sewing. It's available at grocery stores and craft or sewing shops.
- **Measuring tape:** A 25-foot retractable steel tape works best.
- **Nail kit:** Look for a set that includes a variety of sizes for various jobs. Or assemble your own, including fine nails, long nails, short nails, and finishing nails.
- **Notebook:** Pick one that has unlined sheets (for sketching and note-taking) and is small enough to fit inside your tool kit.
- **Picture hangers:** Use these to make hanging art easier.
- **Pins:** Keep straight pins and safety pins for draping and shaping.
- **Plate hangers:** Look for these in different sizes for both small and large plates.
- **Screwdriver set:** Pick a pack that includes several sizes of both standard and Phillips head (cross-shaped head) screwdrivers. Don't use the wrong size or style driver — you'll destroy the screw.
- **Screws:** Choose a variety pack of styles and sizes.
- **Tool kit, tackle box, bucket, or basket:** Use this for storing your gear. Keep it handy for quick fix-its and instant decorating.
- **Velcro:** This comes in handy for making items such as easy-to-remove slipcovers.
- **Wire:** Use wire for hanging, fixing, and holding things.

Quick-Start Decorating

- **Fix your budget!** Spend no more than what you have.
- **Formulate an action plan.** Establish goals. Set priorities. Decide what room or rooms you want finished and in what order. Decorating goes faster when you have a plan.
- **Scope out the job.** Create a floor plan using a computer-aided program or draw one by hand on graph paper.
- **Discover your personal style.** Are you Contemporary or Traditional? Knowing your style eliminates confusion (and wasted time) by steering you toward the best choices.
- **Shop!** Pick stores that stock a large selection for quick delivery or carrying home. Shop by mail. Surf the Internet for information on prices and products from the comfort of your home.
- **Do first things first.** Have all carpentry and wiring performed before you cover your walls and floors. Decorate the ceiling, walls, and floor before you bring in furniture.
- **Buy major pieces of furniture first and accessories last.**
- **Spice up your decor with accessories galore!** Pick pieces with personal meaning.

Furniture Facts

- Furniture is marketed in three distinct price ranges: budget (affordable), moderate, and expensive.
- *To the trade* means that only a decorator or designer can purchase these exclusive home furnishings.
- *Fully-assembled* (or *pre-assembled*) furniture is ready to use right out of the crate.
- *RTA* (ready-to-assemble) and *KD* (knock down) *furniture* come unassembled in flat boxes and must be put together by the buyer. RTA and KD items cost less than fully-assembled furniture.
- *Case goods* are cabinets, tables, or any piece of furniture that has no upholstery.
- *Upholstered furniture* is any furniture that is covered with upholstery, such as sofas and lounge chairs.
- The manufacturer's brochures and hang-tags provide information on whether furniture is fireproof or fire-retardant.
- Quality furniture features good materials, careful construction techniques, and durable finishes.

For Dummies: Bestselling Book Series for Beginners

Home Decorating For Dummies, 2nd Edition

Handy Measurements

- Determine the square footage of your room by multiplying the room's length by its width.
- Establish the total wall area by multiplying the length of each wall by the wall height (from floor to ceiling) and adding those numbers together.
- Find out how many gallons of paint you need by calculating the square footage of paintable areas. First, find the total wall area. Next, determine the area of windows and doors, and subtract that number from the total area. Divide this number by 350 (for smooth surfaces) or 300 (for rough surfaces).
- Keep in mind that tall ceilings range from 10 to 12 feet high (or more), average ceilings are 8 feet, and low ceilings are less than 8 feet. Use color, texture, and pattern to make the most of your space.
- Figure how many gallons of paint you need to paint a ceiling by multiplying your floor's length and width. Divide this number by the spreading rate (see the paint can for this figure).
- To calculate the amount of carpet you need, divide the square footage of the floor by 9 to yield the number of square yards required.
- To determine how many ceramic tiles you need, first find the area (square footage) of the floor. Divide that number as follows: For 4-inch tiles, divide by .1089; for 6-inch tiles, divide by .25; for 9-inch tiles, divide by .5625; for 12-inch tiles, the area equals the number of tiles needed; for 18-inch tiles, divide by 2.25. Add 10 percent to the total for error and replacement.
- Leave walk-around space between furniture to avoid clutter. Allow about 2 to 5 feet for seating and 4 to 5 feet for traffic flow through rooms.

Playing with Pattern

- Mix patterns such as checks with florals or large-scaled patterns with small-scaled patterns.
- Not sure when enough is enough? Play it safe! Use three different patterns that contrast in scale but relate in color.
- More is more when you confidently mix up to five patterns. To do so, let one large-scaled pattern dominate over one medium-scaled floral and another geometric, and toss in two small-scaled accent patterns (your choice of floral or geometric). Make sure the colors in the large-scaled pattern are repeated in all the others.
- Place pattern everywhere! Put the same pattern on the walls, windows, and furnishings.

Toying with Texture

- Traditional rooms look best in refined, smooth textures.
- Contemporary spaces need more textural interest.
- Feminine rooms need elegant and subtle textures.
- Masculine decor calls for nubby, tweedy, and rugged texture.
- The more neutrally colored the room, the more important texture becomes.
- Heavy textures "eat" space, so use them only in large or cozy rooms.

Creating with Color

- Paint small spaces in whispers of a cool, light color.
- Cover big spaces in a cozy, warm, confident color.
- Light, cool colors make walls seem to fade away into the distance, making rooms seem spacious.
- Dark, warm colors make walls seem to come closer.
- For the best color schemes, pick neutral colors that you'll never grow tired of.
- Distribute colors naturally, with dark colors on the floor, medium colors on the walls, and light colors on the ceiling. Use the law of chromatic distribution:
  - Put neutral colors on large surfaces or objects, such as the floor and sofa.
  - Use stronger shades in a smaller amount on smaller spaces or items, such as a short wall or a chair.
  - Employ the strongest accent color in the smallest spaces and places.
  - Scatter accent color around the room to make an impact.

For Dummies: Bestselling Book Series for Beginners

Home Decorating

FOR

DUMMIES®

2ND EDITION

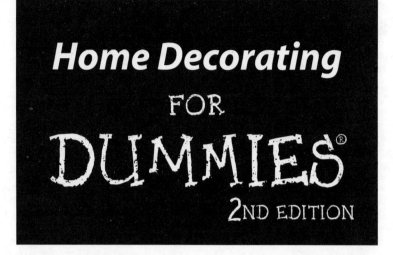

Home Decorating

FOR

DUMMIES®

2ND EDITION

**by Katharine Kaye McMillan and
Patricia Hart McMillan**

WILEY

Wiley Publishing, Inc.

Home Decorating For Dummies,® 2nd Edition

Published by
Wiley Publishing, Inc.
111 River St.
Hoboken, NJ 07030-5774
www.wiley.com

Library of Congress Cataloging-in-Publication Data:

Library of Congress Control Number: 2003113311

ISBN: 0-7645-4156-0

Manufactured in the United States of America

10 9 8 7 6 5 4 3 2 1

 is a trademark of Wiley Publishing, Inc.

About the Authors

Katharine Kaye McMillan, former senior editor of a New York City-based national magazine, is a writer whose work appears regularly in magazines and newspapers. She is a contributing writer to internationally circulated *Florida Design Magazine.* She is the co-author of several books on decorating and design, including *Sun Country Style,* which is the basis for licensed signature collections of furniture and accessories by three leading American manufacturers and importers. A graduate of the University of Texas in Austin, she holds a masters degree in psychology and is a doctoral student in psychology at Florida Atlantic University, Boca Raton, Florida.

Patricia Hart McMillan is a nationally known interior designer, whose interior design work for private clients, designer showcases, and corporations has appeared in publications worldwide, including the *New York Times* and *USA Today.* Known as a trend spotter and for clearly articulated views on design, she is quoted frequently and extensively in both trade and consumer publications. She appears on TV and talk radio. A prolific writer, she is co-author and author of seven books on interior design and decoration, with Sun Country Style signature collections of furniture based on two books. She has taught decorating courses at several colleges and conducted numerous seminars across the U.S. She is decorating editor for *Christian Woman Magazine* and reports on design trends for *The Sun-Sentinel,* a Tribune newspaper based in Ft. Lauderdale, Florida. She has been editor-in-chief of two publications and was head of a New York City-based public relations firm representing some of the most prestigious names in home furnishing and building products. She holds a Bachelor of Arts degree in English, with a minor in art history (with an emphasis in architecture), from the State University of New York (New Paltz). She was awarded a certificate from The New York School of Interior Design.

Dedication

To my cousin, Margaret Walls Ephlin, loving friend and daughter to my late mother and sister to me.

— Patricia Hart McMillan

To Jill, Jon, Naina, and Richard — friends who decorate my life.

— Katharine Kaye McMillan

Authors' Acknowledgments

Our names are on the cover of *Home Decorating For Dummies,* and we get most, if not all, of the credit. But, fortunately for us and for you, dear reader, there is a small army of people who worked enthusiastically and efficiently to place this book in your hands. To these wonderful souls, we give credit where credit is due.

First, our continuing gratitude to acquisitions editor Holly McGuire, who will always have a special place in our hearts and consciousness, and Jennifer Ehrlich, senior project editor par excellence on the first edition. Second Edition editors Tracy Boggier, Jill Burke, and Joan Friedman deserve deep bows. So does our rigorous copy editor, Chad Sievers. Technical editor Rose Bennett Gilbert, herself an author, contributing editor, and syndicated columnist, deserves kudos. And Liz Kurtzman, whose illustrations continue to enliven, enlighten, and entertain should know that we love her work and thank her for sharing it with us, and our readers.

We especially thank those industry leaders whose endorsements appear on the covers of this book. Their kind words mean a great deal to us.

Very special thanks go to Lis King, writer and public relations representative without peer, on whom we always know most certainly that we can rely.

Of great help and worthy of gratitude are officers of many companies, including: Aristokraft's Stephen Mangin and Kathy Parker, Bernhardt's Heather Bloom, DJC Design Studio's D. J. Cole and Karen Carpenter, Garcia Imports' Barbara Garcia and Linda Souza, Kim Shaver of Hooker Furniture Co., Kim Craig Boos of Kraftmaid, Gary McCray of LaneVenture for Raymond Waites, David Petersen of Maine Cottage, Michael Riley of Sphinx by Oriental Weavers, Rudy Santos of RoSan Imports and RoSan Custom Kitchens & Baths, Storehouse President Caroline Hibble, and Tiffany Mullis of Vanguard Furniture.

Perhaps least recognized, but greatly to be thanked, are public relations experts who so ably represent America's top interior and product designers, manufacturers, and importers. These professionals graciously and nimbly responded to our requests for information and photographs. We *must* tell you the names of these who usually serve *incognito*— even at the risk of omitting one, and should that happen, we ask forgiveness. We thank: Brewster Wallcoverings' representative at Lou Hammond & Assoc., Annie Scranton; Bassett's Chris Madden Collection's Janet Schlesinger of the Wm. B . Johns Co.; Glen Eden Wool Carpet representative, Brooke Wilson of Freebairn & Co., who also represents MTI Whirlpools; Hunter-Douglas representative Suzan Zevon of Lou Hammond & Assoc.; Pennsylvania House representatives Andrea Wasiak and Kay Degenhardt of the LC Williams company, Karen McNeill Harris of McNeill Communications for Stanley Furniture and Storehouse, Inc., and James Cross of PR21 for Whirlpool.

Bless you all!

Publisher's Acknowledgments

We're proud of this book; please send us your comments through our Dummies online registration form located at `www.dummies.com/register/`.

Some of the people who helped bring this book to market include the following:

Acquisitions, Editorial, and Media Development

Project Editors: Jill Burke, Joan Friedman

Acquisitions Editor: Tracy Boggier

Copy Editor: Chad Sievers

Technical Editor: Rose Bennett Gilbert

Editorial Managers: Christine Meloy Beck, Michelle Hacker

Editorial Assistant: Melissa Bennett

Cover Photos: © Eric Kamp/Index Stock Imagery/PictureQuest

Cartoons: Rich Tennant, `www.the5thwave.com`

Production

Project Coordinator: Ryan Steffen

Layout and Graphics: Michael Kruzil, Shelley Norris, Barry Offringa, Heather Ryan, Brent Savage, Jacque Schneider, Julie Trippetti, Shae Lynn Wilson, Melanee Wolven

Special Art: Liz Kurtzman

Proofreaders: John Greenough, Angel Perez, Carl William Pierce, TECHBOOKS Production Services

Indexer: Angel Perez, TECHBOOKS Production Services

Publishing and Editorial for Consumer Dummies

Diane Graves Steele, Vice President and Publisher, Consumer Dummies

Joyce Pepple, Acquisitions Director, Consumer Dummies

Kristin A. Cocks, Product Development Director, Consumer Dummies

Michael Spring, Vice President and Publisher, Travel

Brice Gosnell, Publishing Director, Travel

Kelly Regan, Editorial Director, Travel

Publishing for Technology Dummies

Andy Cummings, Vice President and Publisher, Dummies Technology/General User

Composition Services

Gerry Fahey, Vice President of Production Services

Debbie Stailey, Director of Composition Services

Contents at a Glance

Table of Contents

Introduction

. . . .

Do you long to create picture-perfect rooms but can't quite seem to achieve them? Do you want better functioning spaces for working, playing, or living? Do you clamor to express your personal style? If you said "yes" to any of these questions, you've turned to the right source for real answers from the pros. *Home Decorating For Dummies,* 2nd Edition can have you up to speed on what you need to know about decorating with style while staying within your budget. This book contains all the basics — including how to figure out what you can spend; how to spend it; and the latest and greatest in styles, trends, and technology.

About This Book

This book demystifies decorating — it's like having a pro guiding you step by step. At your fingertips, you have one of the best decorating teachers available. *Home Decorating For Dummies,* 2nd Edition is your guide to good decorating decision making. You find tips, tried-and-true techniques, and helpful hints that will have you decorating like a pro. The best part is that you won't be breaking the piggy bank to get a million-dollar look.

What makes this book perfect for decorating novices? It's written by a team with several years' experience decorating and reporting on decorating. We've done all sorts of projects on all sorts of budgets — from creating rooms decorated with penny-saving ideas to adding customized wall coverings and textiles to the New York City townhouse of legendary designer Oleg Cassini (the man who created First Lady Jackie Kennedy's signature look). We've traveled the globe to attend important decorating-related shows. We've interviewed and written about other top designers and decorators, counting them as friends and colleagues. TV appearances — both live (scary!) and taped (not so scary) — and live talk (make that talk-back) radio have beckoned. So have in-store seminars and book signings where we've discussed design. We've designed furniture and accessories for leading manufacturers and importers, too. When it comes to home fashions, we've done — and are still doing — it all.

What's new in this second edition is a lot. We've updated information about appliances, fixtures, lighting, and decorating facts. We've added a whole new chapter (Chapter 29) of great sources for information and resources about products and services. New black-and-white photographs illustrate various chapters, and all-new color photographs offer the latest newsmaking decorating ideas. You'll find dozens more pages of must-read decorating information all written in a fresh, new way.

Who Needs to Read This Book?

Home Decorating For Dummies, 2nd Edition is for very smart people who want to have professional-type knowledge without spending tons of time and effort. If you want your house to look like your dream, this book is for you.

We've written this book for all kinds of people in all kinds of decorating situations:

- ✔ **First-time buyers or renters.** You have a whole new place to decorate. Where do you start? How do you budget? What can you buy that travels well into your next place? This book has the answers so you can keep your sanity.

- ✔ **Second- or third-time home buyers.** You've gone from starter home to bigger home. Or, you've downscaled from a large space to an intimate one. Whether you've gone up or down in size, stayed in the same region or moved to a whole new one, you need to know how to make your old furniture work in a new setting, how to add furnishings, and how to make your style seem fresh.

- ✔ **Newly blended families.** He has furniture, she has furniture, they have furniture. Can it all work together harmoniously? Meshing two or more personal styles into one calls for decorating magic. Decorating can save this household from stylistic splits. Whether you're marrying for the first or second (or third or fourth!) time, merging furniture is oftentimes more difficult than merging families. We can help.

- ✔ **And all the rest of us who love decorating.** This book is for anyone who wants to transform an ordinary space into an extraordinary place, make a small room look larger, an odd room seem normal, an ugly room look pretty — all through the power of decorating. Great decorating results in a great-looking residence and smart-functioning home. This book is for anyone who wants to develop his or her imagination. How do designers and decorators get wonderful ideas? From thin air? Not quite. The answer is, from their imaginations, which they've developed through education and experience. A surprise here and there makes a room uniquely yours. Don't forget: Imagination counts.

What is your decorating situation? Write us at McMillanUS@aol.com or KKMcMillan@aol.com. We're eager to hear from you.

How to Use This Book

We wrote *Home Decorating For Dummies,* 2nd Edition for you to use as a resource, almost as you would use an encyclopedia. You can flip through the book to find the topic that intrigues you most (or gives you the most headaches) and skim those sections first. You can check out the table of contents or the index and go straight to the relevant section to find answers to a specific decorating problem.

If you want to glean every bit of information that you can about home decorating, feel free to read the book from cover to cover. We lay the book out in a series of logical steps and fill it with fun tips designed to give you a basic foundation of understanding. Feel free to take your time exploring, reflecting, and educating yourself about a vitally important subject — your personal taste.

Your copy of *Home Decorating For Dummies,* 2nd Edition is your personal reference to your home, filled with invaluable tidbits of information. You may have so many brainwaves that you'll need to start a file folder and notebook. Take the book (and your files) with you when you shop for home furnishing items. You'll find yourself referring to it frequently for measurements, concepts, and good advice.

How This Book Is Organized

We divide *Home Decorating For Dummies,* 2nd Edition into eight parts, each containing several chapters. Each part deals with a broad area of decorating, and each chapter contains specific and detailed information.

Part 1: Basic Planning

Where do you begin when you want to start decorating? This part opens with an overview of home decorating and has chapters on everything from how to budget to how to draw up a floor plan. You also find information on basic decorating concepts that can help you know why a particular room may look better with one all-over treatment or with wainscoting and wallpaper.

Part 11: Creating Surface Interest

Every room, every piece of furniture, and every object in a room has a surface — surfaces are everywhere! What do you do with huge expanses of space? Or with little swaths of space? This part deals with the effects of color, pattern, and texture, and the common problems created by too much or too little of them.

Part 111: Style and Substance

Style is an integral part of design. It's the look, the mood — and it's more than skin deep. In this part, we introduce you to Historical, Contemporary, and personal styles.

Part IV: Creating Backgrounds

Every room has ceilings, floors, walls, windows, and lighting that form a background. This part covers what you need to know about the special decorating requirements of these elementary parts of a room.

Part V: Tackling the Three Tough Rooms: Kitchen, Bath, and Home Office

This part covers what you need to know to effectively decorate rooms that have special technological and functional requirements. You find copious information, rules, and resources for coping with these rooms that have to be more than just plain pretty.

Part VI: Fixing Up Four Easy Rooms

Find out how to create picture-perfect yet livable rooms. This part covers the special needs for beauty, comfort, and serenity of public and private rooms.

Part VII: Embellishments: Accessorizing with Art and Other Stuff

This part helps you put the finishing touches on every room in the house. Find easy, foolproof advice for adding the final flourishes to every space in your place.

Part VIII: The Part of Tens

Aahh . . . now comes the part of the book that includes power punches of quick ideas for decorating your home. The Part of Tens gives quick advice on great, cost-effective (cheap!), and fun ways to freshen up your home.

Icons Used in This Book

As you work your way around this book, you may notice little pictures, called *icons*, in the margins. Icons alert you to important information.

This icon flags decorating tips from decorators — tips you don't want to miss. With this icon, you find ideas that you can use without taking out a second mortgage. (Your billfold will thank you for checking out these paragraphs!)

This dummy alerts you to technical information, such as the difference between foot-candles and lumens in lighting. You may not need to know these facts, so you can shortcut through these sections if you like.

This symbol alerts you to any dangers or pitfalls that may blow your decorating scheme or budget.

When you see this icon, sit up and take note; you need to remember this important information.

Why work harder than you have to? Take advantage of these shortcuts to success. Don't bother reinventing the wheel. You can always rely on these surefire decorating solutions. Watch out for these guys; you find them next to ideas on how to create a little decorating sleight of hand.

Where to Go from Here

What do you do after you're armed with *Home Decorating For Dummies,* 2nd Edition? Go shopping, of course! Pick up samples and swatches. Read decorating magazines if you want even more hot trends, tips, and information. Log on the Internet and chat about decorating. Pick up brochures, books, and other sources of information. The possibilities are endless.

Part I
Basic Planning

The 5th Wave   By Rich Tennant

"I like the marble vanity and the wall sconces, but I think the Eurostyle fixtures on the whirlpool take away some of its simple country charm."

In this part . . .

Successful decorating is equal parts down-to-earth practical matters and heavenly inspiration. Practically speaking, start your project — no matter how small or large — with three basics. First, figure out your budget. Next, size up the space you're working with (using a tape measure, not your imagination). Then, get a good grasp on tried-and-true design rules (or guidelines). The chapters in this part take you through this basic training. This part prepares you for the true joys of decorating.

Chapter 1

Bringing Your Vision to Life

In This Chapter

▶ Decorating like a pro on a budget

▶ Adding finishing touches and professional flair

A fresh coat of paint for the kitchen, a few throw pillows for the family room, a nice centerpiece for the dining room table . . . how hard can home decorating be? As long as you have a decorating plan, home decorating can be easy and fun. We promise.

So why write an entire book dedicated to the subject? We want to simplify your life by helping you decorate using our quick-and-easy, foolproof approach. You can make some frustrating (and expensive) mistakes if you start your decorating projects without doing your homework. Our friend, HGTV's Chris Casson Madden (host of *Interiors By Design*), calls this book "a must-read" for her staff. That's high praise. Consider this book a really important (and fun!) homework assignment.

Taking the First Steps

So, how do you launch your decorating project? Step one is to make a realistic budget. If that step scares you, turn to Chapter 2 for some helpful pointers.

With a budget in hand, you need to analyze your space. Is it big, small, odd-shaped, or problem-ridden? Brainstorm about the basics: walls, floors, and ceilings. How can you use paint, wallcoverings, and more to create effects? How do you choose the best flooring and the right lighting? Is there any way to dress up a boring ceiling? With all the choices out there, you need a guide to help you decide.

Consider color, patterns, and textures — they need to work together. Color can be tricky to work with. Most people fear using too much or too bold color or bad combinations. Then there's pattern — how do you layer three, four, or more patterns to get the look you want? In this book, you discover that there's nothing to fear, if you understand some very basic decorating rules.

Take some time to become familiar with different decorating styles, such as Traditional, Country, Modern, Cottage, and so on (see Chapters 9 and 10). Compare the different styles and see if your personal style falls into one of the categories, giving you a leg up with planning.

As you can see, home decorating calls for much more than painting walls a pretty color and buying furniture. Decorating is about making your home comfortable, functional, and great looking.

Decorating All Through the House

From a decorating perspective, two types of rooms exist: the easy ones and the tough ones. Decorating a room that needs only pretty furniture in order to feel complete is relatively *easy*. Decorating a room that has appliances, equipment, and fixtures and is used frequently is relatively *tough*.

Tackling the toughies

You need decorating know-how to create the three tough rooms: the kitchen, the bathroom, and the home office. You can add lots of extras to these rooms to make them even more functional and more stylish.

Even if you order pizza and Chinese five nights a week, your kitchen is the most lived-in room in your house. You use it for everything from cooking to entertaining, which means it has to meet a variety of needs for a variety of users. The hearth of the home truly has very special decorating needs.

Just because a room is functional doesn't mean it should be bare-bones basic. The bath — no matter what its size — has morphed into a spa. Whether your bathroom is small or large, turn it into an oasis of comfort.

More and more of us are working out of our homes these days. Your home office (or library or study) needs professional-level function and style. You need solutions that work for you when you go to work!

Fixing up the easies

The bedroom, living room, family room, and other lively places fall into the easy decorating category. They are not without challenges, though.

You spend a third of your life sleeping. Select your bedroom's look while keeping in mind function, fun, and style. You'll make different design choices if you're decorating bedrooms for children and guests.

Your living room is a public room that's also very personal. You want your living room to be a comfortable, relaxing room with maximum style.

Entertaining at home is bigger than ever. Having people over for dining, screening your favorite shows, or playing games is the "in" thing. Some people entertain in the kitchen or the living room. No matter what rooms you entertain your friends in, you want a functional and fun look.

Do you have plenty of space? Get more use out of it! Decorate bonus spaces, such as entryways, attics, basements, porches, hallways, balconies, and lofts, in attractive and functional manners that give your home a new look.

Adding Professional Finishing Touches

You can take your home decor to a whole new level simply by accessorizing. Accessorizing is what makes rooms in magazines and on TV so pretty. As decorators, we've styled plenty of rooms (both sets and real rooms) for magazines. The right accessories and placement can make or break a room.

As professionals, we've learned some little tips that will help you decorate like a pro:

- ✔ **Be prepared.** Research before you buy. Read instructions on products before using them. Keep tools and paints on hand. (See this book's "Cheat Sheet" for how to create your decorator's bag of tricks.)

- ✔ **Plan the work, work the plan.** Establish stages to keep your decorating projects on time and budget.

- ✔ **Ask for help.** Expert help is available — sometimes for free or cheap. Not every project is a DIY (do-it-yourself). Keep a list of decorators, painters, tilers, electricians, and handymen for times when you need a pro's help.

- ✔ **Shop positively.** Don't bring wet blankets with you on a shopping trip (your mom has her taste, you have yours). Pre-shop for a cranky spouse — pick two or three choices you know you can live with to show to him or her.

- ✔ **Done or just begun?** Never consider your place done! Remain open to change.

Decorating is a gift that we give to ourselves and others. With this book, we help you share the gift of gracious living — with your family, friends, and everyone who comes into your life and home.

Chapter 2

Planning Your Budget

. . . .

In This Chapter

▶ Setting your priorities

▶ Counting and cutting costs

▶ Asking the pros for help

. . . .

*F*irst comes the dream, then reality — the budget. Most people skip this step because they're intimated and in denial about their bank account. Bad idea! To plan your work and work your plan, start with your budget.

Budgeting involves not just money, but time and talents (talents can be bartered). The idea is to make the most (and best) use of all your resources. Be honest: How much money can you afford to spend and when?

In this chapter, we guide you through budgeting and making priorities — and figuring out which projects you can delay. We show you how to achieve a look for less by comparing sources and costs, and lastly, how to find designers who won't cost you a fortune.

Coming to Grips with Your Budget

You can start a decorating project in two ways. The first is "the sky's the limit" approach — that takes a stash! The second is the "how much can I get for what I've got?" approach — that takes 1,001 decorating ideas! No matter how much or little money you have, the second approach is more fun — especially for people who love to think creatively.

How much money will you need? Experts tell us that furnishing your first home could cost almost one-third the price of your house or about $10,000 per room, especially if you're buying major appliances, electronic equipment, and big-ticket items. But, no one says you have to spend that much. Check out flea markets, garage sales, even e-Bay and other auction houses for cost-cutting bargains.

If you're starting to hyperventilate, keep this cheery thought in mind: After a first decorating venture, you can budget less money, because you'll have accumulated furniture and accessories that you can use in your new vision.

Simplifying the budgeting process

Budgeting is a two-phase process. First, figure out how much money you have to work with. No matter what figure the experts say is the bare minimum, only *you* can determine what you have. Determine your *total* decorating budget, and be firm! Don't exceed that amount.

Second, consider for what — and then how, when, and where — to spend that money. Now, all you need is to be honest, firm, and diligent! Professional designers work the same way.

Although budgeting is a simple process, you will have unexpected costs. Work a "slush fund" into your budget so you don't have to panic when those costs occur. Count on at least 10 to 15 percent cost overrun.

Now you're ready to sit down with paper and pencil (or spreadsheet program and mouse!) and figure out your budget.

This book deals with decorating, which includes embellishing surfaces and furnishing spaces — basically, working with the structure that you have as it is. Some light remodeling projects, such as wallpapering, fall within that realm. If you're thinking of remodeling — knocking down old walls, building new walls, tearing out the low ceiling to create a high vaulted or volume ceiling — check out *Home Remodeling For Dummies* by Morris and James Carey (Wiley Publishing, Inc.).

As you work up your decorating budget, remember that you want to

- **Be honest.** Tell yourself and your decorator (if you have one) what you can spend. A budget brings out creativity.

- **Be practical.** Have a good idea about where you're spending your money. Top designers find flea markets fun and rewarding. And many count Pier 1, Target, and Marshall's among their best-kept secret sources. Don't waste time being a snob; do spend some time developing an eye for a bargain — wherever you find it — before the professional designers get there!

- **Be realistic.** Set reachable goals. Goal setting lets you get an overview from A to Z. Don't fixate on a few high-priced items that zap your funds and leave you — and your project — hanging.

- **Set comfortable spending guidelines.** Decide whether you want to spend it all at one time or spread payments out over time. Determine how long that time period will be.

✔ **Research typical prices at retail sources.** Look at high- and low-priced options for items of comparable style and value. Check out flea markets, estate sales, auctions, Internet sites, and discount stores.

✔ **Revisit your dream — continually.** Does your decorating dream actually require any architectural changes — tearing down a wall, moving a window, or bumping out a room? Remodeling involves labor costs. If that labor is going to be your own sweat equity, budget your time. If not, factor in the cost of labor.

You can get a champagne look on a beer budget. Magazines feature one room that costs thousands to decorate and its look-alike that costs peanuts. Economical sources, good decorating ideas, and patient shopping can get you a dreamy (and on-budget) look!

Considering basic budget questions

Before you set a budget, think about these key questions:

✔ **Do I own or rent my home?** Why spend megabucks improving someone else's property? You can visually improve your rental in ways that make good budgetary sense.

Buy only items that move when you do: Rugs instead of wall-to-wall carpet; armoires instead of built-in cabinets; stock window treatments instead of custom-made ones. Don't faux-paint walls, unless you find painting and then repainting them white for the next tenant worthwhile.

✔ **What is my house worth?** Expect to recover about 80 percent of the cost of new fixtures and appliances, kitchen cabinets, thermal windows, or flooring. Upgrades keep a house in style and good condition.

✔ **Will my efforts price my house out of the neighborhood?** A general rule is that your house should compare favorably with neighboring ones in style and value. (Buckingham Palace won't fly in suburbia.) If you're in doubt about what improvements to make, ask your friendly realtor. He or she can advise you about what the general public considers tasteful, desirable, and worth paying for.

✔ **Should I decorate for myself or others?** No one can tell you what decorating style, color, or items will make you happy — only you can be the judge. Don't try to please others, except for the other family members whose spaces you might be decorating.

Decorating for resale affects many decisions, especially your color scheme. If you're planning to sell soon, decorate to sell — rely on the "neutral is nice" maxim!

Creating Your Decorating Road Map

Setting goals and ordering your priorities creates a road map to speed your decorating processes. You can organize your projects in two ways. One is to break down large projects into phases that you can execute over time. The second is to gather small, similar activities into larger, more efficient projects. No matter which technique you decide is more appropriate, write down your plan. (We show you how in an upcoming section, "Writing down your decorating plan.")

Breaking down large projects into phases

Large decorating projects are full of many small (and overwhelming) details. Breaking a project into smaller ones reduces stress. You can break a large project into smaller ones in many ways. Deciding which approach is best for you depends upon your personal priorities and those of your family.

One way to approach a whole-house project is room-by-room. Because one room seems more manageable than five or more, this approach cuts a monstrous job down to size. The downside is that it's not the fastest way to get your house in liveable condition.

Another more efficient technique is to gang similar jobs together. For example, painting all wall surfaces (walls and ceilings) throughout the house can be phase one, installing ceramic tile flooring can be phase two. Laying carpeting, installing draperies, and placing furniture (purchased while the other projects are underway) can be phases three, four, and five, respectively. The final phase can be accessorizing.

Grouping small projects together

Gathering small projects into one project or phase of a large decorating job is easy and efficient. Professional decorators save time by shopping for several similar items at one time. Look for fabrics, for example, to recover a chair in the bedroom, a loveseat in the living room, dining room chairs, a family room sofa, and cushions for the front porch all on the same trip.

Make a checklist of the items and notes about color (blue for the bedroom, and so on) and pattern (toile for the bedroom, and so forth). Take your list, along with measurements, sketches, or photographs of the furniture, and any other information you may need, on your search for fabrics. From each fabric shop, get *swatches* (small cuttings) and information about prices (write it on the shop's business card and staple that to your cutting).

After you're home, check potential choices and make your decisions. One more trip to the shop (or shops) to buy, and then you can hand all fabrics and furniture to the upholsterer. Mission accomplished! You can shop for lamps and lighting, floorings and floor coverings, and cabinet hardware — items found in the same shop — for a whole room or whole house in this same efficient way. Not only will you save travel time, you'll also probably find it easier to focus.

Writing down your decorating plan

Be smart. Write down your plan. Even go so far as to post it in plain sight on your home office wall! A worksheet can help you record all the little things you want to keep track of during a project. Remember that nothing is set in stone (unless you're updating your stone patio flooring!).

To create a worksheet, follow these easy plan-writing steps:

1. **Give your project a title.** Write the title at the top of the page — for example, "Redecorate the Living Room for the Holidays."

2. **Record your budget.** Under the project title, enter your budget amount.

3. **List the work to be done.** In the left-hand column, list all the work that needs to be done (such as buying and laying new carpeting). In the second column, enter the estimated costs of these jobs (based on known retail prices).

4. **Prioritize the tasks.** Arrange the tasks in order of priority, based on logical sequence (painting the walls, carpeting the floor) and affordability (saving over time for an expensive item, and buying it last).

5. **Review your priorities.** Have you considered all your priorities before finalizing your decorating plans? You may consider buying a less expensive synthetic instead of costly wool carpeting that will leave too-few funds for finishing your projects.

6. **Add project start and finish dates.** Make your finish date as realistic as possible, which is a great incentive for you and for those people you hire to meet the deadline. Projects that linger on and on lose their luster!

Checking Out Costs

Make a list of items you want for each room. If you don't have a clue about what a sofa or chair costs, check several sources. Newspapers are hot-off-the-press sources. Usually big furniture retailers run full-page ads all on the same day, so comparing prices is easy.

You're not always comparing identical qualities, so you need to know the source and what they're selling. Are both sofas you're considering covered in genuine leather, or is one covered in *pleather* (a synthetic leather look-alike)? Visit several retail stores to find out what is available, at what prices, and what it really looks like!

Check out your favorite flea markets and junk shops. You never know where your next treasure is coming from! In these places, be prepared to buy what you find right then and there — and to carry it home with you. If you're buying an upholstered piece that needs re-covering, know what reupholstering a piece will cost in materials and labor. Only you can decide if your piece is a treasure *and* a bargain.

Internet sites can be good places to check for prices. Many manufacturers and retailers have Web sites where you can see product photographs, find out facts, and place orders. But keep in mind that shipping costs a bundle, and Internet stores don't service your furniture as a retailer would.

Keep those catalogs! Full descriptions of specifications make it easy to compare apples to apples. Great references include Spiegel, Ballard's, Gump's, Crate and Barrel, Sundance, and Lowe's. File your catalogs alphabetically for quick and easy reference.

Add shipping and delivery costs to the prices of direct-mail items. Shipping large, heavy pieces of furniture is expensive when you order items individually. Reduce costs by having your items held to ship with other orders destined for your city. Ask about this when you place your order.

Hunting for Bargains

Who doesn't love the thrill of the real hunt — the bargain! Cost-cutting bargain shopping is a creative game that is both profitable and fun to play. For starters, try some of these tried-and-true techniques:

- ✔ **Be patient.** Patience is a virtue that saves you money. Waiting for seasonal sales can save you hundreds, maybe thousands of dollars. Make a buying calendar with dates of annual sales, dates when you can travel to specialty sources, and so on. Ask your favorite stores to add you to their special customer list for preview sale dates.

- ✔ **Frame art in stock-size frames and mats.** Custom framing and matting can cost an arm and a leg, so save it for truly worthy subjects. Fit everything else to the frame by trimming to size or using oversized mats.

- ✔ **Get crafty.** Faux-paint an old chest that needs a new finish before it makes its debut in your entry hall. Stencil a charming motif on plain doors of tired kitchen cabinets. Paint retailers carry how-to brochures for creating faux finishes. Craft shops stock stenciling kits ready for do-it-yourselfers who didn't descend from Rembrandt. Check out do-it-yourself (DIY) magazines for ideas.

✔ **Get free professional help.** Professionals have a whole bag of cost-cutting tricks, and most are happy to share them. Many furniture stores have a bona fide interior designer on staff whose services come free with your purchase. Home centers (Lowe's, Home Depot, and others) have expert kitchen and bath designers who can assist you by putting your room's info into their computer design system and printing out a floor plan and a materials list. Ask paint, flooring, and lighting store professionals for expert advice — many are certified specialists.

✔ **Go minimal on window treatments.** Less is more, and less costly, too! Leaving beautiful windows bare can save a bundle. If you really need window treatments, buy stock-size vinyl blinds that cost less than aluminum and custom-made ones. Customize stock curtains with trim. Make your own unlined, shirred-on-the-rod curtains by creating rod pockets in the wide hems of sheets.

✔ **Recycle.** Take a good look at all your furniture and accessories before buying new items. Consider reusing old furniture by placing it in a different room. A spruced-up old armoire can be put to good use in almost any room, including your laundry.

✔ **Shop in unorthodox places for interesting, offbeat, inexpensive accessories.** A friend found handsome hardware for her new kitchen cabinets on a boat. If you're interested in the offbeat, stay alert to the possibilities in boating, farming, and even auto supply stores.

✔ **Use one paint for walls throughout your house.** Switching paint colors — especially custom colors — and finishes is more costly. Stick to a good reliable brand, watch for special sales events, choose stock colors (in some cases less than half the cost of custom colors), and buy small quantities of accent colors to differentiate between spaces. Rely on accessories for added color accents.

Calling on the Professionals

Not every designer works just for the rich and famous. Savvy designers know how to stretch a too-tight budget, where the local bargains are, who does what (skilled carpenter, reliable plumber, gifted upholsterer, and so on), and more.

Professional designers work with clients in any number of ways:

✔ **On a fee basis.** Per hour, per day, or per project are common.

✔ **For a percentage markup on furnishings.** Designers buy at *wholesale* (usually about one-half the retail price) from a *to-the-trade* (designers only) source and resell furnishings to you at a markup.

> ✔ **In some combination of these two billing methods.** Negotiate billing before the project begins, and get a written, binding contract.

Interior designers, like doctors and architects, most often receive business by word of mouth. You don't have to wait to *hear* about a great designer. You can find one quickly by consulting the telephone directory or contacting American Society of Interior Designers (www.ASID.org) at 800-610-2743.

You can also contact designers in designer showrooms. Design Center of The Americas (DCOTA) in Dania, Florida (near Ft. Lauderdale) pioneered the *designer-on-call* program. This program gives the walk-in public access to designer showrooms in the company of a professional designer who is authorized to do business there.

To find a center in your area, go to the Interior Design Directory at www.i-d-d.com/designcenters.htm. If your area has a design center, don't hesitate to inquire about a designer-on-call program and any special sale day open to the general public.

Chapter 3

Evaluating Your Space

· ·

· ·

Don't start decorating without an analysis of your space and an accurate floor plan. A floor plan is the easiest way to get a handle on how much space you have, and what that space's strong and weak points are.

In this chapter, we provide you with the tools for creating your floor plan. You see how easy it is to take measurements, draw the plan, and arrange to-scale furniture templates on your paper plan. You can experiment with different ways to arrange a room. What are you waiting for? Read on!

Preparing a Floor Plan

Before you can begin any decorating job, you need to know what that space can do for you. Drawing a floor plan of the room gives you something concrete to work with — and it lets you experiment with different options before you spend the time and money to actually make those changes. Finally, a floor plan helps you map out how much material — paint or carpeting, for example — you need to finish the job.

Poor planning results in poor decorating. Take the time to plan — success is always worth the effort. Measure, draw to scale, and then take your floor plan with you when you shop for a not-too-big-but-just-right sofa and any other furniture you need.

Collecting the right tools

Drawing a floor plan requires the right tools. Before you begin, have the following items on hand:

- ✔ **Binder (or folder):** Use a binder to hold notes, sketches, and floor plans.

- ✔ **Camera:** Take photos of the room from various angles to take with you on shopping expeditions. Bring your camera along to take snapshots of pieces you may buy. (Be sure to get permission from the shop owner.)

- ✔ **Clear plastic furniture template:** Use a furniture template for drawing outlines of furnishings or punch-out shapes to stand for your furnishings when you work with your graph paper floor plan. You can find these at home improvement, office supply, and craft stores.

- ✔ **Clear plastic straightedge or ruler:** Use a straightedge to draw straight lines.

- ✔ **Cloth measuring tape (at least 60 inches):** Used by seamstresses and tailors for areas that can't be measured as well by a steel measuring tape, a cloth measuring tape is useful when measuring any curved surface, like the top of a chair.

- ✔ **French curve:** This plastic or metal template comprising several large and small curves comes in handy for drawing curvy shapes that look "freehand."

- ✔ **Graph paper (with ¼-inch markings):** Graph paper comes in handy when you're actually drawing the plan. Use standard paper (8½ x 11 inches or larger).

- ✔ **Notebook:** Record measurements, ideas, information, and comments. Make plenty of notes, because you can't always rely on your memory.

- ✔ **Sketch pad:** Use a sketch pad for roughing out ideas or drafting interesting items. Even rough pictures are worth a thousand words.

- ✔ **Standard 25-foot retractable steel measuring tape:** Pick a sturdy model with a one-inch-wide blade that stays straight when you're measuring long distances. If you're planning on doing a lot of measuring, invest in a "point-and-shoot" tool.

- ✔ **Writing instruments:** Have on hand pencils, erasers, pens and markers (in various colors and widths), and chalk. Use chalk to make temporary marks on floors or walls when you're measuring distances longer than your measuring tape.

- ✔ **Three-sided scale ruler calibrated with different scales:** This ruler allows you to draw to a larger or smaller scale, if you decide you want a drawing other than the standard "¼ inch equals 1 foot" scale. If the ¼-inch scale suits all your needs, you won't need this ruler.

Measuring your space

Before you start measuring, make a rough sketch of the floor plan on which to note your measurements as you make them. Indicate any openings (such as doors, windows, fireplaces, niches, or built-in bookshelves) and any other irregularities on your sketch. Don't worry about getting it perfect — this is just a rough working drawing.

Use a steel measuring tape (or a point-and-shoot tool) to take the room's measurements, and write down the figures as you go. Rectangular rooms are the easiest to measure. Rooms with odd combinations of walls and features (common in Contemporary homes) are more challenging, but definitely doable. When you finish measuring, you'll be ready to create an accurate, scaled drawing.

To accurately measure a room (you may need someone to hold one end of the tape), follow these steps:

1. **Measure along the baseboard the length of one wall, from one corner of the room to another.**

   For accuracy, measure to the nearest ¼ inch. Record this number on your rough floor plan and in your notebook.

2. **Measure the remaining walls the same way you measured the first.**

   Most rooms have four walls, but if you're measuring an L-shaped room, you have more to measure. Include every wall in your sketch, especially if you plan to give one part of the room a different flooring or wall covering.

3. **Measure the room's doorways and other entries.**

   Note whether the door opens into or out of the room and indicate the direction (with an arc) on your rough floor plan sketch. Also measure the distances of all openings — doors and open archways — from the ends of the walls so that you can accurately locate these openings on your final plan.

4. **Determine the size of the windows.**

   Include the window frame from outside edge to outside edge. Record the measurements for any moldings around the window separately. Gauge the distance from the floor to the bottom of the window frame, from the ceiling to the top of the window molding, and from the window (on each side) to the corner of the wall (or next window or opening).

   If you're also taking measurements for window treatments, see Chapter 16 for more information.

5. **Measure any and all architectural features, including fireplaces, brackets, shelves, and any other built-in features.**

   Measure surrounding space and outside or overall dimensions of these items, and then locate each on your plan.

6. **Measure the walls from side to side and from the floor to the ceiling.**

7. **Measure where the electrical outlets, switches, and other controls are located.**

   Note where heat and air conditioning ducts, radiators, *chases* (coverings for electric wires and plumbing pipes), and exposed pipes are located.

Drawing floor plans

After you finish measuring, you're ready to draw your floor plan to scale. Graph paper works perfectly for this job. The standard graph has four squares to an inch, which translates easily to a scale where a quarter inch — or one square — equals one foot. The following steps guide you through the drawing process:

1. **Lightly pencil in the room's major areas on your graph paper before firmly committing to hard-to-erase dark lines.**

   Include the room's irregularities, such as support columns or any other intrusions.

2. **Note on the paper the room's directional orientation (north, south, east, and west).**

   The quantity and quality of natural light affects a number of decisions. (For more information, see Chapters 16 and 17.)

3. **Draw the room's specifics, using a thicker straight line for walls, windows, and fireplaces.**

   Note also the inside width of the doors and other openings so that you know if your sofa (or other large piece of furniture) can fit through the opening, up the stairs, or around a turn in the hallway. (If you live in an apartment with an elevator, measure to make sure your new sofa fits inside the elevator!)

4. **Indicate where all permanent switches, outlets, controls, TV cable, and phone lines are located (see Figure 3-1).**

   These factors all influence furniture placement. Don't make the mistake of putting bookcases in front of the only phone jack in the room, loading up all the shelves, and then discovering that you can't plug in your phone!

5. **Draw each wall's elevations (see Figure 3-2).**

   The wall elevations are two-dimensional representations that help you figure out art and accessory arrangement or window treatment. Again, remember to mark all the permanent features, such as light switches, electrical outlets, phone and TV cable jacks, air conditioning and heat vents, and so on.

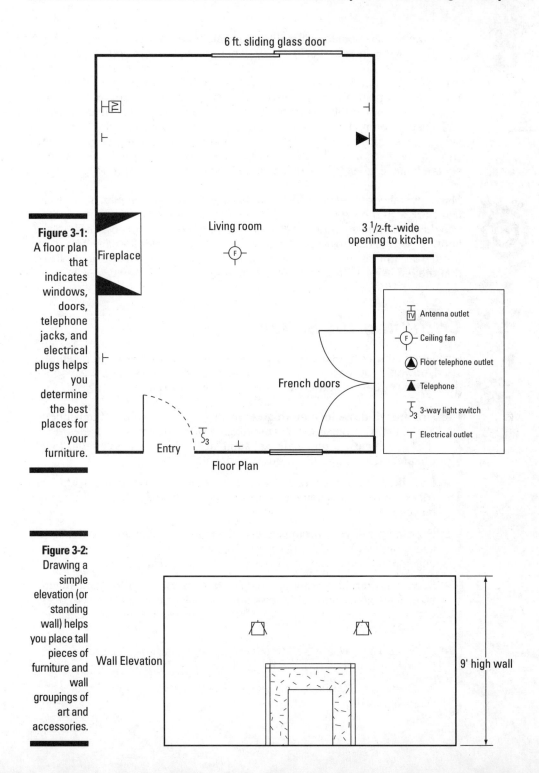

Figure 3-1:
A floor plan that indicates windows, doors, telephone jacks, and electrical plugs helps you determine the best places for your furniture.

6 ft. sliding glass door

Living room

Fireplace

3 ¹/₂-ft.-wide opening to kitchen

French doors

Entry

Floor Plan

TV — Antenna outlet

F — Ceiling fan

▲ — Floor telephone outlet

▲ — Telephone

S₃ — 3-way light switch

⊤ — Electrical outlet

Figure 3-2:
Drawing a simple elevation (or standing wall) helps you place tall pieces of furniture and wall groupings of art and accessories.

Wall Elevation

9' high wall

After you draw each wall's elevations, make several working copies. Keep the original in your file, in case you need to make more copies.

After you've generated a basic floor plan, note the square footage of the room on your plan. Multiply the room's length by its width. For example: A 10-x-15-foot room is 150 square feet (10x15=150) in area. If you're measuring an L-shaped room, break the room into as many four-sided sections as necessary, get the square footage of each area, and add these together for the total. (Do you feel like you're in high school geometry all over again?) You'll refer to square footage when you purchase floor coverings (see Chapter 14).

Make several copies of your plan. Always keep your original plan in your file and work with the copies. Take additional copies along on shopping trips. Use this basic information to estimate how much paint, wall covering, and flooring you need. However, before processing your order for carpeting, window treatments, or other non-returnable items that must fit *exactly,* insist that the retailer send a professional to measure.

Critiquing the space

Evaluating your floor plan helps you decide which features should be emphasized, downplayed, or corrected, and which can stay as they are. Ask yourself the following questions, then note ideas and options that occur to you:

- **Are the windows located in good places?** Is the view from the window attractive? Or does it need camouflaging with draperies or shades? Does the room have a good balance of sunlight? Or do you need blinds? (See Chapter 16 for more on window treatments.)

- **Do I like the room's shape?** Or does the room need correcting with color tricks to create an illusion of better proportions? (See Chapter 5 for more on color.)

    For example, if your room is long and narrow, you may feel like you're in a long hallway rather than a room. To make it a more pleasant place to linger, paint one or both end walls a strongly contrasting color.

- **Does the room have enough wall space to allow room for your furniture?** If so, count your blessings. If not, consider ways in which to deal with this problem, or note whether you may need professional design help in solving it.

- **Does this room relate well to others nearby?** Does the room have easy traffic flow from one room to the next? Or, does the furniture arrangement need to compensate?

✔ **Is the room a good size?** If the room seems small, use the right color scheme. A light palette makes it look larger. Vivid jewel tones play up its gem-like character. (For color tips, turn to Chapter 5.)

✔ **What are the room's strong features?** Does the room have a fireplace or interesting feature you can play up? You can create a *focal point* by installing a fake fireplace, devising a wall mural with paint or paper, or choosing an important piece of furniture. (See Chapter 4 for more about focal points.)

This general analysis is an important step, because the better you know your room, the better your decorating will be!

Considering function and space when selecting furniture

After you've analyzed your floor plan, you're ready to determine the best furniture layout. Follow the professional's technique:

✔ **What is the primary function of this room?** Watching TV, dining, sleeping — all these activities are clues to the kinds of furniture you'll need and where it should go. Don't forget secondary functions your room serves. Does your dining room serve as a home office, too? Listing functions and considering necessary furniture can help you to see whether your demands for this space are reasonable and doable.

✔ **How many people normally use the space?** The number of people who use the room indicates what kind and how much seating you need.

✔ **What's the maximum number of people who may be using the space?** Do you need additional seating, such as folding chairs? What other kinds of furniture, appliances, and/or equipment do you need (for instance, a game table)?

Putting Furniture in Its Place

You've checked your list. You know what pieces of furniture you need to accomplish the functions you've specified. Figuring out where to put furniture for function and beauty can be a difficult job.

Moving furniture on paper

You can arrange your furniture easily — and look at all the different options — by using the plastic or metal templates (to-scale tracing guides for most popular pieces of furniture) or to-scale cardboard cutout pieces of furniture that you can shove around your floor plan. You can find all the most common pieces of furniture in your kit. If not, draw an item to the same scale as your floor plan, using your scale ruler.

Pushing furniture around on paper is much easier than moving the real thing. Your back thanks you in advance! Make two or three possible plans. Weigh the pros and cons of each. To begin, take a look at these suggestions:

- **Find the architectural feature that serves as your room's focal point.** A fireplace fits this starring role, but other possibilities include a picture window, a window wall with a view, or a chandelier. Arrange important seating groups around such focal points. The rest of your room's arrangement will fall into place.

- **If the room has no focal architectural element, make an important piece of furniture stand out.** Usually, the wall opposite the main entry into the room becomes the *focal wall* where the focal point is located. An antique armoire, a beautiful sofa and upholstered chairs and art (see Figure 3-3), or perhaps a grand piano are good substitutes. An entertainment center (TV armoire flanked by bookcases) creates a focal point for a family room. If you don't have any of these pieces of furniture, use a cluster of tall bookshelves. Give them added importance by pulling one or two central units out away from the wall to form a faux breakfront.

Figure 3-3:
A large, important piece of furniture can serve as a focal point.

✔ **Locate traffic paths on your graph.** Use an arrow to indicate an entrance or pathway. If you've lived in your house for a while, you know where these traffic patterns are. Traffic not only must flow through the room (to get from one room to another) but also within the room, so note those pathways if you can.

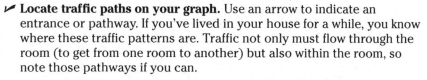

Don't place furniture in traffic paths. Traffic should flow behind and around a sofa and chairs, but not through a conversation or TV viewing area. Some rooms have problem traffic flow situations that make conversation areas almost impossible. Some creative thinking can solve these problems. (For some ideas, see Chapter 8.)

✔ **Allow adequate space around individual pieces of furniture and furniture groupings.** If you're *floating* a large piece of furniture (setting it in the middle of the room), minimum walk-around space is three feet — four feet for wheelchairs. For opening doors, drawers, cabinets, and shelves, allow three feet for the kitchen, and a little less for the living room or bedroom. For seating areas, comfortable conversation distance calls for two (minimum) to ten feet (maximum) between people. Farther spacing is more formal; closer is more intimate. Some furniture pieces require breathing space. The larger the piece (china cabinet or armoire), the more space it needs. Your eye is your judge.

Keep in mind that furniture templates on graph paper look smaller than furniture does in real life. Fight the temptation to cram in more and more furniture. In real life, every piece of furniture needs breathing space, some more than others. For example, a fully upholstered sofa with a skirt to the floor looks larger than a same-sized sofa with legs.

Some Typical Furniture Sizes

Room	Room size: W x D x H
Living Room:	
Armoire	56 x 26 x 89
Chair, Lounge (pillow back)	41 x 36 x 37
Chair, Occasional (open arm)	24 x 25 x 40
Chair, Wing	32 x 31 x 45
Coffee Table (traditional)	48 x 34 x 17
End Table	23 x 27 x 23
Entertainment Unit (3 pieces)	92 x 23 x 54
Sofa (contemporary)	80 x 36 x 36
Sofa (traditional camelback)	80 x 33 x 35

Dining Room:

Chair, Arm	23 x 24 x 40
China Cabinet	61 x 17 x 50
Table (rectangular dining)	70 x 44 x 30

Bedroom:

Bed (4-poster, queen)	73 x 93 x 89
Dresser (triple)	68 x 18 x 35
Nightstand	26 x 17 x 25

Home Office:

Bookcase	34 x 16 x 78
Chair (executive high-back)	23 x 30 x 38
Desk (double pedestal)	58 x 28 x 30
Desk (executive)	78 x 42 x 30

Don't block doorways or passages with sofas that seem to push people away. Your room's first message should be welcoming, and a big sofa blocking the path is hardly a welcome mat.

Evaluating your plan

After your furniture is in place on a floor plan, ask yourself the following questions in order to make sure the plan meets your needs:

- ✔ Does this plan meet all my requirements for function?

- ✔ Is the plan flexible? Does the space offer different situations for different times of day and different circumstances?

- ✔ Does the plan take advantage of the room's good architectural features and correct or disguise the bad ones?

- ✔ Does this plan have the look of openness or intimacy that I want?

- ✔ Will my guests feel welcome to enter this room?

- ✔ Will I enjoy moving about and living in this room?

If you answer "no" to any of these questions, go back to the drawing board. If you create only one plan, you may want to experiment with at least one alternative.

Evaluating your plan is a discovery exercise. You may be amazed at what you discover about your room, your furniture, and yourself as more and more possibilities reveal themselves. So go ahead — create another plan.

Chapter 4

Understanding Design Principles

*I*n cooking, before you make a dish, you usually read the recipe. Decorating is a little like cooking in that respect. Even though you're eager to get started decorating, you need to develop your room recipe. That recipe comprises basic design elements or components that, used in differing quantities, make for different artistic results.

Just as great chefs can all use the same basic ingredients with very different results, all decorators work with the same five basic design elements: color, form, line, mass, and texture. Decorators work with six surfaces — walls, floor, and ceiling — simultaneously, to create an artistic composition.

After you get a good idea what design elements contribute to your decorating composition, you're ready to think about room design. Use the five components of interior design — focal point, scale and proportion, harmony and unity, contrast, and variety — to create a vital point of interest that serves as an anchor around which the rest of the room seems to settle.

We cover these design basics in this chapter. Don't worry — putting these design principles into practice is as easy as whipping up a mud pie!

Deciphering Design

A design is an orderly arrangement of five basic elements:

- ✔ **Color,** the creator of illusion and maker of mood
- ✔ **Form,** the overall shape of any object
- ✔ **Line,** the implied direction or boundary of an object
- ✔ **Mass,** the bulk of an object that occupies space
- ✔ **Texture,** the *touch me, feel me* of matter

We discuss each element in detail in the next section. All artists — whether painters or sculptors, architects or interior decorators — work with these same basic elements to achieve certain effects, all of which must work together to form a unified whole.

But these five elements alone aren't enough to generate a successful design. Five components of composition, which we discuss later in the chapter, round out the list of designer's terms:

- **Focal point.** This is the point of visual reference to which the eye always returns — a "home base."

- **Scale and proportion.** *Scale* refers to overall size, while *proportion* relates the size of parts compared to the whole. Keep these two factors in mind when selecting furniture.

- **Harmony and unity.** *Harmony* refers to the blending of similar elements, while *unity* refers to the overall sense of belonging together. This is a goal, so we keep it in mind as we add each new piece of furniture or accessory.

- **Contrast.** Contrast places opposites side by side, such as black and white or hard and soft. The challenge is to balance contrast, so as to maintain a sense of overall unity. Add contrast in small doses — be careful not to overdo it and thus upset a sense of harmony of parts and overall unity.

- **Variety.** Variety is the spice of life and the spice of interiors. Include variety within a single room as well as within a whole-house design.

Without sufficient and distinct contrast (which can be subtle), a room can look deadly dull. If a room has too much contrast or too much variety, it looks confused. Your job as the decorator is to come up with a recipe that has just enough — but never too much — of the elements that make for a beautiful, functional room.

Consider what you can do with these elements:

- **You can use these design elements as a design vocabulary, building blocks for a strong decorating foundation.** You can judge all your design choices and determine whether they're good, better, or the best solutions to your design problems.

- **With this design vocabulary you can clarify what may in the beginning be a vague vision.** Thinking and speaking clearly about your design is usually a lot more fun — and much less costly — than muddling through blindly.

- **You can use the design elements to get back on track.** Have you ever started a design project and lost your way? You can use these design elements to quickly refocus when you've wandered off track (which happens to us all at one time or another). Thinking your way out of decorating trouble is less costly in time and money than the trial-and-error purchase method.

> ✔ **You can use more of one, less of another element to create your own signature style.** You may use a great deal of pattern and no color, a profusion of color and only one texture, a great deal of texture and very little pattern and color, and so on — all to create your very personal design.

Befriending the Basic Design Elements

The following sections provide an introduction to the five basic design elements: color, form, line, mass, and texture.

Considering color

Color is the decorator's magic wand. Color creates a mood and a wide variety of illusions. When you use color to its best advantage, it reinforces your design idea. Color does so much that it deserves — and gets — its own chapter (see Chapter 5)!

Recognizing form

Form refers to actual shapes in architecture and furniture. Sometimes people say that a room's "bones" are good, which means it has good architectural form. Furniture form is important and should echo the architecture. For example, tall, straight, slender chairs seem somewhat formal and fit well in elegant surroundings. Short, squat, curvy chairs seem casual and fit in rooms with low ceilings and relaxed, casual moods.

Reading between the lines

All lines create movement and establish mood. Lines include real lines and *implied lines* — the lines that the eye naturally follows between two points, or the lines created by planes and surfaces that come together. Stripes of any thinness or thickness, direction, length, and orientation can also indicate lines. Lines used together create various effects, including focal points and a sense of rhythm (see the section "Feeling the rhythm," later in this chapter), as well as pattern (see Chapter 6).

Lines occur everywhere in design, including in doors, windows, columns, arches, plank paneling, and flooring. Furniture, patterned wall coverings, and textiles all add lines to a room. Too many lines can make a room look very busy. Too few lines (in a room without pattern) leave a room looking a little empty. The following sections let you in on the different kinds of lines and their design messages.

Talking straight about lines

Straight lines are considered strong, masculine, and static. Straight lines may be vertical, horizontal, or diagonal:

- ✔ **Vertical lines** draw the eyes up and down, producing alertness. Vertical lines also suggest stability, dignity, and formality.

  A too-vertical (tall, narrow) room is anything but restful. So if you're faced with this problem, introduce some horizontal lines in window treatments, furniture, and accessories, creating a neutralizing, stable square.

- ✔ **Horizontal lines** move the eyes from side to side, creating a sense of restfulness. Horizontal lines are informal. In Figure 4-1, wide logs create repeating horizontal lines, while a strong wallpaper border creates a colorful pattern.

Figure 4-1:
Use horizontal lines to create a restful environment.

Photograph courtesy Blonder Wallcovering
(Eastern Tradition by Westchester Prints)

A room with too many architecturally horizontal lines may be too relaxing. To wake up your room, add vertical stripes, perhaps in wallpaper, tall furniture, torchiers (standing lamps), striped upholstery on tall-back chairs, and so on.

- ✔ **Diagonal lines** promote rapid movement of the eyes and suggest fast movement in general. Use diagonals in entry halls or wherever you don't want people to linger.

Used in excess, diagonal lines are downright disturbing! Be very careful to check wallpapers and fabrics — especially flower-and-vine patterns — for implied lines that aren't drawn in and don't make themselves obvious until they're on the wall or at the window!

Looking at those curves

Curvy lines are natural and feminine. Simple, flowing curves (like those on the front legs of Queen Anne chairs) are gentle. Tighter, more exaggerated curves are more exciting.

Some furniture designs — Victorian, for example — deliberately create tension by pinching the waist of the chair back and exaggerating the curved top. When might you want to use furniture with exaggerated curves and a sense of tension? In any room where you want lively action — perhaps a hallway, a playroom, a game room, or even a laundry room.

Weighing in on mass

All objects have mass, or bulk, which refers to how much space an object occupies — or seems to occupy — and how much weight an object seems to have. Individual objects, such as an 80-inch-long sofa or a grand piano, have mass. Groupings of objects, such as a love seat and two upholstered chairs, also have mass. Figure 4-2 shows a large armoire that has significant mass. (Note that the smooth surface of the polished wood armoire contrasts with the rough texture of the stone wall; we discuss texture in the following section.)

Figure 4-2:
Some individual pieces of furniture have significant, impressive mass.

Photograph courtesy Stanley Furniture, Urban Comfort armoire

Often, people perceive an object's mass not by its weight or how much space it actually takes up, but by its appearance. A sofa with exposed legs, for example, seems light and even delicate compared to the same sofa with a skirt. Objects in dark colors take up more visual space and seem heavier than objects of the same size in light colors.

Be sure to balance mass in your room. For example, balance one heavy object on one side of the room with an equally heavy but not necessarily identical object on the opposite side of the room.

Placing several big, heavy-looking objects together in one end of a room makes that end of the room look as though it's sinking, while the light end seems to fly up, up, and away. Scatter heavy objects around the room for balance.

Touching texture

Texture isn't as visible as color, so people often don't notice texture until they feel it, and then they're surprised. And that's a wonderful way to use texture — as the surface you want yourself and others to enjoy touching, perhaps at first by accident and surprise. Most people appreciate textile surfaces, such as nubby chenille, fine silk, and rough hemp. Many other people enjoy experiencing the coolness of marble, the roughness of certain stone (refer to Figure 4-2), and the warmth of wood.

Texture, like color, is another powerful mood-maker. It exerts a truly vital force in a neutrally colored room with little or no pattern. (Chapter 7 provides more information on working with texture.)

Introducing Yourself to Design Components

Look at a room as though it were an artist's canvas. Maybe a doorway on one side of the wall needs to be balanced with something of equal size and shape (perhaps a tall piece of furniture, a hanging tapestry, or a large rectangular mirror) on the other side. Different-sized windows need to be equalized (you can do this with window treatments). The flooring may seem much richer than the wall material. Perhaps a certain spot in the room needs more or less pattern.

To make the right changes, you need to have a handle on some more components of design: focal point, scale and proportion, harmony and unity, contrast, and variety. We cover each in the following sections.

Focusing on the focal point

All rooms, like paintings, contain points and lines. A *point* is simply a location. Two points, however, create a beginning and an end, or a *line*. A cluster of points or lines helps to create a strong point of interest called a *focal point*.

All compositions need a focal point. Think of a focal point as home base, where the eye can rest. (A focal point occurs architecturally with a fireplace, a bay window, or a built-in bookcase.) You're fortunate when you have one architectural focal point in a room. If your room has two or more focal points, then you need to give one element in the room special status, and all other objects and furnishings should play supporting roles. Don't make secondary areas more interesting by adding stronger colors and patterns that compete with the focal point.

Fireplaces are natural focal points. Big enough to be architecturally impressive, fireplaces are a source of warmth and comfort. Fires are visually interesting, so they're stars. And with mantels to decorate, they easily steal the show. Drawing seating around the fireplace plays up the fireplace and designates it as the star of the room (see Figure 4-3).

Figure 4-3: In this living room, a fireplace is a traditional focal point.

Photograph courtesy of Hunter Douglas (Counterparts)

But what if you don't have a fireplace in your living room and you're not keen on artificial ones? Picture windows or any large windows are natural focal points. Beautiful moldings and trims make them even more interesting. And if you have a gorgeous view, the window really shines. In a modest-sized room, the sofa with a large painting or mirror above it fits in on the wall opposite the window, balancing the window. Pushing furniture templates around your floor plan will reveal options (see Chapter 3).

If you're left without either a fireplace or a beautiful window, you still have hope. A large piece of furniture, such as an armoire or entertainment center, can fill the bill. A lovely sofa, accented with a high stack of pillows and with a large important painting hanging above it, works very nicely as a focal point in any living room.

There is no right or wrong object to use as a focal point. It may be anything that you wish to focus attention on. The choice is up to you. Just be sure that all other furniture and furnishings in a given room help make the focal point stand out.

Keeping size and scale in mind

Size is always relative. People tend to relate everything to the size of their own bodies, and they need a certain amount of space around their bodies for psychological and physical comfort. People also compare the size of objects in a room. These relative size relationships are important. In decoration, absolute size isn't important; relative size is what matters.

Decorating is about *relationships*. Included with the idea of relative size is *scale*, which is the relationship among objects, humans, and the space they all occupy. When furniture scale is too small, an adult may feel like he or she is in a doll's house. And when furniture is too large for a room, both people and the room seem too small. Does this mean that you can never use a large-scaled piece of furniture in a smallish room? No. Go ahead, if it suits you.

In homes with high ceilings, including two-story ceilings, choose furniture that's scaled larger and taller than ordinary furniture. Figure 4-4 shows an example of a high-ceilinged room that is cut down to size with a few well-placed horizontal elements and larger furnishings.

Figure 4-4:
A high-ceilinged room may benefit from larger furnishings.

Photograph courtesy The Rutt Collection, Susan Bates Design

Larger furniture for larger rooms

Welcome to the age of the impressive home — rooms with two-story-high ceilings. These grand rooms call for grand furniture and accessories. If you find yourself in the wonderful predicament of trying to fill a large room, here are a few ways to scale up:

✔ Trade in your low-backed sofa for a high-backed (shelter) sofa.

✔ Make your low-backed sofa look taller by standing a continuous row of extra-large toss pillows along the inside back. Better yet, make sure the pillows have a vertical stripe.

✔ Hang a large, over-scaled picture above the sofa. Group two rows of several smaller pictures on either side for larger scale and dramatic impact.

✔ Hang a collection of three or four tapestries (dressy) or quilts (country) in compatible colors and patterns in a two-story entry or stairwell.

✔ Build your own *wall unit* by grouping three to five bookcases as one single, massive unit, and top your arrangement with a super big container of faux or fresh vines. (We have a friend who used a wicker laundry basket, spray-painted shiny black and filled with dried hydrangeas, on top of a similar arrangement.)

✔ Stack smaller chests or trunks atop larger ones to build a pyramid. Patterned or textured chests and trunks trimmed with eye-catching hardware don't need any other decoration (such as a vase) on top.

✔ Take a tip from retail store display people. Make any piece of furniture — a secretary, armoire, or china cabinet — look more important by placing it atop a simple platform built of 2-x-4s on edge, topped with 5/8-inch-thick plywood and covered to match your flooring or floorcovering.

Creating harmony and variety

Harmony describes how various elements and principles come together to make a total unified look. To use the cooking analogy, when all the ingredients come together, they form an attractive, yummy dish.

If any one general decorating maxim applies, it's "Birds of a feather flock together." Creating a unified design is your hardest job, but keep variety in mind.

Variety is the spice of life — and rooms. Add variety with color, texture, pattern, mass, and line. Use them like good medicine — in small doses throughout. Or, use them in a strong dose as a heavy accent — such as a heap of big red pillows on a white sofa in an all-white room. Whichever tack you take, keep in mind that contrast of various elements, particularly color and values of color, heightens people's perceptions — but you probably don't want to bowl them over.

Feeling the Rhythm

Repeated visual elements establish *rhythm*. Rhythm ensures that the eye moves through the room. Rooms that have a series of columns, arches, doors, openings, niches, or panels have rhythm thanks to their architecture. If your room lacks these built-in rhythms, you can create rhythm in various ways.

Use accessories throughout a room like punctuation marks — or drumbeats — to set up a sense of rhythm as the eye jumps from one group (for example, yellow toss pillows on the sofa and flanking chairs) to another (a group of pictures matted in the same yellow color). For tips on accessorizing, see Chapters 25 and 26.

Don't underdo or overdo it. For example, you probably don't want yellow cushions on *every* chair around the room, but you want them on more than just the sofa. Use a few yellow cushions, some yellow picture mats, yellow lampshades, and so on. Spread a little of that color around the entire room.

If you've got rhythm going — by giving the eye objects to view as it hops about the room — be sure that you have a landing spot for viewers' eyes to come to rest on. Glance around your room, noting spots that need an accessory. Adding that last accessory gives the room its landing spot.

Balancing Your Act

Balance is a sense that everything in a room is placed properly. Balanced rooms are comfortable to be in; unbalanced ones, however, are disturbingly off-kilter. You can achieve balance through classical symmetry or asymmetry.

Classical symmetry achieves a sense of proper relationships by having each half of the room mirror the other. This approach makes the room's center the focal point and works best in rectangular-shaped rooms.

Traditional and Historic settings (see Chapter 9) rely on symmetry because it creates a dignified, stable, and restful feeling.

Asymmetrical balance calls for a *perceived*, not *real*, relationship of balance. Unlike classical symmetry, asymmetry has two unequal (but balanced) halves.

You can bring mismatching elements into equilibrium through clever placement and massing. Balance a heavier object by moving a lighter object farther away from the balance point (think of how a seesaw works). Or, mass lots of smaller objects together. You can use larger areas of light colors and smaller areas of darker colors.

What type of balance is for you? Some rooms lend themselves to classical symmetry due to their architecture. A fireplace flanked by identical windows is a traditional example of such symmetry. Contemporary homes may have irregular, implied room shapes that make asymmetrical balancing acts a must.

Symmetrical balance is considered formal and traditional, and asymmetrical balance is casual and modern.

Part II
Creating Surface Interest

In this part . . .

Decorating is mostly about shaping space and creating surface interest — working with color, pattern, and texture. In these chapters, we point out vital information about each, and we discuss ways in which you can use them all to special advantage. The chapter on trouble-shooting shows you how to analyze spaces and figure your way out of problem situations.

Chapter 5

Eyeing Color Basics

*T*o a decorator, color is a magic wand. Wave your color wand to create optical illusions (make small spaces appear larger and large spaces appear smaller). Magically alter mood — your own and others'. Feeling down? Paint your room a sunny, spirit-lifting yellow. Feeling anxious? Paint your space a calming blue. Hungry for a little drama? Bring on fire-engine red.

Color makes or breaks (well, maybe *bends*) a decorating project. Color sells, or prevents sales. The wrong color on the outside keeps people away from the insides of buildings. (Think curb appeal!) We linger in rooms dressed in eye-appealing, mood-pleasing shades but flee from ones clad in clashing colors.

In this chapter, we explain the principles behind a color wheel so you can confidently create color schemes. Best of all, this chapter helps you to discover your personal color style. Perhaps for the first time, you'll realize that you never liked warm colors — they make you feel fidgety. Or, you may realize that cool colors bring on a big chill that you'd just as soon avoid. Finally, a look at several different color schemes and themes can help you decide what color scheme works for you.

Taking Color 101

What's the right white? Does this yellow go with that blue? How can a problem room be fixed simply by using color? More importantly, how can you make every room in your home reflect your (or the primary occupant's) personality?

When working with colors, think in terms of *color relationships* because colors become even more (or less) powerful when used together. Bright green looks brighter against black than against white, for example. Color can work beautifully and more easily for you after you discover how to wield this magical wand.

Relating to color

Selecting a *color scheme* (a combination of colors) is a real challenge — even to professionals. Start by figuring out what colors you really do and don't like. Hang large paint samples called "chips" on the wall. (Paint companies now make bigger chips that let you experience more of the color.) How do you feel as you look at each? Narrow down the number of colors that you enjoy as you go, until you have the ones that you enjoy the most.

Next, consider the effects of the color on your space. Notice how one color seems to pop out — maybe more than you want. *Advancing* colors (ones that are warm; see "Warm and cool colors" later in the chapter) can create a claustrophobic effect. *Receding* colors (ones that are cool) make surfaces appear to move away. (If you really want to appreciate the effects of color movement, do what the pros do — paint a big poster board.)

What effects do colors have on each other? For example, rowdy colors, such as red, get toned down when accompanied by more sedate colors, such as beige. Quite cool colors seem more brilliant in the company of lively warm colors, such as yellow.

If you want your house to have a serene feel, use a whole-house color scheme that provides a sense of harmony. Sticking to one color scheme throughout can make a small house seem larger and more coherent, too. Mixing and matching *tints* (white added) and *tones* (black added) of one or more colors is an increasingly popular trend because it adds drama. A whole-house approach doesn't mean limiting your palette — it means relating colors so that you (and your guests) don't notice any discordant notes.

The take-home message: Color scheming isn't just about choosing colors you like. Color scheming is about choosing likable, livable colors that produce the right effects.

Finding foolproof color schemes

Any number of color schemes works well in larger spaces. Two very easy color schemes work especially well for small- to medium-sized homes when a space-enlarging sense of unity and serenity is desired:

> ✔ **Unified scheme:** A sense of continuity makes a house seem larger, so use
> the same background color throughout. Introduce variety by using sev-
> eral tints (lighter) and tones (deeper) for background and furnishings,
> and by mixing interesting textures. You can also switch accent colors
> from room to room.
>
> ✔ **Positive/negative color scheme:** One room uses a light background and
> dark accent color, and the adjoining room uses a dark background and
> light accent. You use the same colors (for continuity), but in different
> amounts (for variety). You can easily achieve a dramatic effect.

Some color combinations seem downright wrong — even ugly. When one color
detracts from another, the scheme doesn't work. Paint manufacturers eliminate this problem by arranging colors *sympathetically* — in close relationships
that are mutually enhancing — in their *paint decks* (books of chips that can
be purchased from the paint store). By choosing related colors vertically on
the same page or horizontally as you fan the deck out, you're guaranteed
colors that get along well together. You can avoid one of our pet peeves —
and felony arrest for bad decorating: using pink-based with yellow-based
beiges in the same room.

If it's serenity you want, don't use lots of color schemes throughout the
house, no matter what its size. This is especially true if your house has an
open layout where you can clearly see multiple rooms at a time.

Understanding Color — The Color Wheel

When you first hear of a color wheel, you may have images of amusement
park rides. But a color wheel won't make you dizzy! It starts with a rainbow
bent into a circle.

The color wheel has *primary colors* (red, yellow, and blue) evenly spaced
between *secondary colors* (orange, green, and violet). Mixing *analogous* (adjacent) colors creates *tertiary* (third) and *quaternary* (fourth) colors that usually go by exotic names. Paint decks are color wheels with all the tints and
tones to make color selection foolproof (see the preceding section, "Finding
foolproof color schemes").

The color wheel makes seeing color relationships easier. Colors have relationships to each other. They are next to, across from, and at angles to each
other. Designers talk about color schemes in terms of where colors are in
these relationships.

Analogous colors

Colors next to each other are *analogous* (alike). (A good example of analogous primaries is red and yellow.) Mixing these two colors creates more analogous colors. Because they are so closely related, they always work well together.

Complementary colors

Colors placed opposite each other are *complementary*. Red and green are a good example. Every color has a complement. Don't use equal amounts of complementary colors in your color scheme because it produces an unpleasant tension. Do use a larger amount of one color when using complementary colors.

Warm and cool colors

Colors are either warm or cool; it's the most basic color rule. Warm colors are reds and yellows. Cool colors are greens and blues. Draw a line down the middle of the wheel; warm and cool colors will be on opposite sides. Every warm color has a cool complement.

Warm colors are relaxing, friendly (sometimes even sexy), and associated with easy-going informality and intimacy. These colors seem to advance toward the viewer. Warm colors speed up heart rates and create excitement. Mild warm colors stimulate; intense ones motivate — notice that fast food places use orange to get you in and out in a hurry.

Cool colors are more refreshing and emotionally distant, and they are associated with formality and reserved behavior. They seem to recede away from the viewer, so that walls seem farther away than they actually are. Cool colors slow down heart rates and relieve mental tension. Mild cool colors soothe; intense ones sedate — lots of medical facilities use green to balance their patients' tension.

You can use warm and cool colors to fix problems. Want to cool down a too-warm room? Use colors from the cool side of the color wheel. Want to warm up a space that seems chilly? Use a color from the warm side of the color wheel. Want room temperature not to be a factor? Choose a neutral color (See Chapter 8 for some color troubleshooting tips.)

Using Basic Color Schemes

Use your color wheel to find the perfect color scheme. Some of the most popular and enduring schemes include

- ✔ **One-color neutral.** *Monochromatic* (one-color) schemes come in two varieties — you can use a single color, or tonal variations of one color. Common schemes are based on white or beige, which can be very chic and quite contemporary. Make sure that all your whites and beiges are either cool or warm, and use texture and pattern (subtle ones such as wovens work well) to add interest.

  White and beige tend to announce flaws loudly. Architectural imperfections (not to mention dirt and stains) may seem exaggerated. Hide flawed walls, for example, with a deeper value of beige.

- ✔ **Two colors: Opposites attract.** The *complementary color scheme* contrasts colors that lie on opposite sides of the wheel. Use proportionately more of one color to prevent too much tension. Use soft versions in neutralized shades, such as tan and slate.

- ✔ **Three-of-a-kind.** The *analogous color scheme* uses three colors that lie close to each other on the color wheel. A typical scheme features one primary color plus two supporting colors (secondary or tertiary colors that lie on either side of the main color). For example, you can try red with a red-violet and a red-orange.

- ✔ **Three-of-almost-a-kind.** The *split-complementary color scheme* harmonizes one main color with two colors that are adjacent to the complementary color (but not the direct complement itself). On the color wheel, draw an imaginary line from one main color to its complement. Select a color that is one space to the right of the complement, and then move one space to the left of the complement to find the second color.

- ✔ **Three-part harmony.** The *triad color scheme* uses three colors the same distance apart on the wheel. Start with your main color and draw imaginary lines to colors that are equally spaced from the complement to form a triangle. Examples of triad color schemes are: red, yellow, and blue; and orange, green, and violet.

- ✔ **Four-part harmony.** The *tetrad color scheme* ups the ante by featuring four equally spaced colors. Many Traditional color schemes are neutralized shades. These schemes are tricky to pull off, so base your own scheme on a fabric swatch, for example. Using coordinated upholstery and patterned fabrics makes the effort easier.

Spreading color around

What's the best (and easiest) way to spread color around your room? One time-honored rule says the greater the area to be covered, the lighter the color value should be; the smaller the area, the more *saturated* (brighter, bolder, or stronger) the color should be. As areas shrink, *chromatic intensity* (strength of the color) grows. Figure 5-1 illustrates the differences between a room's primary, secondary, and tertiary areas.

The *primary* areas — the main areas of your floors, walls, and ceilings — should receive neutralized colors in a range of values. Make the floor the darkest surface, the walls medium, and the ceiling the lightest value — it looks the most natural because that's the way Mother Nature spread color. Some situations (big rooms with high ceilings, for example), need color magic. Make a too-high ceiling darker to visually lower it, for example, or make it white to make it seem even higher.

Making color corrections

To make color magic work for you, you could bring in David Copperfield. Or, just try some of these tricks worthy of Houdini:

✔ To make a room look bigger, use light, cool colors to create an atmospheric look. Paint all surfaces the same color. Match the upholstery to the floor. Use contrasting textures to add interest.

✔ To make an average-sized room seem cozier, use medium-tone, warm neutrals. Decorative wall features like *wainscoting* (wood paneling that comes about halfway up the wall) or paneling make great accents. Use contrasting paint for paneling, and either match or contrast the molding.

✔ To make a ceiling look higher, use white paint or a lighter value of the wall color. Keep floors relatively light.

✔ To square off a long, rectangular room, paint or paper the long narrow walls in light, cool colors to make them recede. Make the short walls advance by using a dark, warm color.

✔ To narrow a wide room, use deeper, warm neutrals on long walls, and lighter cool tints on shorter walls.

✔ To darken a high ugly ceiling, use black, dark gray, midnight blue, or even the same dark, intense color (such as hunter green or chocolate brown) you may be using on a wall.

✔ If the room has varying ceiling heights, don't hesitate to paint them different colors. Paint a dropped acoustical tile ceiling the same color as the wall. Paint a raised ceiling white or a light contrasting color. The acoustical tile ceiling will seem to disappear! Hooray.

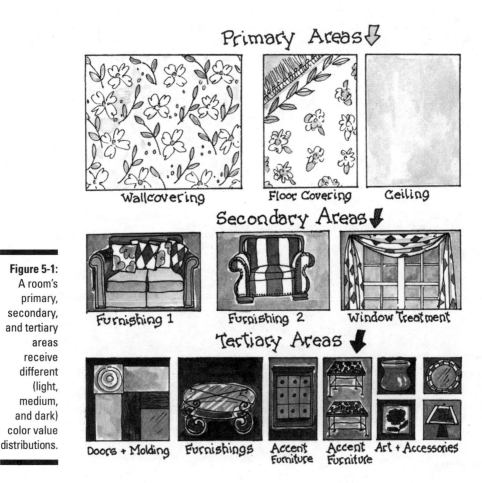

Figure 5-1:
A room's
primary,
secondary,
and tertiary
areas
receive
different
(light,
medium,
and dark)
color value
distributions.

The *secondary* areas, such as area rugs, window treatments, and furnishings, should receive more color intensity than the primary ones. Use more color, pattern, and texture on these areas. (For hints on how to use pattern and texture, see Chapters 6 and 7.)

The *tertiary* (third) areas can take strong accent colors. Use brilliant or dramatic color in art; accessories such as pillows, throws, lamps, and vases; and other decorative and small functional objects. Distribute the colors so that the room has a rhythm. (See Chapter 4 for tips on creating rhythm).

One small whisper of accent color is inaudible, but repeating it turns up the volume. Use apple green, for example, in a series of throw pillows, lamps, and other accessories.

Meeting with the style board

To craft your color scheme, collect samples of fabrics, colors, and inspiring photographs. Arrange them on a *style board,* a large sheet of white paper or poster board (see Figure 5-2). Professional designers use these to show clients how the room might look.

Figure 5-2:
Making a
style board
helps you
plan and
shop.

Collect your color and material swatches from actual samples. You have several options when obtaining samples from retailers:

✔ Some samples (laminate countertops, paint, and so on) are free. You may have to purchase others.

✔ Some retailers allow you to check out samples as long as you return them. They may request a deposit. Many retailers credit deposits to your account when you buy.

✔ Brochures, magazine pictures, or even colored slips of paper (available from art stores) work well. Having actual carpet, paint, and fabric swatches to place together to form relationships is the best option, but pictures will do in a pinch.

If you use foamcore or poster board for your style board, attach your photos, swatches, and so on so that they can be easily removed. You can then reuse your boards.

The larger the sample, the better. Big samples give you a truer idea of how a color will look when it's covering an expanse of wall, floor, or furniture.

 Evaluate your completed plan under the same lighting conditions that you'll be using in your decorated room. (For tips on lighting, see Chapter 17.) What you see will be what you get — your finished room should look as first-class as (and probably even better than) your style boards.

Choosing a stylish color scheme

Selecting a scheme can seem like a difficult test of your decorating ability. An easy way out is to choose a decorating style that comes with a particular color, distinct color palette, or strongly suggested color direction. Some examples include:

- **City Chic.** Think neutral colors — black, white, and beige — in luxurious, high quality textures. Polished chrome, steel, and woods with plenty of sheen and shine add to the glamour. Because colors are muted in this sophisticated, tailored style, texture is supreme; therefore, textiles have woven (not printed) patterns.

- **Coastal Life.** Blue and white seems so right. This Greek Islands approach adds healthy doses of summer-sky blue to a mostly pure-white background. Adding rustic wooden accents, textured textiles, and glazed and decorated pottery makes this look even warmer.

- **Country Cottage.** Ruffles and flourishes in the form of *dressmaker details* (pleats, ribbon, welting, and other trim) distinguish this feminine and pretty look. Colors run the gamut of pastels, both warm and cool. Floral patterns abound, smaller scaled and less imposing than the English Country House look that's a rich kissing cousin.

- **Country French.** Earthy textures and bright calico patterns found in the fabrics make this look enduringly popular. Colors are strong: mustard, rusty red, indigo, and grass green. Fabrics stand up well against white plaster walls. The same patterns in wall coverings make definite style statements for walls.

- **English Manor.** Floral bouquets abound in this classic Traditional style based on English country homes. The jewel-tone colors in brilliant reds, yellows, blues, greens, purples, and oranges are found in the chintz floral bouquet fabric used for draperies, upholstery, and to-the-floor tablecloths.

- ✔ **Lodge Look.** The American West version of this style gets its color direction from American Indian rugs — strong reds, blues, and earth tones. Use rugs on the floor or, in a Contemporary way, as upholstery. Western art — cowboys and Indian chiefs — also provides color direction. The East Coast Adirondack fishing-camp version uses lots of twig furniture, braided rugs, and typical Autumn-in-New England harvest colors in golds, reds, and strong but softened greens. (Don't forget the birch bark canoe!)

- ✔ **Shabby Chic.** This faded-glory style paints everything within sight white — antiqued and softened to ivory or linen white — which resonates strongly with lovers of genteel furnishings that appear to have seen better days. Your paint job doesn't have to be high quality; the more chips, nicks, and dents the better. If your scheme seems color-starved, add discreet accents.

- ✔ **Sun Country.** This Contemporary Country style brings American Country (see Chapter 9) up-to-date, using clear, light, bright, spring and summer colors. No deep pumpkins and russets here. Look to the flowers of spring and summer for a color palette. Simple linens and cottons in solid colors underscore the serenity found in this country-house style.

- ✔ **Villa Style.** Think Old World Tuscany made famous by its earthy, well-weathered gold- and rust-colored stone or plaster walls. These are earth tones with panache. Dark, rich, and rustic woods augment this solid, Mother Earth look with its wrought iron accents and beautifully woven tapestries.

Chapter 6

Applying Pattern Basics

*P*attern — the repetition of line, form, and color — adds interest to a room. Pattern can be as simple as clean, straight lines or as complex as swirling, whorling paisley prints. What's the best way to use pattern for maximal effect?

In this chapter, we guide you through the basics of pattern. Discover how to use patterns in your own home and how to masterfully mix and match them. With so many patterns available, envisioning which one is best for your decorating job isn't always easy. So, we also give you some ideas for ways to practice using patterns before you go all out and decorate a room. This chapter gives you everything you need to use patterns with confidence, so you can make child's play of pattern play!

Considering Pattern

Pattern is everywhere! Certainly you notice pattern in wallpaper and fabrics (see Figure 6-1), and even patterns created by lines in tile floors and wall paneling. Patterns are found in natural stones, such as granite with its all-over spatter effect, and marble, with veins that meander. Pattern adds its own special effects to a room by

✔ Creating instant impact

✔ Giving the eye something intriguing to view

✔ Mediating between two duller, solid, patternless surfaces, which is often described as "getting it together"

✔ Establishing a particular historic style or period or a special playful, elegant, or other mood

✔ Determining the focal point

Figure 6-1:
Wallcoverings such as this Western-inspired pattern from the Navajo Collection offer great character.

Photograph courtesy Carefree Wallcoverings

Pattern is plentiful and often inexpensive. Think of cotton gingham checks — just right for the Country look. (Of course, you can buy big, expensive *silk* gingham checks for a country villa.) Pattern is attention getting, so use it wisely.

Historic patterns

Historic patterns reappear from year to year in fresh, new *colorways* (combinations of colors). Color (see Chapter 5) and scale affect a pattern, making it more or less formal. Some historic patterns, originally seen in monochromatic colorways, look very different in multicolors. (See Chapter 9 for more on Historic styles.)

Below, we list some perennial favorite patterns. Keep in mind that many appear on materials other than textiles:

✔ **Calico.** This cotton fabric is printed with small, brightly colored floral patterns. Cheerful and modest, calico creates a cozy feeling that is a big part of Country-style decorating. This pattern also shows up in china.

✔ **Chintz.** This cotton fabric features generously scaled floral arrangements and comes in many colors. It's typically found in traditional English styles. *Glazing* (a shiny coating) gives it extra pizazz. So do the ribbon-and-flowers patterns that the French add, and broad stripes that seem so typical of English homes.

✔ **Flame stitch.** A pattern that looks like flickering flames, flame stitch is multicolored and, when woven, very textural. You often notice flame stitch with 18th-century furniture. Somewhat masculine in character, it's at home in Traditional settings but looks great as an accent in a Contemporary room.

✔ **Gingham.** This pattern consists of two color checks (blue and white, red and white, yellow and white), usually in a woven cotton fabric. It almost epitomizes humble Country styles. But, a silk gingham — especially in large over-scale checks — acquires an elegance that is at home in any villa or town house.

✔ **Herringbone.** The diagonal ridge that reverses direction periodically in this weave creates a vertical stripe effect. Some people think it looks like a fish skeleton, which is how it earned its name. Herringbone is most often seen in vinyl wall covering replications, especially in commercial interiors. It's tailored and masculine in character.

✔ **Stripes.** Stripes are, obviously, repeated vertical lines, but keep in mind that stripes come in many different varieties, including the following:

  • **Awning stripes:** Big, broad, monochromatic stripes used for awnings, found in upholstery and wall coverings

  • **Rep (or irregular) stripes:** Alternating narrow and wide stripes, often in woven silk fabrics used for upholstering Traditional-style chairs

  • **Roman stripes:** Stripes in alternating bright colors and sometimes of varying widths, found in silk and synthetic fabrics for curtains and upholstery in Traditional-style rooms

  • **Satin stripes:** Alternating matte (dull) and satin (shiny) stripes in silk and silk-like synthetic fabrics (and wall coverings), appropriate for Traditional rooms

  • **Ticking stripes:** Narrow, monochromatic stripes, most often in cotton fabrics used on pillows, but a favorite slipcover fabric for all kinds of Country-style rooms from cottage to Sun Country style

✔ **Toile du Jouy.** This line drawing of a pastoral scene in a single color appears on plain-woven cotton fabric. Designers strongly identify but do not limit toile du Jouy with French furnishings. You can use it in every room in any house.

- ✔ **Tree of Life.** An ancient Oriental rendering of a sprawling tree, you frequently see this pattern with other plants and animals. Usually large in size, you often notice the tree of life in 18th-century printed fabrics and wall coverings. It also seems very much at home in formal and dressy living rooms, dining rooms, and bedrooms.

- ✔ **Trellis.** Garden *trellises* (narrow strips of wood lath joined either in a square or diamond pattern) are the basis of patterns often repeated on fabrics, wall coverings, and area rugs — with and without accompanying flowers and vines. They add a sense of spatial depth, which provides a three-dimensional space-making effect that's very liberating. This pattern is appropriate in any style room.

Contemporary patterns

Geometrics are Contemporary patterns created from basic geometric figures, such as circles, squares, rectangles, triangles, and ovals. (See Chapter 10 for the lowdown on Contemporary styles.) Most Contemporary patterns generally leave out flowers and other recognizable figures (which are considered Historical), but some designers make references to florals by rendering them less realistic by *abstracting* and *stylizing* the design.

Historic patterns are often made Contemporary by updating the colors and scale used in the pattern. Designers call this process *tweaking* the pattern design, because it remains recognizably Traditional but acceptably fashionable. Traditional fabrics and rug patterns become more Contemporary when designs are *edited* to become less complex, more economically manufactured, and more widely available.

It's a jungle out there

The most up-to-date Contemporary patterns today are essentially fresh takes on familiar subjects. For example, animal prints come to mind — jungle creatures, beginning with leopards (on upholstery fabric, sheets, draperies, and more), lions, cheetahs, and zebras. Domestic animals are also quite the rage: cute cats and kittens, dogs (especially pugs), horses, and chickens. Roosters are synonymous with Country styles, from humble-pie Country Cottage style to lord-of-the-manor grand English Country House style, and including the enduring French Provincial style that seems second nature to decorators opting for charm.

Patterns of all sizes and shapes in strong, bold (and boldly contrasting) colors are very Contemporary or "today." See these patterns in textiles by

English designer Trisha Guild (www.DesignersGuild.com), whose textiles are widely available in the U.S. See how such patterns in strong colors work to update interiors by looking at rooms by interior designers Diamond and Barratta, whose work appears in *Architectural Digest*.

Current trends

Woven patterns are very popular, especially brocades in polished cottons and silks. Not as "busy" as printed patterns, they offer a greater sense of serenity. These sophisticated and elegant fabrics work well for large areas (sofas and draperies, for example) because they do not tire the eye.

Complex mixing and matching several patterns with seemingly wild abandon is an ever-increasing trend in upholstery, drapery fabrics, dinnerware, and interiors. Though the effect looks almost as if the complexity happened spontaneously, it is meticulously thought out. Endless potential combinations are possible. Just remember: Mixing and matching requires thoughtfully combining small- and medium-scaled patterns with one large dominant pattern — most often in the same color.

Planning for Pattern

You have tremendous leeway in decorating with pattern. Furthermore, you don't need to pay a lot of attention to the pattern's origin. That is, you don't really need to know whether it's French, English, Indian, or whatnot. Rather ask yourself these questions:

- ✔ Do I like the pattern?
- ✔ Is it the right color for my room?
- ✔ Is the pattern's texture right for my project?
- ✔ Is the pattern compatibly scaled so that it works with my other furnishings?
- ✔ Does this pattern make the statement (not too loud, not too quiet, not too busy, the right style and period, and so on) that I want?

Of course, if you're designing a period room or a movie set, or if you just like to know these tidbits, you probably want to know the pattern's history and whether it's authentic for a particular period and place. But, your home isn't a movie. You make the decisions, so design your room the way you want. However, if you want guidelines, read on.

Picking your pattern

Any pattern that captures your fancy can serve as the basis for a foolproof decorating scheme. A wonderful wallpaper, beautiful bedding, upholstery, an area rug, a plate, or giftwrap can provide inspiration.

One pattern also suggests other companion patterns. Unless you plan to use a particular pattern in a textile, for example, on every piece of upholstery in the room (and perhaps even on the walls), you may want to work in a companion pattern. Traditionally, a large floral print complements a medium-size stripe or other noncompeting geometric. (Two equally big and beautifully colored floral competitors won't make for a happy combo.) Try these other guidelines for selecting and using pattern all through the house:

✔ **Small rooms:** If your room is small to medium in size, choose a pattern with a light background. Use that light background for the largest background areas in the room (the walls and the floor). Repeat the dominant pattern hue on upholstery. Reserve the exciting accent color or colors in the pattern for accessories.

✔ **Large rooms:** In a large room, use the dominant hue in the pattern for large areas such as walls and floor. Use the background color of the pattern for upholstery. Limit exciting accent colors to accessories.

Using pattern as background

Pattern used on walls, floors, and ceilings can create a highly distinctive background for a room (see Figure 6-2). Use it to compensate for inadequate architecture (a vertical stripe raises the too-low ceiling, for example), to make up for the lack of a view (choose a mural), or to add texture to lackluster sheetrock walls (yes, pattern implies texture). The following are general guidelines for using pattern as a background:

✔ **Choose a pattern and its colorway based on the room's size.** An overwhelmingly large pattern in a neon-bright, warm color makes a small room look smaller, while an underwhelming, too-tiny pattern in a bland color makes a large room seem ho-hum. To pick the most helpful pattern (and color) for your room, keep the room's size in mind.

   • **Small rooms:** Select softly colored patterns with light backgrounds. Patterns with three-dimensional effects, such as a trellis pattern, ribbon-and-floral stripes, or toile de Jouy (a scenic pattern), make the room seem larger.

- **Medium rooms:** Pick stronger colored patterns in mid-sized rooms, but stick to light backgrounds to make the room seem larger rather than smaller.

- **Large rooms:** In larger rooms, you can be bold. Choose strong, dramatic patterns with rich, exciting background colors.

✔ **Choose a pattern based on the house's overall style for compatibility.** Don't create a split personality for your house by choosing Traditional patterns for a Contemporary house. Do keep in mind your home's basic architectural orientation and your region of the country.

- **Contemporary rooms:** Stick to geometric patterns in neutral or no colors. Stripes are good. Avoid Traditional (realistic) floral patterns; go for abstract ones instead.

- **Traditional rooms:** For real compatibility, look to Traditional patterns — those based on historic examples called *documents.* They're easy to find and usually created in current colors. And if you really need authentic reproductions of wallpapers and fabrics from a certain period, you can probably find them. Wall-covering retailers, manufacturers, and interior designers are good sources of information. For shock value or Contemporary eclecticism, choose a Contemporary geometric.

✔ **Scale the pattern size to the room size.** Use small patterns in small rooms, medium-sized patterns in medium rooms, and large-scale patterns in large rooms. This rule is a general guideline. However, if you want to use a gigantic floral (perhaps a sunflower) in a small room, (say a laundry or a powder room), go ahead. Whimsy is great fun!

Figure 6-2:
Wallcoverings create great backgrounds in any room and can be the basis for color schemes and themes.

Photograph courtesy Blonder Wallcoverings

Giving upholstery center stage

Pattern steals the show. No one will ever notice how plain-Jane your room's architecture is when you've got a showy display going on. Even if you do live in an architectural gem, showcase a sofa by covering it in show-off fabric. A glazed chintz, a tremendous tree-of-life crewel pattern, and a woven wool buffalo plaid are eye-catching and make very bold statements that exude confidence, encouraging guests to feel at home. When your upholstery is the star, keep backgrounds (walls, floors, and ceilings) relatively plain and non-competing.

Putting one pattern everywhere

Placing the same pattern on the walls and furniture eliminates the problems of color matching and pattern scaling! It's also an ideal solution for rooms with too many lines — attics come to mind. In this instance, consider a small, all-over pattern like calico, which doesn't require intricate matching (and a lot of waste). Using a calico with a light background makes a small attic seem larger and more open, while an all-over small-scale floral motif adds coziness.

The larger the room, the larger the pattern can be, as long as it's not over-whelming. Wall covering and fabric patterns designed to match or coordinate make for an easy, efficient way to create a perfectly coordinated room, because you can cover seating (and a bed, if in an attic bedroom) in the same fabric.

Classic fabric pattern mixes for living rooms

Why reinvent the pattern-mix wheel, when others have done such an excellent job? Exactly! The following are some classic fabric mixes:

✔ **American Country.** Large country quilt pattern (sofa), medium-scale folk-art floral print (lounge chairs), woven checkerboard checks (accent chairs), and medium stripes (window blinds)

✔ **American Southwest.** Navajo-blanket print (sofa), medium scale (1- or 2-inch) woven check (lounge chairs), and woven narrow stripes (draperies)

✔ **English Country.** Large-scale glazed chintz (sofa and draperies), narrow (½-inch) stripes (slipcovered lounge chairs), and small calico or mini-printed pattern (accent chairs, pillows)

✔ **Traditional 18th Century.** Large-scale floral chintz (sofa), crewel-work tree of life (wing chair), woven trellis pattern (lounge chairs), small all-over floral tapestry (accent chairs), and medium satin stripes (draperies)

You can even cover a small room in the same pattern from head to toe. One of the most delightful rooms we have ever seen had the same strawberry pattern on the walls and furniture. The clever homeowner even had the pattern enlarged and made into a needlepoint rug, which covered the room.

Spreading pattern around

You can use a traditional strategy and combine a plain background on the walls and floor with patterned furniture. Then spread coordinating patterns around the room on the draperies, decorative pillows, Oriental lamps, or an area rug. This technique commonly combines several patterns in one room, which usually calls for clever mixing and matching of fabrics so that they relate (for unity) and contrast (for interest).

Mixing patterns with confidence

After you get the hang of it, mixing patterns is fun. The following are some general guidelines that remove some of the guesswork from successfully mixing patterns. Use this list as a jumping-off point, and experiment fearlessly.

Some of the classic fabric mixes — like the French use of big cotton checks on the backsides of solid velvet-covered chairs — probably happened because the upholsterer ran out of velvet or the client was too stingy to put velvet on the back. Consider these tips when mixing patterns:

- ✔ **Create magic with a simple color scheme.** White plus a color is easy: Cobalt blue and white, rose pink and white, or apple green and white. Or go for real drama — choose black and white! With your one-color scheme, you can either stick to one scale or vary scales of motifs.

- ✔ **Limit the number of patterns in a room, if you're a novice.** Curb the number of patterns in a given room to three, until you're more familiar with using and mixing patterns. (Figure 6-3 illustrates an example of a three-pattern scheme and a five-pattern scheme.)

- ✔ **Play the trim game.** Gain additional unity by using the same trim for your pattern mix. For example, if you're making toss pillows in four different patterns, use the same moss fringe on each.

    Or for both variety and unity, make your own *welting* (a covered cord trim) for pillows or upholstery by covering a rope-like cord (available in fabric and upholstery shops) in one fabric and using it as trim for the companion fabric, and vice versa.

✔ **Practice your scales.** Whether you're using three or five patterns, choose one large dominant pattern for the largest area. Accompany the dominant pattern with medium- and small-scale secondary patterns.

✔ **Think positively — or negatively.** A *positive* printed fabric places dark motifs (such as flowers or geometrics) on a white or light background. A *negative* printed fabric (like a film negative) places light floral or geometric motifs on a dark background. Using the positive and negative prints in the same or adjoining rooms is a quick and easy way to decorate.

✔ **Up the ante.** If you're using five patterns, start with a large-scale dominant pattern — perhaps a big floral bouquet. Choose two medium-scale patterns (one floral, one geometric) in the same colors as the dominant fabric. Finally, choose two small-scale accent patterns (each in a different pattern or accent color).

Figure 6-3: To combine several patterns in one room, consider a three-pattern or five-pattern scheme.

Practicing Makes Perfect

When you're mixing and matching patterns, let your eye be the final judge. Don't be afraid to try out combinations that you think may be over the top. The following sections provide some tried-and-true methods for experimenting without penalty.

Making sample boards

Creating sample or swatch boards lets you experiment to your heart's content. An 8½-x-11-inch sheet of bond paper or white cardboard works well. Clip a bunch of 3-x-5-inch samples of wall coverings and fabrics. Add photographs of area rugs, patterned synthetic flooring, or decorative ceramic tiles — all patterned materials you're considering using. Move samples, swatches, and photographs around until you find the mix of three to five patterns that pleases you most. Paste or tape those samples onto your sample board. (Let the sizes of your swatches represent their roles in your room; for example, large-scale patterns get larger swatches.)

Studying magazine pictures

Magazines are chock-full of photographs that are invaluable when you're decorating. Patterns occur on many areas in the same room, providing great opportunities to study "the mix" (the number, size, and scale of the patterns, and the use of similar or contrasting backgrounds). Check out our favorite magazines — *Architectural Digest, House & Garden, Veranda,* and *Traditional Homes* — which show wonderfully diverse styles and periods.

When you're looking at a picture you especially like, take note of what captures your fancy. Observe where patterns are used (on the wall, the floor, or the furniture, for example). Notice how they're used — as a quiet or dramatic background, a bold attention-getter, or a gentle accent. Clip these sources of inspiration; perhaps start a scrapbook.

Scanning wallcovering sample books

Wallcovering pattern books have room settings that illustrate the art of mixing and matching many patterns. Study these illustrations, and look especially at those rooms that concern you most, such as the living room, dining room, bedroom, kitchen, and entry hall. Notice especially

- ✔ The variety of ways in which several wallpaper patterns are *mixed and matched* in different living rooms of different styles and periods
- ✔ The ways in which different designers *distribute* pattern differently, even in Traditional rooms
- ✔ How designers *combine* patterned art, area rugs, and numerous accessories in rooms with as many as five different wall covering patterns, including busy borders

Room settings in wallcovering sample books (especially by our favorites, including Brunschwig & Fils, Brewster, Scalamandre, Schumacher, and Waverly) are great lessons in ways to decorate with pattern. And the patterns you see in the books are immediately available, too, which saves you shopping time. After you look through a few wallcovering books, you can't help but have some good ideas on how to furnish your rooms with pattern.

Chapter 7

Feeling Your Way Through Textures

*W*hat would the legendary glamorous Hollywood bedroom be without lustrous satin bedding, or the city-slick New York living room be without a shining mirror, polished marble, and glinting steel? Can you imagine a mountain cabin without raw-wood log walls and a rough fieldstone fireplace?

All too often, people take texture for granted, enjoying its contributions without giving it much credit. Although texture often plays second fiddle to the more obvious color, texture — and especially textural contrast — is another of decorating's magic wands, ready for the waving.

In this chapter, we show you how to use texture on your walls, floors, ceilings, and furniture. We also provide some general decorating tips for using texture to add both visual and tactile appeal throughout your home.

Getting to Know Texture

Texture, the very visible characteristic physical structure of a material, appeals strongly to the senses of sight and touch. Figure 7-1 illustrates two very different textural effects — one in a living room and the other in a bedroom. The roughness of the heavy-looking stone fireplace in the living room contrasts sharply with the smooth and shiny, light and lively satin sheets and tieback curtains in the bedroom.

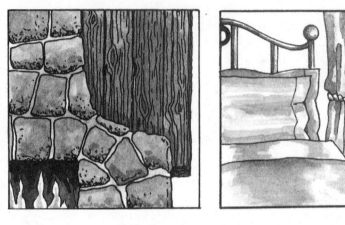

Figure 7-1:
Different
textures
create
contrasting
visual and
tactile
effects.

As you decorate, plan to take full advantage of texture. Make sure that your room has enough contrast between smooth and rough, hard and soft, shiny and dull surfaces to provide visual and tactile interest.

Texture has feelings, too

First, people see texture, and then they touch it. People talk about texture in both *visual* and *tactile* terms — how a material looks and feels. For example, a surface is smooth, rough, prickly, rugged, and so on. Handling textile fabrics gives rise to the notion of its *hand.* For example, people talk about velvet's soft hand, silk's smooth hand, and linen's rough, almost scratchy hand.

Paint textures or finishes have names, such as *satin, matte,* and *eggshell,* which describe how the paint feels to the touch and how it reflects light (called *sheen*).

Sheen, whether it's in a shiny satin fabric or paint finish, implies lightness. A satin paint finish seems lighter in weight and more ethereal than a matte finish, which seems heavier and earthier. Generally, matte finishes relate to casual, rustic interiors and satin finishes to finer, dressier rooms.

Throwing its weight around

Texture contributes to the perception of an object's physical weight — which affects where and when it's used. For example, a polished marble tile floor with its lean-and-light look is at home in an elegant room. That same marble tile, tumbled for a more rustic, heavier look, works well in a Country-style setting. The same principle applies to upholstery fabrics. For example, corduroy seems heavy and bulky, partly because it reflects less light than a silk fabric, which seems lighter, finer, and richer. Traditionally, corduroy is a natural choice for a robust family room couch, and silk is ideal for a fine, formal living room sofa.

Texture is also important on the floor, a major part of any interior. By comparison, a shaggy rug looks duller and heavier than a velvet carpet, needlepoint rug, or marble tile floor and is more stylistically appropriate for a casual room. For more about flooring, head on over to Chapter 14.

Making Magic with Texture

Texture plays several roles — supporting background, dramatic accent, or strong star. Consider the ideas here for making the most of texture. Always give texture a clear role to play in your decoration, and it will add a sense of vitality.

Planning the background

Walls, floors, and ceilings are your rooms' background. Some people give more thought to the color of these surfaces than the texture. Think of them as equally important. Color can create spatial illusions, but the tactile sense adds another, unique dimension to style.

Traditionally, texture is distributed in the following way:

- ✔ Use a fine texture on the ceiling (so that it never seems heavy or as though it's falling).
- ✔ Use a medium texture on walls (so that they seem supportive).
- ✔ Use a heavier-looking (hard, smooth, and even) texture on the floor (so that it appears sturdy and people can walk on it).

Applying texture in this way establishes a great background for sensuously soft upholstery and hand-waxed, almost matte-finished wood furniture. But you can also get creative with texture — maybe you'll like furry ceilings, for example.

Table 7-1 provides examples of textures that are often used together on walls, floors, and upholstery in a given room.

Table 7-1: Typically Paired Living Room Textures

Wall	Floor	Upholstery
Period wood paneling	Marble, parquet	Silk, velvet, tapestry
Pine planks	Plank, tumbled stone	Woven cottons
Wallpaper	Parquet, woven rugs	Brocade, linen
Paint	Low-pile carpet	Velveteen, cottons
Faux paint	Marble, wood, carpet	Chintz, silk, cotton
Stone, brick	Plank, deep-pile carpet	Woven wools, cottons

Lining the walls with texture

Certain textures and styles traditionally go together. You may pair:

✔ Antique brick with a Traditional family room or a city loft

✔ Barnboard siding with a Country family room

✔ Decorative ceramic tile with a French kitchen

✔ Grasscloth with a tropical room

✔ Stucco with any room in a Southwestern or Tuscan style

✔ Knotty pine boards with an Early American or Country-style interior

✔ Mirror and other glass with a penthouse

✔ Shirred cotton fabric with a room with ethnic origins

Newer pairings often involve faux paint finishes that add texture and character to walls. Ralph Lauren paint and other paint brands make it easy to create fascinating textures with the right paints, brushes, and techniques. How-to brochures show you how to give your walls the look of suede, denim, linen, and more. They explain how to rag, roll, sponge, and drip your walls to new-found beauty. Check out your home improvement store for free seminars.

Textured painted walls can be boldly colored. Bolder colors — such as sunflower yellow, chartreuse, purple, and any hue of red — are the rule, even for older, Traditional-style homes. New colors are deep, *hey-look-at-me* tones of lemon yellow, Bristol blue, fuchsia, and hibiscus pink. (Forget about the old prim and proper greyed-down pastels!) And, the trend is anything but monochromatic. Call this the *Polychrome Age* — and follow the lead of the avant-garde in mixing and matching textured bright colors such as Monet's famous French Provincial yellow and blue, pimento red and Tuscan gold, and more, with as much glee as designers use to mix and match patterned fabrics.

In Traditional interiors, textural contrasts are controlled — that is, not too strong or bold. Elements may surprise and delight, but they should never seem in violent opposition.

Some Contemporary styles call for using textured backgrounds daringly, in a surprising mix of strong, sometimes even warring, opposites. This technique requires a very good eye for dramatic couplings that seem contradictory but work because of at least one common element such as color.

For example, consider covering walls with barnboard siding in a formal, eclectic dining room. With the grayed-to-silver barnboard, hang an elaborate crystal and silver (not gold) chandelier that's entirely at odds with the barnboard's informality. Then restate the case for elegance from the chandelier by choosing chairs upholstered in gray silk and trimmed with silver nailheads. Pit the chairs against a glass-and-chrome dining table. Tie it all together with a soft, luxuriously thick, gray, velvet-like wool rug, which relates in color to the barnboard and other furnishings, but offers textural contrast to all other elements.

Dare to use texture in a Contemporary way. Tip the balance one way (informal) or another (formal). Don't use equal amounts of opposites, or you end up with a room that seems confused and static.

Laying texture on the floors

Floors are for walking on, so no matter how rustic they look, they must have flat, smooth surfaces. This still leaves room for plenty of textural interest. Consider the differences between rough quarry tile, glazed ceramic tile, brick, wood, wool carpeting, resilient flooring, and wood flooring. Each material has a distinctive texture that traditionally works well with one or more wall textures. For example,

- ✔ Brick contrasts richly with wood paneling and wallpaper and adds a slightly rustic, vintage note.

- ✔ Ceramic tile contrasts nicely with many wall coverings, such as paneled and faux-painted walls, and can look dressy or relaxed, Historic or Contemporary.

- ✔ Quarry tile works well with a variety of wall textures, including barnboard, linen-textured wallpaper, and fine or lightly textured paint in a casual room.

- ✔ Resilient flooring pairs nicely with wall coverings, paneling, plaster, and painted wall finishes and, depending on its pattern, is at home in a variety of room styles and periods.

✔ Wood flooring offers mild contrast, so it relates well to all wall materials and is appropriate for all decorating styles — whether the pattern is dressy or casual.

✔ Wool carpeting with a cut pile provides a contrast to wall coverings, wood paneling, and plaster walls, and wool carpeting generally looks urbane, whether the room style is Traditional or Contemporary.

Adding textures to ceilings

Country-style rooms, like the one in Figure 7-2, often have interesting textured ceilings (with wooden beams that contrast texturally) that need no other decoration. Ceiling textures in Traditional and most Contemporary style interiors are generally smooth, which makes them ideally suited to any number of decorative treatments, ranging from an interesting paint color and texture (achieved by combing, swirling, or adding sand) to *anaglypta* (molded plaster carvings), murals, wall covering, and tenting with a variety of suitable fabrics.

Figure 7-2:
A ceiling places visual and tactile textural interest overhead by the use of contrasting materials.

Using texture in furniture

In Traditional and Contemporary homes, mixing upholstery textures adds interest and drama. Traditional schemes call for textures that are subtly different. Choose some sturdy fabric with the boldest, wooliest, and shiniest texture — woven wool, velvet, quilted cotton or linen, or leather — for the sofa, which is usually the largest upholstered piece. Accent and lounge chair fabrics should be a little finer and lighter in weight. Diversity livens up the mix.

Contemporary mixes tend to be more extreme, pitting opposites against each other. What all these textures have in common is color or mood. Pair a sofa in matte velvet with sleek lounge chairs in lacquered leather in the same scarlet red, for example. Or, cover the sofa in red and the chairs in white, but use the same type of city-slick upholstery.

Contemporary interiors might stick to one texture . . . in a variety of materials. Think that's not textural interest? Wrong! Consider an ultra-modern kitchen with satin-smooth maple cabinets; a polished stainless steel hood, appliances, and fixtures; a polished marble floor and countertops; and glass chairs and table. Very slick. Ultra cool.

Furniture frames count, too! Many pieces of upholstered furniture have exposed frames made of wood or metal. Count them, along with upholstery fabric, into your texture mix.

Other materials, such as woven wire, aluminum, wrought iron, and wicker (see Figure 7-3), are very textured. Woven wicker furniture is even more texturally interesting when bamboo is mixed with sea grasses and other unique textures, or when one of these materials is woven in a distinctive chevron, cable knit (like the sweater), big basket check, or trellis pattern.

Figure 7-3:
Wicker furniture adds complex textural interest that makes it a natural star.

Applying texture as an accent

One of the quickest ways to spice up a ho-hum room, where just about every item has the same safe texture (not too rough, not too shiny, not too smooth, or not too *anything*), is to bring in accessories that beg to be touched and handled.

Hand-thrown pottery, straw baskets, dried plants, palette knife paintings, wooden carvings, quilts, macramé hangings, pillows and throws — any of these accessories do a great job of adding texture to your home.

Use texture with respect. A little may go a long way, so proceed with caution. Don't overdo it. When in doubt, add one major highly textured accessory at a time until your eye tells you that you have enough.

Making texture the star

Try using one strongly textured decorative item as a *focal point* or an accent for an *architectural focal area*. A very large antique ceramic urn, its rough clay surface highlighted by an aged finish, amidst polished urbane furnishings serves as a focal point, for example. A mantel — an architectural focal point — is often highlighted by a highly textured decorative item such as sparkling crystal vases.

Think in terms of opposites: smooth versus rough, bumpy versus prickly, hard versus soft, an undulating line versus a straight line, or multidepthed versus a plane. Use this technique in a Contemporary room where people expect to see surprising juxtapositions and daring extremes.

Country-style rooms also welcome exaggerated textural focal points, such as quilts or woven wall hangings with stones, features, and interesting bits and pieces of wood incorporated. Baskets also provide textural interest.

Historically, Traditional rooms can handle strong but not too strong texture. Tapestries, embroidered wall hangings, and sculpture are some examples that work well. You can update such rooms with exciting colors and stronger textures for a look that's more *today*. First you learn the rules, then you learn how to break them — aesthetically!

Working with texture

You want texture to work with, not against, your decorating plans. So consider some of the following tips for using texture in your house:

- ✔ Texture is all about contrasts. Remember, more contrast means less unity. And with less unity, the space seems smaller. So, keep contrasts subtle in small spaces, but go bolder in larger spaces.

- ✔ Window shades and blinds in natural wood and metal are relatively high-contrast textures. In small rooms, reduce contrast by visually blending window treatments with walls with the same color.

- ✔ Shag rugs with furry textures seem bulky, even in light colors. Use them to make big rooms seem smaller. Avoid shags in small rooms.

- ✔ Sleek textures seem streamlined, lightweight, and Contemporary — they appear to take up very little space. That's what makes them ideal for small spaces. Rooms with backgrounds in these textures may need help from more heavily textured furniture and accessories that add depth, warmth, and comfort.

- ✔ A great method for selecting textures is to create a *swatch board.* On a large piece of white cardboard, paste samples of fabrics, wood finishes, mica surfacing, wall coverings, and any other materials you like. Pasting them on the board helps you see how these textures relate. If you don't like what you see, keep experimenting until you find the combination that makes you happy.

- ✔ Some textures reflect all light, creating luminous, ethereal moods. Other, rougher textures capture and hold some of the light, creating shadows that add a sense of mystery. Contemporary interiors celebrate light; Traditional interiors embody great light-shadow play, which is an effect that occurs between textures that absorb light and those that reflect light.

Texture is key to style. Be as subtle or bold as you want, just don't forget that this powerful tool is part of your decorating bag of tricks — ready, when you are, to rev up excitement and add more interest to that too-quiet room.

Chapter 8

Troubleshooting Basics

nyone can walk into a room and say, "I don't like this room." To fix a problem-laden room, you need to step back and figure out what went wrong. A little distance can help you find the solution to make that problem go away.

In this chapter, you find all the tools you need to rescue your room gone wrong, or one that's merely languishing in the decorating doldrums. We take you step-by-step through the process of figuring out what's wrong. You also discover how to solve its problems by applying a few simple rules and guidelines. Finally, we provide three case studies — real-life examples of decorating problems and solutions.

Asking "What's My Room's Problem?"

When you walk into a room and you don't love it, follow these two easy steps:

1. **Zero in on the problem.** Ask yourself three main questions:

   • Do I like the color of the room? *(Blue gives me chills.)*

   • Do I like the room's lines (or patterns)? Does the room have too many lines (making it seem too busy)? Too few (making it seem boring)?

   • Do I like the room's combination of textures? Are there too many? Too few? Are they incompatible or just tasteless? *(That too-rough stone makes me think I'm in a dark, dank cave.)*

After you answer these questions, take the second step.

2. **Seek solutions.** Take a close-up look at the area (color, line, or texture) where the problem seems to be. Come up with some decorating ideas to improve this facet of your room's design.

Keep in mind some very basic decorating guidelines. You don't need to consult an encyclopedia of interior decorating; just check out Chapter 4 for planning basics, Chapter 5 for color ideas, Chapter 6 for pattern information, and Chapter 7 for tips on texture.

Apply these guidelines one-by-one — like an automobile mechanic using a checklist. If you check the list and find that one item is okay, just keep going to the next item, until you find the problem.

Zeroing In on a Sound Solution

After you've spotted the problem and generated some possible decorating improvements, you're ready to take decorating action by following these easy steps:

1. **Choose a solution.** To find a solution to an unsatisfactory color scheme, narrow your problem down. Then apply some simple color rules to solve your problem (see Chapter 5). Ask yourself the following questions:

   • Is the room too warm, making you feel overstimulated and unable to relax? If so, apply the "cool colors are calming" rule by adding cool-color accents of blues and greens.

   • Is the room so cool that you feel depressed? Apply the "warm colors are stimulating" rule. Cheer up the cold room with accents from the warm side of the color wheel, such as oranges and yellows.

   • Is the color bland and boring? Spice it up with complementary colors (colors from the opposite side of the color wheel, such as orange and blue, or green and red).

2. **Apply the rule.** Work in steps, gauging your response as you work.

   For example, what if your walls are too red and make you feel hot and jumpy? To simmer it down a bit, cool the room by degrees:

   • Switch to a cool-colored, neutral upholstery. Beige, taupe, white, and any dampened-down blue or green should do the trick.

   • Add a neutral rug. Soft earth tones, for example, look natural underfoot.

- Hang cool-colored art with white mats for more relief. A leafy land-scape or an atmospheric seascape, for example, brings a breath of fresh air into any room. Any too-hot floral can be matted in crisp white or other cool colors for a breezier feel.

Your eye and body can tell you when you've cooled your room down to your comfort level. You'll feel more serene (your pulse rate, blood pressure, and body temperature will drop!) in a room that's balanced.

Considering Case Studies

Sometimes the best way to solve your own decorating problems is by looking at real-life examples. The following sections let you do just that.

C is for color

A longtime client's new Contemporary-style home was impressive. The rooms had gracious lines and a mesmerizing view of the bay. White walls and smooth wooden floors added to the home's Contemporary, art-gallery mood that meant to be sophisticated and view-oriented. So, what was wrong?

Could the problem be the color — or the lack of it? Ah, yes. All white was too white and competed with the wonderful atmospheric blue of the sea and sky. The room needed a color. But what color? Fortunately, you always have a color cue (and clue!). By looking around, we found ours in the sea and sky. The obvious solution for walls and ceiling was an atmospheric blue — not too light, not too dark, slightly grayed, and just right. The result: a modern masterpiece.

L is for line

We were called in to rescue a party room in a Florida condominium. (It could have been anyone's living room.) The white walls and ceiling should have made it light and airy, right? Wrong! It was a dark, ugly cave crowded with yellowing rattan furniture that created so many crisscrossing lines that we felt dizzy. The sofas and chairs were boring. Lamps were too dressy. Our first reaction: Run! Instead of making a mad dash, we took a deep breath.

The main problem was line — too much of it. Other problems included bad color, poor furniture arrangement, and dingy upholstery and finishes.

First, we laid out the furniture in a more functional and attractive way. Tables and dining chairs were moved toward the windows to take advantage of pool and garden views. Two new, comfortable loveseats and recovered lounge chairs were placed near the bar and TV. Changing the floor plan changed the way the lines of the furnishings worked together (see Chapter 3).

Next, we applied color to visually alter the space. The color cue came from a fairly new blue-green rug. Walls were painted a matching shade of blue-green, and the acoustical tile ceiling was painted the same shade to blend with the walls. Blending the floor, walls, and ceiling with a cool color made them visually recede and created an instant tropical mood.

Painting almost all the trim — ceiling molding, doors, and window frames — a crisp stark white added contrast and uplifting mood. The baseboard molding, however, was kept the same blue-green as the wall, to blend wall and floor. (A white baseboard would have broken the flow.) We added crisp white, slim-line window blinds in a country wood texture in order to dress up windows and control sunlight.

To add glam and glitz (and make the room seem more spacious), the wall in the dance floor area was mirrored. Freestanding support columns — big visual barricades — were mirrored to make them magically vanish. (Mirrors are among magicians' and decorators' best tricks!)

To tone down the dizzy lines of the dingy rattan furniture, it was painted the same blue-green color as the walls. Lounge chairs were recovered in a vibrant red and green tropical bark cloth fabric that coordinated with two striped loveseats. The finishing accents were two paintings and a big bouquet of silk tropical flowers. The result: A tranquil tropical paradise.

T is for texture

Texture is like the Broadway understudy — present, prepared, seldom needed, but occasionally called on to play a starring role. A longtime friend and client's Boca Raton home was a study in what is referred to by locals as "Boca beige." Joan, an artist, had worked hard to furnish her home. She gave serious thought to the selection of every item. She should have been happy with the results, but when she entered her home, her heart didn't beat faster. What was missing? Joan took a truly critical look at her living room — just as though it were a canvas. Using our suggestions, she examined the room's color, line, and texture.

As Joan studied her room, she was happy with the colors and lines. But she realized, to her amazement, that all surfaces were equally smooth and matte.

The Oriental rug, painted walls, velvet and soft brocade fabrics, and even the painted ceramic accessories were all smooth — too smooth! The room had no textural contrast.

Introducing a variety of textures was as easy as bringing in accessories: a small collection of shiny brass candlesticks for the mantel, baskets beautifully woven in a variety of smooth and rough grasses to hold magazines and mail, a clutch of small mirrors in a variety of carved and gilded frames to hang over a small chest, and a bouquet of flowers made of sparkling crystal in a richly carved wooden vase. The result: A sophisticated Contemporary environment.

Adding texture is a remedy you can easily and inexpensively apply and one that brings its very own, very special decorating pleasure.

Part III
Style and Substance

The 5th Wave   By Rich Tennant

"Well, it _does_ make the room look larger."

In this part . . .

*E*ven professional designers admit that it's often easier to design for others than for themselves. "To thine own self be true" is not so easy. One day your favorite color is green; the next, it's red. Or, one moment Contemporary furniture seems the style of choice; the next, your best friend's Cottage style is the only look that will satisfy. Fickle? Confused? Unsure? In these chapters, we guide you through the process of self-discovery, so that the room you end up with is the one *you* wanted all along!

Chapter 9

Living with Historic Decorating Styles

· ·

· ·

Many Historic *styles* (named for people) and *periods* (named for eras) remain popular. Furniture from most styles and periods, updated for today's requirements, works equally well in authentically recreated historic environments, paired with other updated fabrics and accessories, and as an accent piece with Contemporary furnishings.

In this chapter, we review Historic styles. We show you how you can use these styles traditionally in your own home, as well as how you can use them to create your own personal look.

Considering Lasting Styles

A whole world of Historic style is available for you to discover and enjoy — and maybe even use in your own home. Mixing compatible Historic styles — from Classic to Modern — permits you to develop a unique personal style and still adhere to what historians and teachers consider good design principles.

You may love the look of super-sleek Contemporary accented by a few clean-lined Neoclassical Louis XVI pieces. Go right ahead; both styles emphasize pure line. Or you may adore the *inherited-over-generations* look typified by English Country. For this look, feel free to mix a range of fine wood pieces from different periods — just don't forget the important accessories like instant ancestor portraits, appropriate fabrics, and great colors that pull the whole look together.

Historic styles continue to influence everyone, including architects, interior decorators, and homeowners. Most homes feature one or several historic influences. By playing up the architecture's design with the right historic-style furnishings, you can create a dramatic and consistent mood. Ignoring the architecture and doing something eclectic (or mixed) demands a more knowing eye — one that this book helps you to develop and use.

For firsthand experience of the styles of bygone eras, conduct research that entertains as well as educates you. Go to grand museums and stately mansions. Don't pass up a chance to visit houses open to the public. And look at books on these subjects.

Understanding Historic style helps you develop a real appreciation for good, better, and best in design. Some call that *taste*. This awareness may help you avoid decorating blunders because no one can simply mix and match everything successfully. Why not? Because the message of designs is different. Some furniture, for example, looks more serious, and some looks more fun. But by knowing which style is which (and what its message is), you can develop your own judgment about what is good, what you like, and ultimately, your own personal style. Discernment — the ability to tell good from better from best (forget right and wrong) — is fundamental to developing personal style.

Using Historic Styles in Your Home

You can select furniture using at least two easy approaches. One approach involves choosing a style and sticking with it throughout the house. This results in a great sense of continuity and harmony. The second approach involves using one style in the public rooms and at least one other style in the private rooms. This approach is a little trickier to pull off successfully because you have to balance elements, such as line, color, and texture, in the quest for harmony.

Transition from public to private areas by using distinct styles best suited for each purpose and your individual style. Select more formal, dressy styles for main public areas, and more casual and relaxed styles for private rooms. You may choose, for example, 18th Century Traditional (a mix of English, French, and American furniture) in the living and dining rooms. You may even carry this style into the master bedroom. Or you may switch over to Louis XV (French Provincial) in the master bedroom.

A natural for a young girl's bedroom is a painted French Provincial or American Country style. For a young boy, Arts and Crafts (Mission) and Southwestern (a ranch house style) work well. (We discuss all these styles later in the chapter.) Variety offers something for everyone by meeting everyone's need to express personal style (see Figure 9-1).

Photograph courtesy Blonder Wallcoverings

Figure 9-1: Murals, like this one from the *Coming to America* collection, can introduce a sense of history to any room.

Nothing is wrong (and plenty is right) with using one style throughout your house. If you like the idea of choosing one style as your very own, but you're not sure which is right for you, we suggest that you take a good look at the furniture styles that interest you. Check your impression against our descriptions of the design philosophy. (For example, is the style too fine, too rustic, too formal, or too friendly?) Keep narrowing down your selection until you find the one style that fills your decorating bill. Even then, you may introduce variety in a number of ways. For example, if you were to choose Louis XV furniture, you may use gilded furniture frames in the living room, painted woods in the bedroom, and fruitwoods in the den, family room, and dining room.

Understanding Styles of the Past

When you hear the phrases *Neo-Renaissance* or *Post Modern,* do you have any idea what they mean? When you hear *Louis Quinze* (Louis XV is pronounced *louey canz*), do you think that people are talking about the latest recycling plan? If you're in a quandary about which style is which, read on.

The phrase *Old World* probably makes you think of permanence and elegance. Old World influences (rounded archways, richly textured rustic wall surfaces, and Spanish tile roofs, for example) add a sense of splendor to Contemporary homes. *Old World* refers to an amalgam of European styles — Gothic, Renaissance, and Mediterranean. A trendy look, Old World is just one current example of hybrid Historic styles.

Gothic design (12th to 16th centuries) is characterized by the pointed arch and vault, a technical development that made taller ceilings and larger windows possible. The great hall also emerged during this time. Designers continue to adapt Gothic design today. Gothic designs from England, France, Germany, Italy, and Spain vary. Spanish design, with its elaborate decoration inspired by myth, allegory, and religious themes, was heavily influenced by Islamic art. Gothic-inspired furniture and accessories (including stained glass windows) are available for every room in your house.

Italy

Designers through the ages have returned to the Renaissance's greatness. Today's interpretations are updated, streamlined versions of elaborate Renaissance design: Chairs have wider seats, sizes are scaled to homes and not palaces, and there's less fussiness.

The 15th Century Early Renaissance *(Quattrocento)* was a transitional period between Gothic and Classical. Medieval austerity meant homes were minimally furnished. Today we see some mixed use of Gothic and Renaissance elements in both architecture and furniture.

The 16th Century High Renaissance *(Cinquecento)* was the high point of the Renaissance. Classical order based on Greek and Roman ideals dominated design. The great architect Palladio (1508–1580) reinterpreted Classicism for this new era. (He's famous for the Palladian window, a central window flanked by two shorter ones and topped by a sunburst.) Furniture became more specialized and detailed. Storage cabinets, for example, were designed to hold personal and valuable objects. Walls featured painted scenery and lifelike *trompe l'oeil* (fool-the-eye) paintings, which are very popular now.

Current-day versions alter proportions and color schemes, or simplify the heavy carving or detailed painting. Architectural elements — classic Palladian windows or embellished columns — may inspire you to add Renaissance touches.

To get that Renaissance look, wrap your walls in deep reds, hang plenty of tapestries, pile on gold and other metal accessories, and add stained glass and jewel-covered ornaments. Renaissance touches are suited to Contemporary houses that feature Palladian windows. (Check out Versace's Home Collection for a few pointers.)

France (17th and 18th centuries)

All French styles convey the love of romance, order, and *joie de vivre* (life's happiness). The French adapted Italian styles by lightening and brightening dark colors and making furniture designs more delicate, formal, and feminine. (The French were the first to think of women's special needs.) The key French periods include:

- **Louis XIV:** Under the Sun King (1638–1715), large-scale furniture, excessive ornamentation, and strong color contrast reigned. This style is revived from time to time.

- **Regency:** An economy in architecture and decoration characterized the Regency style, a transitional style that lasted from 1700 until 1730. France's version of Baroque was elaborately decorative but still based on classically ordered character. Graceful scrolls and curves display the restraints and classical discipline of characteristic Rococo design.

- **Louis XV:** This style (1710–1774) was feminine, sentimental, and delicate. Smaller rooms and smaller furniture ruled right along with delicate color schemes, curved forms, and Oriental influence. Louis XV chairs have never left fashion.

- **Louis XVI (Neoclassic):** Greek and Roman design was rediscovered and reinterpreted. From 1760 to 1789, Louis XVI's clean lines and balanced decoration dominated. Naturalism, simplicity in decorative forms, straight lines, compass curves, classical order, and Pompeii, Greek, and Adam influence was keenly felt. (For more about the Adam influence, see "England" later in this chapter.) For people who love French period furniture, many of the original cabinet-making companies continue to produce original designs precisely as they were made during their heyday. The Louis XVI chair is everywhere.

- **Empire:** Seen from 1804 until 1820, Napoleon commissioned this style to reflect the masculine military symbols of his victories, including Egyptian motifs and Roman allegorical influences. Color schemes tended toward pale neutral tints for walls, floors, and ceilings, and pretty pastels for fabrics. Napoleon's wife, Josephine, influenced color sensibility with her muted blues, grayed purples, soft browns, and fleshy tones. The curved, saber chair leg and Campaign furniture (folding beds, chairs, and chests designed for easy moving about the countryside) remain popular.

French style is always elegant, refined, feminine, and a bit more formal than many other styles. Add flair by bringing in a bit of the glorious touches of French period style. Look for hand-painted tables, commodes, or other accent pieces to lend instant grace and delicate charm. If you have a creative bent, try your hand at fooling the eye with paint on furniture or walls.

England

During Tudor and Elizabethan times, when the Renaissance trend finally hit England (it was out of style in Italy), people didn't get it — at first. Inigo Jones, who brought Palladian architecture back with him from Italy during the1600s, and Sir Christopher Wren, the leading influence in the arts (leaving some to speak of England's *Wrennaissance*), had great impact on architecture and design.

TIP

The design of chair and table legs is a clue to the style of a particular piece of furniture (see Figure 9-2), indicating where it can successfully be used.

Figure 9-2:
The designs of exposed legs of chairs and tables are quick indicators of Historic style and period.

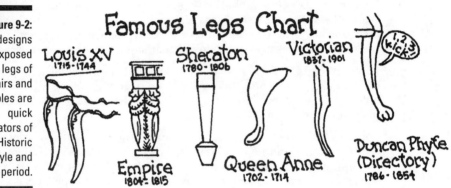

The important styles of England (usually lumped together by furniture retailers as *Traditional*) are the following:

- ✔ **Adam:** French Rococo and ancient Roman styles of Pompeii influenced the Adams brothers, furniture makers and trend-setting designers. The brothers reveled in finely designed, delicately scaled, elaborately detailed interiors and furnishings. They covered their furnishings in rich distinctive colors of dulled blue, pale yellow-green, light gray, and lavender.

- ✔ **Chippendale and Rococo:** These styles featured generous scale and chairs with generally straight legs. Some chair backs reflected Oriental influence in the shape of the top of the chair and in fret-like patterns in lieu of back splats. By contrast, Chippendale chairs (named for a furniture maker) seem more masculine than the curvy Queen Anne chairs and the lighter-scaled Sheraton and Hepplewhite chairs. Colors popular with Chippendale's furniture were neutralized color schemes that were deeper than the French colors of the same time.

- **Georgian:** Classical details from Greece and Rome influenced the great furniture designers of the Georgian era (named for England's king). The tendency was toward heavy proportion and detail. Designers still imitate and use this style today.

- **Hepplewhite:** Well-scaled chairs with a distinctive shield-shaped back characterize this style, created by and named for the furniture maker.

- **Queen Anne:** Seen from 1702 until 1714, this style (named for the reigning monarch of England) featured curvilinear design and Oriental influence. The Queen Anne chair, with its generous curved (sometimes called *cabriole*) leg, is an enduring favorite, especially for dining chairs.

- **Sheraton:** This style, named for the furniture maker who created it, includes more delicately scaled furniture with Neoclassical elements and design motifs.

- **Victorian:** This period of decorative excess was also known as the *mauve decade,* thanks to the dramatic wine-pink and aubergine (eggplant) colors that were widely used. Factory-made furniture was available in abundance. Victorian-era design incorporated nostalgic renderings of Gothic, Renaissance, Moorish, and Oriental designs.

Discovering Historic-style designers

A few designers in the 20th and 21st centuries have contributed to the enduring popularity of Traditional styles. Here are a few:

- **Sybil Colefax,** the renowned English designer, established chintz as the essential element in the grand English Country House look. Mario Buatta, the New York City–based Prince of Chintz, carries on the Colefax and Fowler (Colefax's partner) tradition in the United States, adding his own innovations and signature in the process.

- **Syrie Maugham,** wife of writer Somerset, is credited with painting Traditional furniture (and everything else) white — a radical departure from heavy, dark, cluttered Victorian furniture and furnishings — bringing Historic style very up-to-date. The late Sister Parish, noted New York designer, carried on this tradition, creating the current American Country style.

- **Elsie de Wolfe** is considered the inventor of the decorating profession. She began her own career as an interior designer in 1905, when she was 40 years old and not doing very well as an actress. With instincts and charm, she printed up cards, was commissioned to design Manhattan's Colony Club, became famous for its trellis room, and went on to her career of making everything around her beautiful. An American, she loved 18th Century French design.

Lacy curtains, layers of patterns, and armloads of accessories create the Victorian feel. Your home needn't be Victorian to be decorated in the style, but it does work best in older homes (or in newer homes that lack a distinct style).

Germany

Named for a popular cartoon character, Biedermeier (early 19th century) is a solidly masculine furniture style based on French and English Empire and Neoclassical elements. Biedermeier's most distinctive feature is its dramatic use of light- and dark-colored woods. For stylistic impact, mahogany, ebony, or ebonized *fruitwoods* (woods from various fruit trees) were offset by blond or light-colored fruitwoods. Inlays of dark wood accented light wood, and sometimes vice versa. Heavy gold hardware was sometimes used as drawer pulls or decoration.

The simple but bold elegance of Biedermeier makes it very well suited for people who favor masculine style. Add eclectic touches to a contemporary home with Biedermeier. You can use the style in any room, depending on your preference.

America

American style, with its cleaner, simpler design approach, came about by necessity. Furniture makers had limited materials to work with and were isolated from European trends. They created regional or vernacular styles by adapting trends seen in cabinetmakers' books from Chippendale and others.

American political idealism (democracy and equality) affected more than the government; it influenced designers to create furniture that could be used by everyone. The rocking chair, one of the earliest American furniture designs, has been used by everyone and in almost every room from President Kennedy's Oval Office to grandma's front porch. Basic American style (before the 20th century, when everything became international) is characterized by its lack of pretentiousness.

Early American styles

You can break down Early American style into the following categories:

- ✓ **Colonial Gothic:** Early settlers brought their homeland's traditions with them. Homes and furnishings were based on Gothic and Tudor style. As affluence grew and more aristocrats moved here, more refined English styles began to influence style. Today people may use Gothic-inspired Windsor chairs in a mostly Modern kitchen.

- ✔ **Gothic Revival:** Carpenter Gothic architecture, with pointed arches, tracery ceilings, and stained glass windows, kept Gothic's influence alive.

- ✔ **Greek Revival:** *Federal style* is the name given furniture designed for the Greek Revival houses during the early years of the United States. Classic Greek ideals and art inspired these 18th century furnishings. Duncan Phyfe (1768–1854), whose name was given to a saber-legged chair and a distinctive pedestal table with three saber legs, is one of the best-known furniture designers. The clean, simple lines of a modern tester bed have their origins in Classic design, so they can be eclectically mixed with historic Classic styles such as Greek Revival (see Figure 9-3).

Touches of pure Americana can add decorative — and patriotic — appeal. Scour antique and junk stores for eagles, flags, and other icons of independence. Think red, white, and blue for a dynamic color scheme. Don't think your interior needs be Traditional either. Some very Contemporary Americana continues to be created by artists like Jasper Johns (famous for his American flags). Some collectors display Americana austerely, in a gallery-like manner and with contemporary furniture.

Figure 9-3:
A modern tester bed can be mixed with historic Classic styles such as Greek Revival.

Photograph courtesy Brewster Wallcoverings

Styles may come and go suddenly. Any style that makes a comeback is generally tagged with the terms *Neo, Retro,* or *Revival,* to distinguish it from its predecessor.

American Country

Around the time of America's bicentennial in 1976, a new decorating style was developing that borrowed from European provincial styles. This casual look used up-to-date fabrics and furnishings with old mix-and-match furniture. Painted and distressed finishes added a lighthearted note. Accessories were practical — baskets and quilts. American Country continues to evolve, but comfort, casual informality, country accessories, and a lack of pretense remain characteristic. See Figure 9-4 for an example of Contemporary American Country.

Figure 9-4:
America's Contemporary Country Style is casual and comfortable.

Photograph courtesy Blonder Wallcoverings

Don't confuse the American Country style with the English Country style. Simple, carefree, and relaxed, American Country style is down-home living at its best. Formal, fussy, and distinctly floral English Country style, on the other hand, is based on the lifestyle of the aristocracy.

Country is a state of mind. Enrich any room with views of country landscapes for an instant breath of fresh air. You can use idyllic scenes in virtually any interior — simply match the mood and level of formality.

China

Two Chinese furniture styles are perennial favorites — Ming (1368–1640s) and Qing (1640s to the early 1900s). Both styles are elegantly restrained. Embellishment always underscores that the simple lines of these pieces were designed for beauty, function, and contemplation.

Antiques, usually less expensive than European antiques, are increasingly difficult to find, but you can easily notice the influence of antique Chinese furniture. The lacquered finishes *(japanning)* found on Chinese furniture (red from the 14th century and black popularized in Europe and America during the 17th century) prompted many copies then and now called *Chinoiserie.*

Creating Your Own History-Based Style

Many manufacturers offer furniture based on the styles in this chapter. Some even make reproductions of authentic pieces. Chances are you'll decide that one is just right for your decorating project.

Most of the new versions of Historic styles are designed to meet the needs of our technology-driven homes. As a society, we're far more interested in comfort, convenience, and function than people of the past. We're also just a bit larger in height and weight. So our homes tend to have higher ceilings and more space in general. Keep all these factors — and your preference for personal style — in mind when choosing period-style furniture.

For the happiest mix of styles, remember the old maxim, "Birds of a feather flock together." Combine large-scale furniture with other large-scale styles, fine with fine, formal with formal, dark with other dark woods, and fancy with fancy styles. Don't mix casual (pine or oak) and formal (mahogany or cherry) furniture in the same room.

You don't have to treat Historic-styled furniture with awe. Draping a big-scaled buffalo plaid blanket over a Louis XIV chair, or a Navajo rug over a Louis XV chair can look very of-the-moment. Or, spray-paint Victorian wicker chairs, make bold-colored raw silk cushions, and place them around a glass-topped dining table for an exciting mix.

Chapter 10

Decorating with Contemporary Styles

*N*ever has so much been available to so many as in today's decorating world. We divide decorating into two parts, Historic (see Chapter 9) and Contemporary (this chapter). The term *Contemporary* separates today's designs (named for people, places, and things and meant for a broad public) from older Historic styles (named for kings, queens, and furniture designers and intended for royalty and elites).

In this chapter, we consider the origins of Contemporary style (a little history makes for a lot of understanding and easier choosing). We zero in on popular Contemporary furniture and decorating styles. We also tell you about trend-setting furniture designers.

Moving from Historic to Contemporary Style

The clean-lined, unfussy look most often associated with the modern age actually began with freethinkers — from Shakers and Utopians to artists and intellectuals — who saw the need for a new way of furnishing the home. Driven by lofty ideals, artisans, craftsmen, and designers began making furniture and everyday household items that reflected (or reacted to) social conditions, technology, and values of a growing middle class. More honest (no fancy veneers over cheaper woods), simple (no extravagant carvings), and utilitarian (function first) styles emerged.

Tracking Contemporary style

Following are the most popular styles created after 1800 — not for royalty or the elite, but for the common man. We gather them here under the Contemporary style umbrella (as opposed to ornate earlier styles called *Historic*). Although the Modern or Contemporary design age begins roughly with the start of the 20th century, we begin with designs that prompted the move from Historic to Contemporary style and continue to be favorites.

✔ **Shaker (1830–1850):** Traditional furniture designs stripped to bare essentials (few turnings, no decorations), producing furniture plain in appearance. Natural materials; no ornamentation; strong emphasis on function. Today, familiar rush-seat Shaker style chairs are available as antiques or as reproductions and copies.

✔ **Gothic Revival (1851–1914):** Emphasized natural materials. Designs based on nature. Handcrafting versus machine-made. Arched-top chair crests, rails and knobs, and lots of turnings show up today in side chairs for the dining room and kitchen.

✔ **Adirondack (1890s–present):** Rustic, natural, often made of bark-covered logs or simple planks. Look for junk shop finds when in the country (for authenticity), or purchase hand-made new versions of these comfy furnishings, which translate into today's Lodge Look that also contains Western motifs and icons.

✔ **Art Nouveau (circa 1900):** The first new style not using any historical reference was based on flowing lines of leaves and vines and influenced by Japanese art. Designs today show up most often in lamp bases, mirrors, and candlesticks.

✔ **Arts and Crafts/Mission in America (circa 1900):** Simple designs executed in natural wood. Emphasized hand craftsmanship, quality materials, and strong, clean lines. Also called *Golden Oak*. Widely seen in today's Stickley chairs and other furniture that uses the same designs as earlier origins.

✔ **Art Deco (1918–1939):** Fashion-oriented. Influenced by primitive art and cubism. More color, pattern, and grand ornamentation, including motifs such as zigzags, electricity bolts, and skyscrapers. Often seen today in headboards and accent chairs.

✔ **Bauhaus (1919–1933):** Design based on unifying art and technology. Little ornamentation. Function, form, and materials (metal tubing, glass, and other technological, machine-made materials) most important. Emphasis placed on machine-made, efficient production. Knoll (www.knoll.com) and others produce the original designs.

✔ **International Modern (1925–1947; currently updated):** No regional influences, historic references, ornamentation, or unnecessary elements is what made Modern furniture so radical in its time. Details come from the interesting use of modern materials. Emphasis is on machine-age technology — the house as a machine for living. (To see great examples of Modern and Contemporary design, go to www.artandculture.com.)

✔ **High Tech (1980–1990s):** Emphasis on exploitation and exposure of elements of science and technology for home use. Shows the construction of the interior. Uses industrial materials for the home. Electronic and space-age details important. Celebrates and makes room for the machine.

✔ **Contemporary:** Contemporary (meaning "of the moment") combines influences, trends, and new technologies without strict adherence to any one design philosophy. Current trends include designs that blend styles and periods but are streamlined for today's taste. (Designs based on Traditional styles are considered Contemporary interpretations.)

Shaker furniture, for example, was based on *spiritually correct* mathematical proportions and emphasized their "cleanliness is next to Godliness" values. Shaker chairs were designed to be hung on wall pegs for accessible storage and easy floor cleaning.

The Arts and Crafts Movement, launched in the late 19th century by William Morris, spurred the development of furnishings and textiles designed by artists (hence Arts) that were handmade (hence Crafts) and nature-based (anti-mass production). Morris's designs are still in production. These Gothic-inspired designs were a revolt against overwrought (tasteless) Victorian furniture. Machine-made embellishments on poor quality materials rankled artist-designers such as Charles Eastlake, another important taste-maker of the Arts and Crafts movement, who called for less ornamentation and more discernment in design.

Mission style in the United States, inspired by Arts and Crafts, brought artists and artisans together to hand-craft furnishings with an emphasis on naturally-finished woods, honest skilled craftsmanship, and simplified ornamentation. Today, new generations continue to discover and respect Mission style's strong masculine, natural look, thanks to Stickley (www.Stickley.com) and other manufacturers who keep this style alive and easily available.

Focusing on Modern Style

At the start of the 20th century, several design movements began the radical shift from the ornate styles for the elite (discussed in Chapter 9) to sleek, machine-age furniture for everyman. Modern style encompasses many schools, including International Modern, but we usually just use the short term *Modern.*

Architects and designers, such as Frank Lloyd Wright, Walter Gropius, Ludwig Mies van der Rohe, Le Corbusier, and Marcel Bruer, pioneered Modern as a distinct architectural style. Many also designed furniture. Structural qualities were emphasized — the furniture was as much a sculpture as it was a chair (see Figure 10-1). All details were strictly abstract — not derived from nature, and certainly not symbolic. Technology and economy (maximum value, minimum expenditure) were important, as were comfort and convenience. No ornamentation — no carving, hand-painting, or form of decoration — was introduced into these pure designs.

Charles Eames and his wife, Ray, also a designer, created furniture that emphasized comfort. Their Executive Chair (Herman Miller, www.hermanmiller.com) with its five-leg metal base and padded plywood shell seat (with matching ottoman) was the first design in history that fully supported each area of the human body from head to toe. The trend-setting style continues to be manufactured in its original design and in many copies.

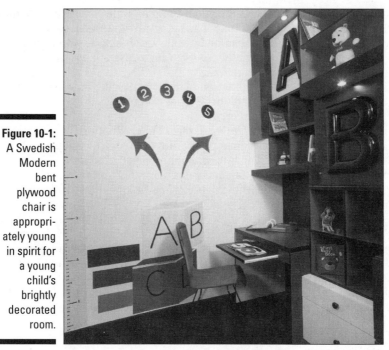

Figure 10-1:
A Swedish
Modern
bent
plywood
chair is
appropri-
ately young
in spirit for
a young
child's
brightly
decorated
room.

Photography courtesy Susan Huckvale Arann, ASID, Staten Island, NY

Modern — now frozen in time and place — is historic, but don't confuse that with Historic styles. Modern style falls under the Contemporary style umbrella (see the sidebar "Tracking Contemporary style" in this chapter).

Catching Up with Contemporary Today

Contemporary designs encompass a wide range of looks loosely based on updates on Modern, French, English, and other styles (see Figure 10-2). Current trends, fads, and fashions under the Contemporary umbrella are referred to as *styles*.

Modern-inspired styles

Design styles based on Modern style depart from its strict rules. Two major differences are more curvilinear shapes and more colorful upholstery and finishes. One current version of Modern, for example, is Romantic Modern. This furniture boasts frankly sensuous curves and pretty pastel-colored upholstery, a sexy style we credit to renowned designer Vladimir Kagan (he's famous for the iconic kidney-shaped coffee table). The Romantic Modern decorating style chooses pastel colors over stark white, gray, or black for walls and furniture; substitutes frosted and decorated for clear glass; and may add a crystal chandelier for elegant fun and whimsy.

Figure 10-2:
Designer
Robert
Lidsky's
kitchen
blends
cherry
woods, blue
glass tile
walls,
stainless
steel
appliances,
and stones
for a
distinctive
Contem-
porary feel.

Photography courtesy Rutt of Bergen County, NJ & The Hammer & Nail, Wycoff, NJ

Historic-inspired styles

Contemporary styles inspired by Historic ones show their design heritage. English Manor (or Country) House décor keeps the original ideas found in grand English country houses of the past, but updates Chippendale, Georgian, and Queen Anne furniture by increasing chair sizes for today's bottoms. Upholstery and other fabrics may stay true to Historic patterns, but they feature fresh, new colors that appeal today.

To differentiate between authentic reproductions and "in the style of" pieces that lack specific names, furniture retailers refer to the latter group as *Traditional,* because they keep the traditions of the past alive.

Contemporary versions of Historic-style chairs are made current in several ways, including larger, more comfortable seats and upholstery fabrics in fresh, today colors and patterns. Furniture dealers refer to these generically as *Traditional.*

Discovering some of the latest decorating styles

Change is everywhere, so we check in with our favorite sources — trade shows, store displays, magazines, TV shows, and showcase houses — to keep up with breaking decorating news. Following are some leading decorating styles.

- **American Country.** American Country style (see Chapter 9) is evolving. Romantic American Country (with pastel colors and more frills) sticks mainly to English and American Country furniture styles, but a few dressy pieces may creep in. Modern American Country mixes Modern and Contemporary pieces with country furniture and accessories.

- **Island Chic.** A style developed by the fictitious Tommy Bahama (the figment of a lifestyle marketing company's imagination), whose philosophy is expressed as "life is a beach" and whose motifs are mainly tropical in a mass-market neutral color palette. Furniture adds wicker, metal, and other materials to dark woods in a vaguely British Colonial style.

- **Lodge Look.** Westward Ho! Cowboy style gets all dressed up and rolls across the country, replete with touches of silver and turquoise and lots of Navajo rugs. Furniture even includes twig, pole, and Adirondack chairs mixed with more Contemporary pieces.

- **Organic Modern.** Newer versions of Modern design don't use straight lines or surfaces. Instead they show plenty of lifelike curves and shapes but are not as feminine or romantic as Romantic Modern. These designs may be made of plastic, glass, metal, or leather. Whatever the materials, these soft-edge designs have a cutting-edge look.

- **Shabby Chic.** Designer Rachel Ashwell's (www.shabbychic.com) ode to peeling paint on antique frames in historic styles and periods. All-white objects are placed in all-white interiors for a foolproof, feminine approach to decorating on a shoestring that manages to look enchantingly elegant and like Snow White's fairy tale cottage.

- **Sun Country Style.** Designer Patricia Hart McMillan's trend-spotting name for the new International Country style. Created by several designers, the look celebrates the mood of summer in relaxed, elegant country house style that mixes Contemporary and Traditional furniture.

Designers making furnishings news

Call them current (or *au courant*) — designers whose furniture and accessories collections are making news. We list some of our favorites — names you may want to know if you're interested in what's happening now:

- **Ransom Cullar,** a young designer for Thayer Coggin (www.ThayerCoggin.com), one of the United States' first manufacturers to create both International (or Classic) Modern and current or Contemporary seating that harkens back to Modern influences.

- **Michael Graves** (www.MichaelGraves.com), architect turned product designer, whose housewares items for Target bring Neo-Modern design to the masses.

✔ **Cecil Hayes,** a Florida interior designer to the stars, whose furniture designs — executed in her own facility — are beautiful renditions of her own and her clients' personal expressions and are available in to-the-trade showrooms.

✔ **Dakota Jackson** (www.DakotaJackson.com), a former circus performer whose magic now is in clean-lined, smartly designed furniture available in his own New York City showroom and in to-the-trade showrooms nationwide.

✔ **Vladamir Kagan** (www.VladimirKagan.com), a New York City designer of curvy, Romantic Modern furniture who continues to inspire droves of imitators. He is well known for making a splash with his iconic 1950s kidney-shaped tables.

✔ **Ross Lovegrove** (www.rosslovegrove.com), a London-based designer who pioneered plastics in furniture and high-tech computers, including Apple Computers. He has won many awards for his ultra Modern furniture. He currently designs a line of modernist furniture for manufacturer Bernhardt.

✔ **Patricia Hart McMillan,** an interior designer whose clean-lined Sun Country Style furniture for Garcia Imports (available in leading furniture stores) was hailed as fresh and innovative by *Furniture Today.* The Palm Tree armoire (available through Robb & Stucky, www.robbstucky.com) is an instant classic.

✔ **Chris Casson Madden** (www.chrismadden.com), whose furniture designs for Bassett and accessories for other manufacturers, available through J.C. Penney and other retailers, keep Traditional designs desirable, available, and affordable.

✔ **Todd Oldham** (www.ToddOldham.com), former fashion designer turned product designer for Target. His high-spirited, mostly Modern furnishings for young people make beanbags newsworthy again.

✔ **Karim Rashid** (www.KarimRashid.com), now based in New York City, who has been heralded as a genius for his groundbreaking designs. He eschews hard edges and lines and opts for curved lines and surfaces. His design goal (and name of his book) is *I Want to Change the World.*

✔ **Phillipe Starck** (www.Phillipe-Starck.com), a Paris-based designer whose trendy designs are now widely available. Hailed as "original and influential," he is noted for his witty and bold styling of boutique hotels, restaurants, and other public places.

✔ **Martha Stewart** (www.MarthaStewart.com), whose collection of Traditional furniture for Bernhardt updates mostly English and American styles, keeping it current and appropriate for today.

✔ **Michael Weiss** (www.veryvanguard.com/MichaelWeiss), whose Modernism collection distributed by Vanguard makes clean-lined, well thought-out, mix-and-match pieces widely available through furniture stores across the United States.

Chapter 11

Determining Your Personal Decorating Style

*B*uying complete rooms-to-go is easy decorating — all the choices are made for you. Hiring a decorator to make your place look like a show-room is also easy your designer will choose everything for you. Only one problem: It's not your style!

When you face the task of decorating — whether starting from scratch or redecorating after 20 years — you may not be sure where to start. The most important aspect of home decorating is figuring out what *you* want.

In this chapter, we guide you through the process of figuring out what style you can call your own. You can take a quiz to get you thinking about likes and dislikes. We also show you how to develop your own personal style. Decorating is about making a space reflect your style — not someone else's. This chapter shows you some little touches that make a huge difference in turning a house into your home.

Discovering Personal Style

In Chapters 9 and 10, we discuss specific styles — Historic and Contemporary — that each have a distinctive look and mood. Historic styles (see Chapter 9) tend toward the formal and conservative, while Contemporary styles (see Chapter 10) veer toward the informal and progressive. So now that you've got some background in the evolution of design, you may be asking yourself: Which style would work best in my home?

The general style of your home should relate to your home's architecture (or lack thereof), your region of the country, and a room's function. We don't often see an all-white Louis XV den in a Long Island split ranch, for example. (But, for the person who embraces that look and personalizes it, it's possible. Achieving that look in very practical materials is even possible!) Whether *you* like the look of the past (the fancy or practical version) or the look of the now is a personal choice. How you make any broad category of style your own is your personal style.

Designer Karim Rashid warns that style tends to be too much about surface appearances and not enough about how well your room functions. Don't get so carried away about making your personal style statement that you forget about function, safety, comfort, and convenience. We've seen more than one design statement that had surface glitz but was completely unusable, hazardous, and ultimately a disaster.

Defining personal style

In decorating, your personal style is the expression of your total life experiences. Your style reflects your education, experiences, travels, and (most importantly) your hopes, dreams, and wishes. It's a look, a mood, a statement that grows out of personal needs.

Most of us have to fix something that we see as horribly wrong with our homes. How you inventively create an entryway where none existed, or make the most out of too little space, demonstrates your creativity at work. Personal style reveals your own unique solutions to these design problems.

Taste test

Don't know if you're an introvert or extrovert? Drop some lemon juice on your tongue. Is your mouth dry? Or, are you salivating? Introverts tend to salivate to dilute the acidity and stimulatory effect of the lemon. Extroverts tend to keep a dry mouth — the acidity and external stimulation aren't a bother to them. So, next time you have a party and serve Lemon Drops (a slice of lemon, a dollop of sugar, and vodka), you can perform a quick and scientifically valid psychology test! In the meantime, you can test yourself before proceeding with your decorating plans.

Your personality is reflected in your personal style. Experts agree that we each have a personality and that it affects how you approach decorating your home. If you're an introvert (shy and retiring), your level of internal stimulation is high, so you prefer a calming environment. Introverts feel better surrounded by subdued colors, textures, and pattern. If you're an extrovert (outgoing and gregarious), your level of internal stimulation is low. Extroverts prefer a stimulating environment characterized by strong colors, textures, and patterns. (See the "Taste test" sidebar in this chapter for a quick way to determine if you're an introvert or an extrovert.)

Who's who of personal style

Over the past few years, many designers and so-called experts have written plenty about personal style without offering a whole lot of useful definition. Examples are often helpful.

Excellent examples include a few leading decorators known for their distinctively styled room settings. These style geniuses also design furnishings and accessories that almost anyone can acquire. When you come across their work in your favorite magazines, books, and television shows, take a close look at the elements that constitute their personal, much publicized styles. You can follow the lead of these decorating stars:

- **Barbara Barry,** the "queen of serene," has designed some of the most tranquil yet up-to-the-minute interiors for rock and movie stars. Her designs are noteworthy for their livable, Contemporary look that features plenty of grace notes and glamour.

- **Mario Buatta,** dubbed the "Prince of Chintz," looks to lush layerings of floral patterns. His over-the-top luxury has made him the designer of choice for people who treasure the English Manor House look.

- **Orlando Diaz-Azcuy** designs minimalist-inspired interiors that incorporate elements of the romantic and exotic. His cutting-edge, ultra-luxurious take on modernist design has made him a favorite for everyone from dot-com millionaires to celebrities.

- **Ralph Lauren** remains the king of American style. His beddings raised the standards of quality; his furnishings and accessories scream quiet good taste. His flair for combining old-money American and English Country House styles and making them relevant, even for rap stars, has made him a star in his own right.

- **Larry Lazlo's** glamorous interpretations of Art Deco style and standout modernist designs have earned him an international reputation. Lazlo's opulent modernism is immediately noticeable in the fabrics, furniture, and art accessories he creates.

- ✔ **Adam Tihany's** trademark isn't so much a look as a feel — the feel of mega luxury. His amazing designs for some of the world's best restaurants have earned him an international reputation. He believes comfort comes first, no matter if it's Contemporary or Traditional.

- ✔ **Vicente Wolf** is the premier designer of modernist-inspired interiors. His artful room settings seem to transcend time and place. His romantic, tailored rooms appear in numerous magazines, and he's consistently named one of the top 100 interior designers year after year.

Finding Your Personal Style

You can easily feel overloaded with input from so many sources. You've heard so many "shoulds" and "oughts," "outs" and "ins," that you've never taken the time to decide something as basic as whether warm colors or cool colors make you feel better. Do the hot citrus colors of Provence turn you on, or is beige more beautiful? Are you torn between Country and other Contemporary rooms (see Figure 11-1)? If you don't know the answers to these questions, never fear: In this section, you'll find the answers you need.

Figure 11-1:
Choosing a personal style, such as Country, Modern, or Country Modern is about selecting a look that makes you feel happy and productive.

Country   vs.   Modern

The numerous options you have can make choosing just one style — or even two or three — difficult. When you're having trouble making up your mind about which decorating styles you want to include in your home, knowing more about yourself may help. So take a few minutes to answer the questions in the following quiz.

Taking a personal style quiz

Section I: Personal Style Pursuit

To get an idea of your decorating mood, answer the following questions (circle your responses, then total your scores):

1. **My favorite mood is:**

   A. Buttoned up

   B. In charge

   C. With it

   D. At peace

   E. In love

2. **My favorite historic site is:**

   A. Monticello

   B. Falling Water by Frank Lloyd Wright

   C. The Louvre

   D. The King Ranch

   E. The Taj Mahal

3. **If I had to live with only one color, I would choose:**

   A. Royal blue

   B. Pure white

   C. Beige

   D. Hunter green

   E. Dusty rose

4. **If I could pick only one pattern, it would be:**

   A. Paisley

   B. Solid color woven design

   C. Leopard print

   D. Laura-Ashley-type miniprint

   E. English chintz

5. **If I could choose only one piece of furniture, it would be:**

   A. A wing chair

   B. A white sectional sofa

   C. A hutch

   D. An entertainment center

   E. A canopy bed

Now total up the number of responses you had for each letter and enter the totals here:

A _____ B _____ C _____ D _____ E _____

Mostly A: You're a Traditionalist. Warm woods and colors and interesting printed fabrics enrich your life.

Mostly B: You're a Modernist. Streamlined furniture and fabrics with woven patterns add up to the "clean" look of Contemporary that satisfies you.

Mostly C: You're Eclectic. The mix is what matters to you. To make mixing easier, try to limit your furniture to two or three compatible styles.

Mostly D: You're Country. A great gathering of friendly objects and the heart-warming look of timeworn furnishings appeal to your instincts.

Mostly E: You're Romantic. Gorgeous colors, soft fabrics, and pretty objects provide the environment that you need in order to flourish.

Section II: Frills or No Frills?

To see whether you prefer more or less frilliness, circle any of the following items that you especially like:

Category A	*Category B*
Florals	Stripes
Pretty colors	Neutrals
Lots of pillows and throws	Important accessories only
Several different collectibles	Investment collections
Several patterns	Textures
Fresh flowers	Bowls of green apples
Displays of keepsakes	Leather
Paintings of mother and child	Still-life paintings
Rooms with a view	Rooms with a television
Painted furniture	Natural fine woods
Sleek surfaces	Glass and chrome
Total A _____	Total B _____

If you answered mostly A, add plenty of frills and flourishes to your home. If you answered mostly B, go for rooms that are tailored to perfection.

Section III: Am I Formal or Informal?

To determine whether your taste leans toward the formal or the informal, answer the following items (circle either "Like me" or "Not like me"):

1. **I feel it's best for the host or hostess to serve his or her guests.**
   Like me or Not like me?

2. **I prefer lots of texture and easy-to-care-for, durable materials.**
   Like me or Not like me?

3. **I prefer meals served in the dining room.** Like me or Not like me?

4. **I prefer fine fabrics and luxury materials.** Like me or Not like me?

5. **I like touches of wit, humor, and whimsy in my rooms.**
   Like me or Not like me?

6. **I most often entertain guests in the kitchen and family room.**
   Like me or Not like me?

7. **I most often entertain my guests in the living room.**
   Like me or Not like me?

8. **I prefer symmetrical room arrangements.** Like me or Not like me?

9. **I like lots of furniture groupings placed around a room.**
   Like me or Not like me?

10. **I like very serious interiors.** Like me or Not like me?

11. **When others are in my home I encourage them to put their feet up
    and help themselves to whatever they want.** Like me or Not like me?

12. **Every day is Casual Friday.** Like me or Not like me?

For questions 1, 3, 4, 7, 8, and 10, give yourself 1 for "Like me," 0 for "Not like me." For questions 2, 5, 6, 9, 11, and 12, give yourself 0 for "Like me," 1 for "Not like me." The higher your score, the more formal you tend to be.

Section IV: Dimensions of Style

To diagnose key aspects of your personality, answer the following items (circle either "Like me" or Not like me"):

1. **I like to be the center of attention.** Like me or Not like me?

2. **The world would be a better place if I ruled it — or at least decorated
   it.** Like me or Not like me?

3. **I feel I am a person of worth, at least on par with others.**
   Like me or Not like me?

4. **I am proud of my accomplishments.** Like me or Not like me?

5. **It bugs me when people are late for appointments.**
   Like me or Not like me?

6. **I like to plan events ahead of time.** Like me or Not like me?

7. **I insist that there's a place for everything, everything in its place.**
   Like me or Not like me?

8. **I would like to be a flower arranger.** Like me or Not like me?

9. **I stay at home a great deal.** Like me or Not like me?

10. **I prefer tranquility to excitement.** Like me or Not like me?

11. **Too many colors and objects make me nervous.**
    Like me or Not like me?

12. **My views of myself change rapidly.** Like me or Not like me?

13. **I have different friends from different walks of life.**
    Like me or Not like me?

14. **I act very differently when I am in different situations.**
    Like me or Not like me?

15. **I crave adventure and excitement.** Like me or Not like me?

For questions 1 through 4, if you answered "Like me" more often than "Not," you have a healthy ego. Use plenty of accessories that show who you are and where you've been in life. Don't be afraid to have an ego wall of your degrees, awards, and photo ops with politicians and celebs.

For questions 5 through 7, if you answered "Like me" more often than "Not," it's a safe bet that you're just shy of being a control freak — and no one is saying that's bad. You need storage space and super functional design with key accessories that show you're in control.

For questions 8 through 11, if you answered "Like me" more often than "Not," you're probably an introvert. Pick quiet, calming colors and keep fuss and muss to a minimum. Do add one or two upbeat accessories — a knockout silk flower arrangement, for example — to keep yourself from going into the doldrums. If you're an extrovert, take risks, go bold — snap up that orange sofa. Don't play it safe, or you'll be sorry.

For questions 12 through 15, if you answered "Like me" more often than "Not," you tend to like so many things that pinning yourself and your room down to one look is difficult. You're more willing to go out on a limb with the latest in fashion trends. For you, a good neutral is red! You need to change accessories frequently — just buy more!

Section V: I Know It's Good, But Why Do I Like It?

Grab every decorating and design magazine you can. Clip out pictures of rooms you like and hate. (If you're looking at books, simply flag pages with sticky notes.) Now write down exactly what it is you love or loathe about these rooms. (If you have speech recognition software, then you can talk right to your computer! Or, just talk into your tape recorder.) Discuss your likes and dislikes with your partner, friends, and family. Invite them to do the same.

The important part of this exercise is learning how to verbalize your preferences. Putting into words those fuzzy feelings and vague thoughts can help you hone your taste. You'll be forced to master decorating lingo, too. Sam Rosenberg, a West Palm Beach-based conceptual designer, says this exercise is especially good if you're preparing to do a major decorating job; he makes this task a requirement for his clients.

Stating your style

Now that you've taken the quiz (hooray, you scored 100!), you should have a better idea of your style. You may remain torn between two looks (that means you're complex). Happily, personal style isn't either/or. Express various facets of your personal style in different rooms (tailored living room, frilly bedroom; both still in your favorite color or color scheme) or in different homes (a primary residence and vacation place).

Writing out your ideas about your personal style in the form of a statement usually helps to make it more concrete. Your statement may be short and sweet ("I like a *casual, eclectic* style, with *frilly* touches") or go on for pages. Take your personal style statement with you when you go shopping. If you're torn between two choices, look at your statement and let it help you decide.

Exploring Your Personal Style

Not absolutely sure why you likes some styles, not others? Try some of the following techniques for developing your personal style:

- ✔ **Continue looking for new decorating books.** Glance through the books in the bookstore and add the best to your bookshelf for ready reference.

- ✔ **Experiment with color.** Tape a large piece of colored fabric or paper to the wall. Reenter the room, gauging your immediate response to the color. Then repeat the process with other colors. How does each color make you feel? Happy? Sad? Calm? Depressed? Better? Worse? Rate each color, beginning with the one that makes you feel best.

- ✔ **Keep a file of all the magazine pictures you like.** Observe how elements work together to create a look. Note special architectural features (such as moldings, windows, fireplaces, and doors), surface treatments, furniture styles, color schemes, and other nuances.

- ✔ **Look at department- and furniture-store room settings.** Take note of the relationships between furniture, backgrounds, and accessories that underscore a particular theme. Make a note of the ones that appeal strongly to you. What did you like best or least about the room? Getting a sense of your most extreme likes and dislikes is important.

- ✔ **Make short lists of colors, furniture, and accessories that you like.** Take your lists with you on shopping trips so that you don't become overwhelmed by all the options.

- ✔ **Store all your notes and ideas together in a folder.** Review your ideas from time to time, especially after you've seen a showcase house or room that strongly appeals to you. You can adapt these things to your own rooms.

- ✔ **Treat a small room (hallway, laundry, or playroom) as your "color lab."** If you want to experiment with a color, but you don't want to use your living room as a guinea pig, paint one or all four walls of a smaller room in the new color. Because paint is easily and inexpensively changed, if you decide you can't abide by that color, you can paint the walls a safe color again. All you've lost is a couple of bucks and a little energy (and look what you've gained!).

- ✔ **Visit designer showcase houses for avant-garde ideas and daring pairings of furniture and accessories.** Take a notebook and jot down your likes, dislikes, and criticisms. Review your notes occasionally as you continue decorating and redecorating your home.

Admitting that you're crazy about a certain color today doesn't mean you're stuck with it for life. Expect your personal style to evolve as your awareness grows, your knowledge builds, and your taste develops. Above all, don't be afraid to experiment (especially when you can do it easily and inexpensively).

Personalizing Your World

Every item you select for a room is an expression of your personal style. For example, if you love pattern, chances are you'll seize every opportunity to express that love, starting with walls and including curtains and other fabrics. Wall covering offers up pattern galore, especially if you choose coordinating patterns.

If too much pattern isn't your taste, decide just how much is enough. None? Or just a little, for relief from plain and simple surfaces? Or perhaps a lot, like in Figure 11-2? If this themed, *Out of Africa*–style appeals to you, chances are that a "more-the-merrier" approach to accessories is essential to your own style.

Figure 11-2:
You don't actually have to go on safari to make Safari your own personal style.

Photograph courtesy Blonder Wallcoverings

Whether you like few or many accessories, personal expressions make your house feel like your home. If you're not sure how many accessories are enough, add just a few items at a time. You'll be able to tell when you've reached your limit by your level of emotional and intellectual satisfaction.

You may hesitate to add personal touches for several reasons. Perhaps you plan on selling your house in the near future, you're renting and the lease forbids you from painting the walls, or you want to ease into a personal style. We offer the following tips and techniques for adding exciting personal touches that only *seem* permanent, allowing change without penalty:

✔ **Choose fabrics in your favorite color for draperies and upholstery.**
These portable pleasures leave when you do.

✔ **Display collections in a distinctive cabinet.** Forget about built-ins and
choose a cabinet or other piece of furniture that both establishes your
interests and enthusiasms and is a good traveler (a large piece of furniture made of parts that disassemble for easy transport).

✔ **Leave large spaces neutral and satisfy your craving for powerful
colors by using those colors in a smaller room.** Such rooms are easily
repainted in an innocuous neutral tone.

✔ **Look to accessories, such as area rugs, baskets, and slipcovers, for
strong textures.** All these items are quick and easy to add or subtract
when you move or improve.

✔ **Make a color statement with a large, room-size rug and then repeat
the colors throughout the room in accessories.** It's one background surface you can roll up and take with you to your next destination.

✔ **Paint just one focal wall your signature color.** Painting one wall is
easier than painting four. You can paint it white later, if you need.

✔ **Repeat your signature color around a neutral room or all through the
house.** Add the color (such as tulip yellow or cornflower blue) by using
various accessories, such as toss pillows, picture mats, and lamps.

If your work requires moving frequently, stick to the same neutral color for
walls and background. Add important elements in your signature color that
allow you to "grow" your portable collection of personal style elements over
time. Rome wasn't built in a day, nor is personal style!

Chapter 12

Finding Out about Furniture

· ·

· ·

Furniture shopping can be confusing and time consuming. Should you buy furniture already assembled (and pay more)? Or, opt for pieces you have to put together (and pay less, but spend a lot of sweat equity)? How do you tell if furniture is well constructed? If the wood frame is worth the money you're paying for it? And what about upholstery? Should you look only at new pieces, or consider reupholstering a garage sale or flea market piece? What about making an accent piece yourself?

In this chapter, we answer all these questions and more. You discover tips for buying furniture. You also see how you can make an old piece of furniture seem like new again with just a little creativity. This chapter has all the information you need to make your next furniture-buying excursion less of a bother and more of an adventure.

Sizing Up Different Furniture Types

Furniture can easily be divided into two categories: pre-assembled and ready to assemble (see Figure 12-1). If budget is a consideration, knowing the differences between the two, as well as the advantages and disadvantages of each kind, is a good place to start. In this section, we provide you enough material to make an informed decision about what kind of furniture to buy.

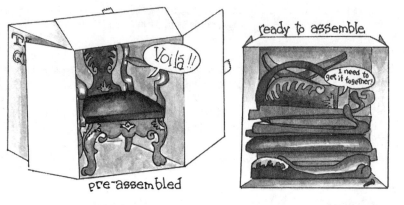

Figure 12-1: You can purchase furniture fully assembled (pre-assembled) or ready to assemble.

Pre-assembled or ready-made furniture

Pre-assembled furniture is furniture that is delivered in one piece, ready for use. Occasionally, a pre-assembled sofa's legs may need to be removed so that the sofa can fit through the door of your house. (The delivery person attaches those parts upon delivery.) You, the buyer, get involved with the furniture only after it has been completely assembled.

You can find pre-assembled furniture in a variety of price ranges. The prices vary based on the materials used in construction, the construction techniques, and the kind of finishes used on the frame. You can generally figure that furniture that costs more is of higher quality. High-quality furniture has several distinguishing characteristics, including the following:

- ✔ The frame is made of strong hardwoods. Typical hardwoods are ash, maple, and oak. Softwoods, such as pine, can't stand up to wear and tear.

- ✔ The *veneer* (a decorative finish that covers the surface of a lower quality wood that's used in all price points) is made from the finest hardwoods such as mahogany or oak. Veneers consist of five to seven thin layers of wood sandwiched together and are actually stronger than plain wood of the same type. They won't split or crack. They also allow for matching the grain or creating decorative grain treatments.

- ✔ Multiple coats of finish cover the wood frame. More coats mean more durability.

- ✔ The hardware for drawer pulls and glide rails is sturdy and has a protective finish for long wear.

If you want your furniture to last for years, buy the best furniture you can afford. Spending more now can translate into furniture that looks just as good ten years (or more) from now as it does today.

You can buy brand new pre-assembled furniture in furniture stores. But for pre-owned — used but usable — furniture, don't forget to check out other sources, including estate, garage, and moving sales; flea markets; auctions; consignment shops; and charity outlets. Don't forget furniture sales by fine furniture retailers — check your local newspapers and TV ads for clearances. Shop around for the best prices before you buy. You can also check the Internet. Many online stores offer rock-bottom prices for high quality pieces — just be sure you know exactly what you want before you have that 8-foot sectional shipped cross-country. Be advised: Online and discount stores may not offer any service if your furniture needs repairs.

If you live near an alternative source of furniture (a charity outlet or second-hand store) that benefits from the castoffs of the wealthy, you can find some especially good deals. Get to know the people who run the store and ask them to alert you to new arrivals. Many experienced shoppers — even antique dealers — know to shop in these places, so competition can be fierce.

You may buy furniture from these secondhand sources with the intention of refinishing and restoring your new find. Refinishing *case goods* furniture (chests, dressers, and other all-wood or laminate pieces) isn't as difficult as you may think. Paint and craft shops carry kits that make the job easier and faster. Buying used upholstery depends on whether it's clean and serviceable or whether you need to re-upholster it. Before deciding to re-upholster a piece, investigate the cost of fabric and labor to recover a piece. You can find names of upholsters in the Yellow Pages and through furniture stores.

To make an odd assortment of furniture seem less odd, paint all the pieces white or black (both are classics) or refinish them in the same stain (these come in many colors). Color unifies all the disparate styles and makes the pieces work together instantly. (Don't paint valuable antiques — the paint destroys the piece's resale value.) To make a unique piece stand out, decoratively paint it or cover it in a mosaic material.

Ready-to-assemble furniture

Ready-to-assemble (RTA) furniture is furniture that you put together. It's more available and more acceptable now than it has ever been. Ready-to-assemble furniture is popular mainly because it's less expensive than pre-assembled furniture. Plus, it's instantly available — you carry it home in the box, and you don't have to wait for delivery.

The most popular kinds of ready-to-assemble furniture are bookshelves, desks, and other office furniture. They can be made from a variety of materials, but laminates are the easiest to assemble. The range of styles available is broad.

Even if you're a do-it-yourselfer, before you buy, find out how the piece is assembled. Some ready-to-assemble furniture requires more work than others. Check to see whether you have all the tools you need to finish the job. (Some manufacturers include some of the tools you need in the box, but others don't.) So be sure you know what you're getting into before you get your new furniture home and discover the need for a professional assembler.

Think twice before buying inexpensive, ready-to-assemble pine case goods that need finishing — especially those that require a lot of effort to finish. Think about where, when, and how often you'll use these pieces, as well as how long you want them to last. Inexpensive pine case goods don't stand up to hard use. So you may not want to spend much time or money on them. Consider these pieces somewhat temporary (they're great if you like to hand-paint creatively) and not heirloom pieces.

Buying Quality Case Goods

The term *case goods* refers to furniture that isn't upholstered and is usually made of wood or metal, such as dressers, tables, chests, and armoires (mainly storage pieces). When you're buying furniture, the quality of the case goods plays a huge part in determining the price. Several factors affect the overall quality of case goods, including the following construction techniques:

- ✔ Wood pieces should be joined in either a *mortise and tendon* (one piece fits into a pocket on the other) or a *dovetail* (in which the pieces fit together like meshing gears). Then the pieces should be glued together for greatest strength.

- ✔ Drawers should glide easily on heavy-duty glide rails. Drawers shouldn't move or wobble from side to side.

- ✔ The insides of drawers should be smoothly sanded.

Ask the salesperson to point out these and other excellent furniture construction features so you know what you're getting.

Good-quality case goods come in a range of prices (due to differing construction techniques, materials, and finishes), so if your budget is limited, you're not limited to cheap furniture. You may even find high quality case goods in your favorite style, *and* at a price you can afford. Check out the section called

"Pre-assembled or ready-made furniture" earlier in this chapter for information on nontraditional places to buy furniture.

Case goods come in a variety of materials, including wicker, chrome, stainless steel, wrought iron, wire, plastic, glass, and laminates. Take a look at the following tips on some different case good materials before you choose which one you want to buy:

✔ **Glass:** Usually used as tops for tables and for shelving, the glass should be at least ¾-inch thick for durability. For safety's sake, make sure you buy only *tempered* glass (which won't break into dangerous shards — check the label to make sure). Glass now comes in beautiful colors that are especially decorative and great accent pieces even in Traditional settings. We once used modern Curvet glass chairs in a remodeled barn.

✔ **Laminates:** A plastic surface bonded to particleboard substrate, laminates are durable and affordable, and they usually look very modern. You can find them in a variety of patterns and textures (some carry photographic reproductions of wood) that are highly decorative. Though a far cry from early inexpensive surfacing materials, think of laminates as cost-effective furniture.

✔ **Metal:** You can choose from a variety of metals, including chrome, stainless steel, wrought iron, and wire. Make sure the metal you select is smooth and has no sharp edges. If you live in a high humidity area, make sure new metals have a protective coating that prevents bubbling, peeling, and rusting. Follow manufacturer's care recommendations.

✔ **Mosaic.** Once restricted to floors and walls, this art form of using small bits of tile, glass, or other interesting materials arranged decoratively is showing up more and more in furniture. Mosaic materials include broken bits of china, stone, and shell.

Furniture in one material may be accented with mosaics of other materials, including shells used for elaborate inset designs, jewels, gold, silver, and bits of colored or stained glass. Furniture treated with these exciting accents most often is itself an arresting accent in any room.

✔ **Plastic:** Make sure the plastic is smooth and without obvious seams. You can choose from many kinds of plastics; construction makes a difference between inexpensive and expensive plastics, such as Lucite.

✔ **Wicker:** Check that the wicker you buy is smoothly woven. The heavier the wicker, the better the quality. If a secondhand piece of wicker is unraveling, you can reglue it. Ask your paint or hardware store dealer to recommend the best adhesive for this job.

Speaking the language of wood

You can shop easier in furniture shops if you know the language, according to Jackie Hirschhaut of the American Furniture Manufacturers Association (AFMA). (For more information, visit www.afma4U.org.) Use these terms on your next furniture-shopping safari:

✔ **All wood.** This term means that all components are wood — solid, engineered, or a combination.

✔ **Hardwoods.** These trees lose their leaves in winter, including ash, cherry, maple, oak, poplar, and walnut.

✔ **Engineered wood.** This term refers to wood made from slices of lumber (plywood) or chips and fibers remaining after a tree is milled into lumber.

✔ **Medium-density fiberboard.** This material is made by breaking wood chips into fibers, mixing fibers with glue, and fusing the two under heat and pressure to produce boards. Fiberboard is generally stiffer and thicker than particleboard and is often covered in laminate or engineered wood.

✔ **Particleboard.** This material is made by mixing wood chips and glue and pressing the mixture into boards. Particleboard is often thin and used on furniture backs.

Double-check whether you're buying the wood you think you're buying. Many manufacturers stain less expensive woods to look like a pricey mahogany, cherry, or fruitwood. This cost-cutting, style-making solution lets you have the look of a rich wood at a more affordable price. Usually the price of the furniture is an obvious clue — if you find a piece that looks like mahogany for a relatively low price, check to be sure what you're buying.

Finding Quality Upholstered Furniture

You can find upholstered furniture at secondhand sources. But for sanitary reasons, you may want to strip off the old upholstery and padding down to the frame, and then rebuild with new padding and upholstery. If you plan to reupholster, choosing furniture without exposed wood frames can save a lot of money in labor charges, because exposed wood frames are more difficult to cover. If upholstering is a skill you have, there's no limit on the pieces you may want to re-do.

When buying upholstered furniture, keep the following points in mind:

✔ High-quality upholstery frames are made of kiln-dried hardwood, as opposed to lower-quality frames made of less durable pine. Because it's impossible to see a frame, manufacturers supply this information.

✔ Steel coil springs should be hand tied (not machine clamped) in as many as eight different places where the adjoining coils and the frame meet, for greatest stability. Some newer technology uses flat S-curves. New furniture supplies this information on a hangtag. If not, ask the dealer.

✔ Layers of cotton batting or polyester fiberfill, a quilted pillow of high-quality foam, and a layer of muslin should cover the steel coil springs. (Ask a salesperson to explain the differences in foam quality.)

✔ You can specify the degree of softness of your sofa seat if you have it custom-made. Otherwise, take the time to try out every sofa until you find the one that seems most comfortable. Expect sleeper sofas to be harder, more rigid, and heavier than other types of sofas.

✔ Upholstery fabric should be upholstery-weight velvet, tapestry, woven wool, leather, or another heavy-duty material.

If you're choosing a fabric, look at fabrics available in all price ranges. Compare the *thread count* (threads per square inch). The greater the density (the higher the count, the more tightly woven the thread), the stronger the fabric. A quick test of density is to hold the fabric sample to the light. The less light that passes through, the denser — and therefore stronger — the fabric is.

✔ Your sofa and chairs don't need to be the same style or covered in the same material. They should have compatible styles and coordinating coverings, for the sake of unity. To flank a sofa, for example, pick two side chairs in different styles, perhaps a straight-backed Queen Anne and a shield back covered in identical fabric (see Chapter 9 for more on chair styles). The effect offers both unity and diversity.

✔ For longevity, choose neutral-colored upholstery coverings in durable materials. Neutral colors never go out of style. Add a dash of color with patterned pillows (they can easily and inexpensively be changed).

✔ If you choose a distinctive pattern (such as a bold stripe) for your sofa and chairs, the pattern should match at the seams and align on the pillows and skirt (if there is one) to create an unbroken pattern.

✔ Sofa pillow edges should align smoothly, without gaps between pillows or the sofa back and arms.

✔ Make sure the frame of the furniture is sturdy. The sofa shouldn't flex in the middle when it's lifted by the ends.

✔ All exposed wood parts should be smooth, without any discernible air bubbles (indicating a poorly cured varnish) or blemishes (indicating poor quality wood).

Understanding upholstery-speak

When shopping for upholstery, the American Furniture Manufacturers Association (AFMA) suggests using these terms so that you and the salesperson are speaking the same language:

✔ **Corner blocks.** This term refers to small blocks of wood used to strengthen and keep aligned the corners of seat frames. Blocks are glued or screwed (or both) into place.

✔ **Down.** Soft, fluffy feathers are used in seat cushions for added plushness. Used alone, they mash down when sat on and must be plumped back into position each time. Plumping them all the time can get old, so down is most often used to top off other materials (foam) that have position memory and don't need constant fluffing.

✔ **Flexible polyurethane foam (FPF).** Almost all upholstered furniture uses this shape-keeping, comfortable under-cover material. The higher the density, the more durable the foam and the more expensive the cushion or sofa.

✔ **Synthetic fibers.** Most upholstery fabric is man-made and extremely durable, and often looks like natural fibers and materials. Most popular are acetate, acrylic, nylon, rayon, and polypropylene.

✔ **UFAC.** The Upholstered Furniture Action Council (www.furninfo.com) is a voluntary upholstery industry "safety-first" organization banded together to create manufacturing standards to reduce flammability in upholstery.

Working Furniture Magic

Decorating old or unfinished furniture lets you make a creative statement. Take a look at the following decorating tips. Try some out on *your* furniture:

✔ **Consider new uses for old furniture and unique items.** We bought an old combination radio/phonograph in a beautifully veneered cabinet for $5 from the Salvation Army. Now we use it as an elegant foyer console. Try using drums as tables; bunch together a trio of tribal drums and use them as individual coffee tables. See Figure 12-2 for an example of old and unique furniture used in a new way.

✔ **Create an instant slipcover by throwing a king-size sheet, quilt, or bedspread over an unsightly sofa.** Tie it in place with rope or grosgrain ribbon.

✔ **Decorate an old chest for a teenage boy's room with discarded license plates.** Garage sales and junk stores are good sources. Just decide where to add them. Nail them into place.

✔ **Decoupage an old dresser or dressing table with motifs cut from wallpaper.** Safeguard with a finishing glaze or coat of polyurethane.

✔ **Dress up a plain-Jane, upholstered side chair.** Get out the trusty hot-glue gun to attach interesting *gimp* (an ornamental braid or cord), fringe, or other trim along the bottom of the seat.

✔ **Faux paint old wooden furniture.** Paint stores have rows of booklets describing various techniques step-by-step. They also carry kits. Everything you need is right there in store.

✔ **Individualize dining room chairs for your children.** Paint mismatched chairs bold colors (all the same or coordinating colors). Stencil your children's names on the chair backs, or add a motif. Craft shops have small glue-on toys, animals, numbers, and initials.

✔ **Paint a wooden chair with an interesting shape different colors and patterns, like a Victorian house.** For color combination ideas, pick the colors already in your scheme. Some paint companies put out booklets of historic color combinations — check these out for instant inspiration.

✔ **Paint vertical stripes on an old or RTA chest or nightstand.** All you need is tape (you can buy special masking tape at the paint store), a brilliant color or two, and a very steady hand wielding a paintbrush. Measure off the stripes using a ruler and a pencil to make light marks.

✔ **Take a tip from Colonial homemakers — cover tables in flat-weave rugs.** Dhurries, needlepoints, or chainstitch rugs transform tables into desks and display areas for framed family photos.

✔ **Use a deep, glass-fronted china cabinet to hold a small TV or serve as a minibar in the living room.** Punch a hole in the back to slip through the wires for any appliances. Display glasses and ice buckets.

✔ **Use pillows to convert lumber into a sofa of sorts — outside or inside.** Use flatter pillows for seats and backs and fluffier ones for decoration and added comfort.

Figure 12-2:
Discreet furniture never reveals its source (garage sale or heirloom?), but adds to a room's overall beauty and comfort.

Photograph courtesy Hunter Douglas

Part IV
Creating Backgrounds

The 5th Wave   By Rich Tennant

I love how you've handled the lighting in here.

In this part . . .

Walls, floors, and ceilings are the background against which furniture, accessories, and you star! As you decorate each — with the others in mind — you build toward a setting worthy of the furnishings you'll place in this space. These chapters, including one on lighting (which, in the movies, precedes camera and action), provide the essential information you need for creating the perfect background.

Chapter 13

Creating Wonderful Walls

In This Chapter

▶ Designing unity all through the house

▶ Respecting your house's architectural style

▶ Discovering great wall coverings

*T*hink of walls as a background for living — much as you would a stage set, with you and your family as the stars. What sort of background works?

In this chapter, you discover that walls can be changed almost as quickly as your mood. We show you how to create a sense of unity by using your walls as the tie that binds rooms together. We encourage you to consider your house's style — do you want to stick with tradition or radically depart from it? You'll find all the guidelines here to help you decide. Finally, you find out about the many possibilities for wall covering.

Forming a Unified Look

Walls are the largest surface area of any room. These backdrops for all your daily dramas can be as bold as you want. Or, if you prefer, walls can just fade away. Either way, they're the starting point for decorating — for creating that special mood that reflects the real you.

Not all walls are created equal. Traditional walls are square, symmetrically arranged, and broken up by symmetrically placed doors and windows. If that sounds uncreative, even boring, you can introduce some diversity with color, pattern, and texture without disrupting a much-desired sense of unity. (For more tips on working with these elements, see Chapters 5, 6, and 7, respectively.)

Contemporary interiors are anything but symmetrical. The Contemporary open floor plan — rooms with few, oddly placed walls — is a horse (or house) of a different color. To create a sense of unity that flows from space to space, make walls, floors, and ceilings all white or all beige. Actually, this situation isn't bad and doesn't have to be boring. Add interest with colorful, texture-full furniture or strong and attention-getting art (see Figure 13-1).

Figure 13-1:
For a serene look of unity throughout your home, use the same color. For variety, use varying tones and tints of the same color for the walls, ceiling, and furnishings.

Photograph courtesy Hunter Douglas, Duette ® Duolite® Shades

If you're a decorating daredevil jumping at the chance to paint every wall a different color in a Contemporary home, you still need a unifying element. Moldings and trim can take on this role. Paint all moldings and trim the same color — perhaps crisp white. A strong color repeated throughout in upholstery — sofa, dining chairs, chaise — also serves as a unifying thread.

If you want to create a unified look, all background elements — walls, floors, and ceilings — should make one another look better. (For creative ideas for floors and ceilings, see Chapters 14 and 15.) Don't allow any of these elements to compete unfairly for attention. Each should contribute to the particular mood (expressed in color, texture, and line) of the room as a whole. For example, if one surface is formal, then the other two will look more unified if they're also formal.

Decorating with Architecture in Mind

If you don't know where to start with decorating your walls, let your house be your guide. Start by looking at your house's architectural style. Architectural styles come with a whole menu of tried-and-true furnishing ideas, past and present.

Traditional wall design

Typically, Traditional rooms are boxlike, with a few doors and small windows. These rooms have plenty of wall space against which to place furniture. Often, the architect creates a focal wall by including a fireplace, which is a decorating plus. (See Chapter 4 for more on focal points.) The walls can be broken into three areas: the lower wall, a mid-height chair rail, and the top of the wall. Traditionalists panel the lower part of the wall, paint the chair rail a contrasting color, and then add paint or paper to the top. Traditional color distribution calls for a dark color on the bottom, a medium color in the middle, and a light color on the top.

If your Traditional room is spacious and the walls are high, you can create a sensational room with beautifully colored paneling, a boldly contrasting or complementary-colored chair rail, a heroically scaled and patterned wall covering, and a magic mix of patterned fabrics (see Figure 13-2).

Figure 13-2:
Large rooms with high ceilings make it possible to divide walls by using wall coverings, borders, paint, or paneling.

Photograph courtesy Brewster Wallcoverings,
The Carriage Trade by Kenneth James

If you want to make a Traditional room seem more Contemporary, any of the following techniques work well:

- ✔ Eliminate the Traditional three wall areas, and paper the wall floor-to-ceiling in a Contemporary textured or patterned wallpaper. Forego using a traditional chair rail or paint it to blend with the background.
- ✔ Flip-flop the color scheme, placing darker elements on top and lighter elements nearer the floor.
- ✔ Paint the entire wall the same color.

Traditional decorating doesn't work well with restless (Contemporary) diagonal lines, so don't introduce them in graphics, wall coverings, or chevron-patterned planks.

Abracadabra! Creating wall magic

In the best of all decorating worlds, a terrific wall treatment almost magically makes problem areas vanish. Consider some of our favorite decorating tricks in the following list:

✔ Cut too-high walls down to size by dividing them into three horizontal bands. You may even decide to paint ceiling moldings a different color and make the ceiling appear lower by adding color to it, too. Or you can bring the ceiling color down onto the ceiling molding and even several inches below the molding along the top of the wall to achieve a stronger effect.

✔ In a Contemporary room, create three distinct areas by applying two horizontal bands of wood or metal molding. Paint the areas between the bands contrasting colors.

✔ Make too-low walls seem higher by keeping the wall all one light color. In Traditional rooms, keep wainscot paneling, a narrow chair rail, and the paint above the chair rail all the same light color. If you use wallpaper instead of paint above the chair rail, choose a narrow stripe with a light background color that matches the light-colored paint used on the chair rail and paneling. Use a simple narrow baseboard and ceiling molding.

✔ You can also stretch any short wall to new heights by adding vertical lines from the floor to the ceiling. Do this by painting stripes, applying striped wall covering, applying planks vertically, or installing *bead board* (a paneling that looks like narrow planks) vertically.

✔ Transform an awkward rectangular room into a more graceful square by painting the shorter end walls a much darker, warmer color than the two longer side walls. This technique makes the end walls seem to advance toward the room's center, and, as a result, the room seems less rectangular.

✔ Make a square room seem less static by painting one focal wall a brilliant color. For small rooms, keep your palette light and cool, such as an apple green and crisp white. For large rooms, go for warmer, darker colors, such as Venetian red against gold.

✔ Calm down busy walls by painting all the moldings and trims (including the mechanical devices, like vents) the same color as the wall.

✔ Create interest in an otherwise dull room by outlining moldings in a color that's complementary to that of the wall.

✔ Eliminate the feeling that a room has too many doors by painting the doors and trim the same color as the walls. (Unfinished wood doors and white doors can be sore thumbs.)

✔ Accentuate beautiful doors and make the surrounding walls recede by painting the walls a plain neutral color and the doors a strongly contrasting antique color. We recommend an antique color kit to achieve this effect.

✔ Make unattractive trim around the doors and windows less obvious by painting it to match the walls.

Contemporary wall design

Contemporary rooms are irregularly shaped, with more doors, huge windows, and not much wall space against which to place furniture. These large spaces can look like an airport waiting area or hotel lobby. They demand skillful furniture arrangement. (See Chapter 22 for tips on arranging living rooms.) Baseboards and ceiling moldings, devices used to divide walls into three areas, are dispensed with in very Contemporary rooms. The few walls in these houses (which feature open floor plans) are often short or high (perhaps two stories high). Tall walls, when long or wide enough, are great backgrounds for hanging large artworks, which help visually divide the wall into more interesting areas.

Sometimes, the little wall space in a Contemporary room competes with the view through *window walls* (exterior walls devoted almost entirely to windows) or a large expanse of sliding glass doors. In this case, take into account the visible exterior walls. Relate or contrast your interior walls with the exterior walls.

If you're unsure what color to use in a Contemporary house, take your cue from the local color. For example, we chose atmospheric blue-gray paint for the walls of a New York City high-rise apartment so that the colors wouldn't compete with the daytime sky. We kept the flooring and furniture in the same blue-gray family so that the window view and the sky beyond seemed like a soothing extension of the room. Bright artwork on the wall opposite the windows provided ample color and accents. For a Florida living room with a similar wall of windows, we chose hibiscus pink paint that made the view of the bright blue sky and ocean pop out by contrast.

Texture also can make materials seem lighter or heavier. Mirror, for example, can make walls seem light and airy. Stones and boulders make for a heavy-looking wall. Take care that a textured wall (fieldstone, for example) doesn't look heavier than the floor. For example, a stone wall against a bleached-white plank floor could look top-heavy, upsetting the sense of balance.

Considering Your Material Options

An abundance of materials is available for walls. This section gives you a brief look at old favorites and their special virtues. Consider using old favorites in new ways (exterior siding on the inside) or combinations to create walls with the look you're after.

Ceramic tile and natural stones

Ceramic tile has long been a natural choice for bathrooms. Increasingly, ceramic tile is also a popular choice for kitchens with Old World or Vintage charm — for small areas, such as *backsplashes* (the space between the sink and wall-hung cabinets), and entire wall areas (floor to ceiling).

Tile makes good sense in areas that must stand up to heavy traffic and cleaning (see Figure 13-3), including entry halls and mudrooms. Porcelain tile has color throughout which makes it an excellent choice for heavy wear areas. Porcelain's *vitreous* (glasslike) nature makes it nonabsorbent so it's stainproof and sanitary. Glazed and porcelain tile come in an endless array of colors, patterns, textures, and sizes. Use small sizes in Traditional settings and large ones in Contemporary styles.

Figure 13-3:
Using tile for important wall areas creates interesting pattern, color, and texture.

*Photograph courtesy Rutt Cabinets,
Design by George Rallis*

Marble, a fine material in its polished state, is usually seen on walls and floors in formal settings. Lately, marble is taking on a rustic look because it's being *tumbled* (placed in a rotating bin with an abrasive that roughs it up) instead of *polished* (creating a smooth surface). In Old World kitchens, tumbled marble (which is treated with a sealant to keep it clean) adds rustic yet sophisticated charm.

Fabrics

Fabric is a favorite wall covering for almost any room in the house. Certain historic houses have velvet-covered walls, while others have linen. Fabric, such as polished cotton, works well for *tenting* (covering the walls and ceiling) powder rooms, fancy bathrooms, and even bedrooms. But fabrics are impractical for use in kitchens, where they're a fire hazard. Generally, in living rooms and other public areas, fabrics are professionally mounted on a backing material that makes them easier to install (by professionals). Consider having fabric treated with a protective coating that makes it easier to maintain.

Fabrics used in bedrooms are often gathered or sheared at the top and bottom on curtain rods that are attached to the wall. Sometimes fabric is gathered on wood slats, which are screwed or nailed into the wall. Another method is to gather and staple fabric directly onto the wall.

Tenting bedrooms and bathrooms is a romantic and practical way to disguise disfigured walls and ceilings.

Favorite fabrics for walls are velvet, linen, silk, cotton chintz, and cotton corduroy. Some fabrics, like corduroy, don't drape very well. Silk does.

Fabrics come in standard widths: dressmaker, 35-inch; drapery, 45-inch; and upholstery, 54-inch. To measure fabric for wall covering, follow these steps:

1. **Determine the number of widths you need per wall by placing a full 35-, 45- or 54-inch-wide piece in the center of the wall, and then adding widths to either side to cover the wall.** Deduct 1 inch from each side to allow for cutting away selvage and room for a ⅝-inch seam. (Consider 54-inch-wide as 52-inch-wide fabric.) This prevents awkwardly placed seams or motifs.

2. **Measure your wall's height and translate that figure into yards.**

3. **Multiply the number of widths by number of yards for total yardage needed to cover your wall or walls.** (For example: A 13-foot-wide by 12-foot-high wall needs three widths of 54-inch fabric, multiplied by 4 yards, for a total of 12 yards of fabric.)

Mirror

Mirrors do marvels: They visually expand small spaces and reflect light and views. Use mirrors in wall-to-wall, floor-to-ceiling applications in Contemporary rooms. Mirroring a wall above a *wainscot* (wood paneling) or *dado* (the area below a chair rail) in a Traditional room, such as a small- or medium-sized dining room, is a brilliant idea.

If you want to mirror a whole wall in a Traditional setting, consider using mirror tiles with beveled edges. Beveled edges give mirror tiles a richer, heavier look. You can also purchase mirror in large sheets and have professionals install it in wall-to-wall applications. Do-it-yourselfers find that mirror strips (in various widths and lengths) and large mirror tiles are easier to handle. Both are available in plain or beveled edges.

Paint

Paint offers so much for so little cost. You can choose any color, starting with the thousands offered by leading paint companies. If you don't see the one you want, just take an example of the color you want (maybe your favorite shirt) with you to the paint store, and the store's computer can match it perfectly.

Many paint companies have developed collections of color combinations, labeling them with romantic or historic names that hint at a way to use them. But no color police are going to stop you from using a collection called Seashore in your suburban ranch house. If the brochures of color combinations aren't the solution, some stores have computerized aids for selecting just the right color scheme for any room. (For some tips, check out Chapter 5.)

Want a texture as well? No problem. New faux-finish and special decorative effects come in a kit, complete with instruction booklets (see Figure 13-4).

Figure 13-4:
You can apply paint in a number of different ways to achieve very different effects.

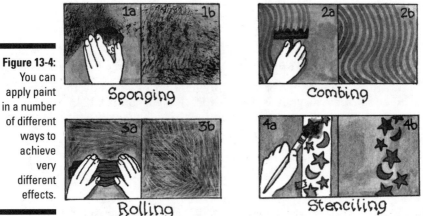

If yours is a high-traffic household, pick a finish that's not only beautiful but also washable. Paint technology is always improving, so that one coat of quality paint over a tinted primer is sufficient. You may have to pay a little more, but you save in labor.

The sidebar "Generating special effects with paint" provides suggestions for using paint in creative ways. For even more information about paint and painting techniques, check out *Home Improvement For Dummies* by Gene and Katie Hamilton (Wiley Publishing, Inc.).

Estimating the quantity of paint you need is as easy as going online to www.gliddenpaint.com. If you really want to do it yourself, use this three-step process: First determine your room's total square footage by multiplying wall width by wall height by number of walls. Next, if areas such as doors and windows will be a separate color, calculate that area and subtract it from your total square footage. Finally, divide the total square footage by the coverage per gallon as noted on the can.

Stucco

Stucco (a textured plaster) is a great traditional finish for all types of Country and Old World-style walls. Ask your paint dealer about stuccos that come premixed, ready to spread from the can. One of the newest is Spatula Stuhhi Venetian Stucco available from Janovic in New York City (see Chapter 29). Practice your spreading technique on a piece of plywood or gypsum wallboard so that you get the precise texture you're aiming for.

Wallpaper and wallcoverings

Most wallpaper really isn't paper — it's vinyl or vinyl-coated, so it's tougher, longer wearing, and washable. Some (unwashable) wallcoverings are grasscloth, silk, linen, or other kinds of material. Visit the Wallcoverings Association's Web site (www.wallcoverings.org) for lots of facts about wallcoverings.

No other material does what a well-designed wallcovering does for any room — it introduces unique pattern, color, and texture simultaneously. The range of patterns is so vast that you're certain to find anything you want. Many wallcoverings come pre-pasted for easier installation.

You need patience when shopping for wallcovering. Give yourself time to search through the enormous number of wallcovering books. Most home improvement stores carry popular wallcoverings. Specialty wallcovering stores carry a greater range of products, including designer lines.

You may need a specific wallcovering pattern to solve a difficult decorating problem. For example, you may need a tiny geometric on a light background to create a sense of unity and dimension in a small attic room. You may need a large floral pattern to make a big bedroom look better scaled. You may need just the right pattern to visually furnish a hallway that's too small for furniture and but large enough to look empty. Certain embossed wallcoverings take on the look of leather, carved wood, and ornate plaster (and they can be painted), which adds desirable texture to Contemporary spaces where Traditional pattern wouldn't work.

Generating special effects with paint

Paint, the least expensive wall covering, is also the most versatile. Try these special decorative paint effects to enliven your walls:

✔ **Classic faux finishes.** Faux paint finishes have never been more popular. They include sponging, ragging, rolling, combing, feathering, stippling, spattering, masking, marbleizing, and tortoise and bamboo finishes. All are do-it-yourself projects, and kits and instructions are readily available at home improvement shops.

✔ **Other faux finishes.** If traditional faux finishes aren't your cup of tea, check out the Ralph Lauren Paint "Techniques" booklet and discover step-by-step how to make a painted wall look like denim, chambray, linen, suede, or antiqued leather. If you want more, consider the historic crackle or aging finishes, or unique finishes that simulate such sophisticated textures as gray flannel, duchesse satin, and river rock. Kits, how-to booklets, and videos are available in paint stores and home centers.

✔ **Stenciling.** Stenciling is a classic art form that seems to grow more popular every year. It's a charming touch to Colonial, Early American, Country, and Romantic rooms. And it's easy to do, even for amateurs. Books and kits abound (you'll find them at craft shops).

Table 13-1 offers handy estimates for the number of wallpaper (or other wall-covering) rolls you can expect to use in your room.

Table 13-1	**Estimating Typical Wallpaper Rollage**		
Room width by length	*Rolls for room with 8-foot ceiling*	*Rolls for room with 9-foot ceiling*	*Rolls for covering ceiling*
8 x 10	9	10	3
10 x 12	11	12	4
12 x 12	12	14	5
14 x 20	17	19	9
16 x 20	18	20	10

Wood

Unless you have a log home, logs probably aren't something you want to add to your walls. But wood paneling may be (and it's come a long way since the 1970s).

Paneling ranges from extraordinarily expensive, solid wood, traditional, English-style paneling (and French *boiserie,* which is fancy wood paneling), to knotty pine planks and more familiar, less expensive, 4-x-8-foot sheets in a wide variety of woods and wood looks. Paneling is available in a huge variety of natural wood colors and textures, painted finishes, and antique colors.

Reclaimed barnboard is wonderful for Country-style rooms. Sometimes, it's free for the taking. Just ask the farmer or landowner for his or her permission to tear down a crumbling barn for its boards! And ask your builder or carpenter about the proper way to de-bug recycled wood before bringing it into your house. Ask your local paint dealer for suggestions about refinishing old barnboard.

Shop around for the paneling that adds the look you want. Generally, paneling with raised grounds and trims, which look like boxes, is dressier. Plank styles, with vertical grooves, tend to look casual and are at home in informal rooms. You may like paneling used as wainscot, usually about 30 inches high in Early American, Victorian, and Country-style rooms and even higher in Arts and Crafts interiors.

When shopping for wood wall coverings, keep these pointers in mind:

 ✔ Paneling comes in 4-x-8-foot sizes for easy, efficient installation.

 ✔ Bead board resembles tongue-and-groove planks that feature a distinctive thin vertical stripe. It's particularly good-looking in Cottage-style interiors. It can be used in just about every room in the house, beginning with the front entry and ending with the kitchen. (You can even apply bead board to ceilings.)

 ✔ Real planks — especially knotty pine — are popular wall surfaces. They're great for Cottage and Lodge interiors, dens, and family rooms.

 ✔ Wood moldings create designs on walls that simulate or enhance paneling. You can paint these moldings to blend or contrast with painted walls or stain them to match wood paneling or planks.

Chapter 14

Finding Fabulous Floors

*F*looring and floorcovering are two different items. *Flooring* is the hard, finished surface, such as wood, tile, or stone, that is permanently attached to, and an important part of, a building. *Floorcovering* is a material, such as an area rug, that goes on top of finished flooring. Many rooms use flooring and a floorcovering together — for example, a rug over wood.

In this chapter, we show you some of the most popular of these materials — wood, stone, synthetics, carpeting, and rugs. We highlight some of the advantages and disadvantages of each material. And, of course, we explain various ways you can decorate with them.

Installing Hard Surfaces

Hard-surface flooring is a favorite for homeowners who want flooring to last forever. You can find it in a wide range of materials, including wood, natural stone, and ceramic tile (see Figure 14-1). Some designers have used concrete flooring for Contemporary rooms. Synthetic flooring (either resilient vinyl or laminate flooring) is less expensive than other materials. And linoleum, an early man-made floorcovering, is making a comeback.

Figure 14-1:
Hard-
surface
flooring
adds charm
to almost
any room in
the house.

*Photograph courtesy Brewster Wallcoverings'
King's Road collection*

Walking on wood

Wood flooring is available in two forms: *traditional* (which professionals install and finish) and *engineered* or *prefinished* (which you can install your-self). For more facts about wood, go to www.hardwoodinfo.com.

Traditional wood flooring comes in two configurations: planks (in wide or narrow widths, and in same-size or random widths and lengths) and parquet patterns. Planks come with either straight or beveled edges with real or faux pegs. Beveled edges create a rich-looking, recessed groove, but those grooves are dirt-catchers that can slow down a vacuuming job.

Traditional wood flooring costs more than its prefinished counterpart. But you can refinish wood flooring several times, so it lasts for many years. After installations, telling traditional flooring from prefinished is difficult. The only thing you notice is the characteristic warmth of a wood floor (see Figure 14-2).

Both traditional and prefinished wood flooring are available in a variety of colors, wood grain patterning, textures, and finishes. Hardwoods (maple, oak, and walnut) are common favorites because they wear well and come in a range of light to dark finishes. Brazilian cherry, an especially fine hardwood, is very dressy looking. Exotic hardwoods, such as santos mahogany, wenge, and bamboo, are becoming popular. Bamboo doesn't hold up well in wet areas, but you can use it in living, dining, and family rooms. All hardwoods stand the test of time — they're durable.

Pine, a favorite in Country-style interiors, is a softer wood in a medium color. Pine does show the effects of hard wear, but if you like the lived-in look, this wood is for you. Pine doesn't refinish as well as hardwood. However, some people like to install pine (because it's relatively inexpensive) and then paint it or stencil patterns on it. Doing so adds old-fashioned charm. Cover painted or stenciled surfaces with a protective coat of polyurethane.

Figure 14-2:
Ceramic tile, carpeting, painted or natural wood, stone, mosaic — almost anything goes for bedroom flooring.

Photograph courtesy Brewster Wallcoverings'
Kindred Spirits collection

You can fancy up plank floors with elaborate borders and decorative medallions, thanks to laser-cutting technology that makes manufacturing more affordable than ever. Ask your dealer about these exciting options.

Parquet patterns — available in a wide range of woods — are available in numerous styles in traditional wood flooring and in a limited number of styles in prefinished floorings. You can choose simple trellis patterns as well as historic styles based on those from famous chateaux and mansions. The more elaborate the parquet, the more at home it is in a grand room — and the higher the price. Simple parquet patterns in more rustic, less finely grained woods are at home in cottages, too.

Wood reflects sound. If a quiet atmosphere is your main goal, wood isn't your best bet. However, adding padded carpeting in walkways lowers the boom on wooden floor noise and adds pattern and color to a plain surface.

Casting a stone floor

Durable and elegant stone brings to mind images of palaces and huge houses. But you don't need a mansion to incorporate stone in your home (see Figure 14-3). Many different kinds of natural stones are available and they all must be properly sealed and maintained. (Ask your dealer for more specific information about the stone that interests you.) The following are some of the more popular varieties:

- **Brick:** Brick is a handsome material that looks great in Traditional and Contemporary settings. Like many natural stones and some Mexican tiles, brick is porous and must be sealed against stains to make cleaning easier. More popular places for using it are ground-level kitchen floors, mudrooms, and back entry halls.

- **Concrete:** Once the stuff of subfloors and basements, concrete is now trendy in homes, thanks to new colors, textures, and finishes. Color can be added to ready-mix concrete, applied to the top of a still-moist concrete slab, or acid-stained by professionals. Concrete can be stamped with brick, slate, and other patterns. It must be sealed to protect the color and finish. Less costly than natural stones, concrete is easier to maintain.

- **Ceramic tile:** Available in an endless number of colors and in patterns that mimic other materials such as natural stone, ceramic tile is a great option. A wide range of tile sizes and shapes, as well as different colored grouts, makes ceramic tile one of the most versatile decorating tools.

- *Porcelain tiles* have color throughout, so that the color and pattern aren't lost if the tile is chipped or worn. Porcelain tile is particularly great for kitchens because it doesn't stain. But porcelain tiles do cost more than glazed tiles. Porcelain tiles mimic real stone beautifully but don't have to be sealed.

   Tiles are classified according to use for walls, floors, and countertops. Make sure that your tile dealer knows what surface you're buying the tiles for, and follow the dealer's advice for installing them.

- **Granite:** Making its way into today's homes, especially as kitchen counters, granite is the hardest of the natural stones. It's also durable and relatively expensive, but becoming competitively priced. At $65 to $100 per square foot installed, it compares favorably to man-made, solid-surface materials. Granite comes in fascinating colors and patterns, ranging from casual earthy looks to fine and formal colors, and in textures from polished to *honed* (rough).

- **Limestone:** Limestone, commonly used to build monuments and museums (such as the U.S. Holocaust Memorial Museum, the Empire State Building, and the Biltmore Estate) is available for inside use. For use in interiors (where it's popular as entry hall flooring), the porous stone needs proper sealing. Because it reacts adversely to acids, don't use it in your kitchen.

- **Marble:** Available in a variety of colors, marble is usually highly polished, fine, and formal. You can create elaborate patterns in contrasting colors of marble for Traditional interiors or in pale, sophisticated colors in Contemporary interiors. *Tumbled* varieties (whose finish is more casual) are at home in Old World kitchens. Marble is relatively soft, scratches easily, and isn't good for heavily used areas. You can purchase marble in about the same price range as granite.

✔ **Mosaic:** Made of tiny pieces of cut natural stone or ceramic tile, mosaic can be pricey. Every piece is hand-cut and applied to a backer. Some mosaics are applied to a cement backer board that's good for use in damp areas, such as the shower and kitchen backsplash. Mosaic is also pre-grouted, so you can easily and quickly install it without losing any of the tiny pieces. Mosaic can be used as a border, wall mural, or floor medallion.

✔ **Slate:** Sometimes called *flagstone,* slate was once reserved for hallways and garden rooms. Now it's finding its way to other parts of the home, including kitchens. It comes in several natural colors, including dark gray, red, green, and variegated purple. Usually cut in large rectangles, grout lines add pattern to this surface. Slate is handsome in Traditional, Country, and Contemporary rooms. Some designers combine slate with limestone tiles for an interesting contrast. Slate costs less than marble or granite.

✔ **Soapstone:** This stone is well named, because to the touch, it feels soapy. Soapstone is a favorite surface in science laboratories because it's heat-, acid-, and water-resistant. The Scandinavians make stoves out of it. You can find it in Country-style sinks, and it's reasonably priced compared to other stone.

✔ **Terrazzo:** A poured concrete with inset marble chips, terrazzo was popular years ago, especially in Florida and other warm-weather climates. Originally, terrazzo was an inexpensive alternative, but today it's not all that cheap. Terrazzo is a distinctive material with great appeal, and it lasts forever. It works with Traditional and Contemporary interiors.

Figure 14-3:
Natural stone — especially with complementary mosaic stone trims — creates an upscale look that's well worth the investment.

Photograph courtesy Rudy Santos, Designer & CEO, RoSan Imports and RoSan Custom Kitchens & Baths

Sizing up synthetics

Synthetic flooring is available in a number of materials. It comes in two varieties: *resilient* and *laminate.* Resilient flooring has been around for some time, while laminate flooring is relatively new.

Resilient flooring

Resilient flooring is sometimes called *vinyl flooring,* but to qualify as a solid vinyl product, it must contain at least 40 percent polyvinyl chloride (PVC). Once considered an inexpensive flooring alternative, vinyl isn't necessarily the lowest-priced material anymore thanks to new materials and manufacturing techniques.

Resilient flooring wears well, as long as you don't wear stiletto heels on this impressionable surface. Cushioning makes resilient flooring easy on feet and legs. This kind of flooring is a favorite material for kitchens and baths because it cleans easily. Patterns are based on granny quilts, porcelain china, and authentic-looking natural stones.

Laminate flooring

Laminate flooring is a relatively new facet of synthetic flooring. It's made by layering printed paper and coatings, and then fusing them together under high heat and pressure. Laminate flooring comes in strips, planks, and squares, and it's made to look like wood (or sometimes, like stone). In the past, this kind of flooring had to be carefully and properly installed because water (from mopping and cleaning) could damage the edges. For this reason, you may not have wanted to use it in a kitchen, bath, or entry hall. New technology has improved this material so that laminate is now wet-area safe. Laminate flooring is also easier than ever to install.

Wilsonart International (www.wilsonart.com) has introduced its Duolink system featuring the Tap-N-Lock method of connecting the "planks." Because the planks are tongue-and-groove, they lock together with a tap (and no glue), which makes it easy to install yourself. Like prefinished, do-it-yourself (DIY) wood floors, laminate can be installed as a *floating floor* (not attached to the wall at the edges) over most existing floorings. Many other companies, such as Pergo, offer similar DIY flooring. Check your home improvement stores.

Stepping on Soft Surfaces

Although hard surfaces last longer, you may prefer softness underfoot. You can have it in the form of wall-to-wall carpeting — considered a flooring because it's installed as part of the building — or a rug that covers most of the floor.

Choosing carpeting

Wall-to-wall carpeting fills the floor area with pattern, color, and texture. When properly padded, it's extremely comfortable and among the least expensive floorcoverings. As if that weren't enough, carpeting muffles noise and doubles as a sound controller. Go to www.carpet-rug.com, the carpet industry's Web site, for information.

Most carpet is *tufted*, meaning the yarn is embedded in the backing. Give a second thought to buying a continuous loop rug carpet, because after a loop starts to unravel, it has no natural stopping point. (Continuous loop is a construction technique, not a style. Other construction techniques include woven and needlepunch.) We know, because our puppy started pulling on a loose thread in a living room carpet. Before anyone noticed, a large part of the rug had become one long and very loose thread, lying in a heap at his paws while he tugged away at the connected end, delighting in his new game!

Carpeting can assume either a very laid-back or a very in-your-face role. If you pick a show-off pattern, keep the upholstery and window treatments in a solid or all-over pattern or texture that doesn't compete with the carpeting.

Commercial-grade carpeting, in handsome stripes and geometrics, not only looks good but also works hard in heavy wear-and-tear areas like family rooms. If you haven't considered commercial-grade carpeting before, be sure to look it over. Note that tightly woven, no-pile commercial carpets often feature novelty weave patterns. Ask your carpet dealer whether the pattern can be installed so that seams don't show. An all-over printed pattern hides seams, and so do low and high pile surfaces. (*Pile* refers to the height of the carpet's fibers.)

Commercial-grade carpeting is slightly more expensive than residential-grade carpeting, but it's well worth the price if you intend to keep it for a long time.

Don't use ordinary carpeting in baths and kitchens. Look for bathroom carpeting (which can be laundered) and kitchen carpeting (which doesn't allow water to pass through to the floor beneath). If you're happier scrubbing hard-wear areas, combining kitchen carpeting in the kitchen/dining area with ceramic or vinyl tile in a sink and stove work area can be a great idea.

Be sure to use the correct padding with the carpeting you choose. Ask the salesperson for guidance in choosing the right one. And, to protect your investment, ask your carpet dealer about a stain-resistant protective coating to prolong your carpeting's life.

Resting on your rugs

Rugs come in many different sizes. But generally, a *rug* covers most of the floor, while an *area rug* defines a smaller area.

An area rug is an accessory that defines a special spot in a room (see Figure 14-4). You can use area rugs just about anywhere in a house — in the entry hall, bedrooms, the den, and even the kitchen. Our friend placed a watermelon red Oriental rug in front of the sink in her Traditional kitchen, with a black-and-white vinyl tile floor. She painted the insides of the white cabinets the same luscious fruity red as her rug, so that opening the cabinet doors was a feast for the eyes. Put padding under your area rug to keep it from slipping.

Figure 14-4: Wood and carpeting — or wood and an area rug — are great for a dining room. Generally, the busier a wallcovering, the quieter the floor.

Photograph courtesy Brewster Wallcoverings, Toile Impressions collection

The larger the room, the larger your area rug can be. For example, we placed a 10-x-12-foot rug on a diagonal angle in the middle of a long, rectangular, combination living and dining room. A sofa, coffee table, and two easy chairs sit on top of the rug. As a result, the rug defines a conversational area and orients the seating toward a TV set and window with an ocean view. Although seating faces more toward one end of the long room, the angled rug directs the eye to both ends of the room so that no area seems neglected.

Rugs are manufactured in several different ways: machine-made, handmade, and homemade. Machine-made rugs are the most plentiful and least expensive. Handmade rugs are costly but may increase in value over time. Homemade rugs have tremendous charm — perfect for Country and Cottage interiors.

Machine-made rugs

Many more people can own handsome rugs now than in the past because of machines. Machines produce rugs quickly, eliminating the high cost of labor. Traditional weaves include the following:

- **Axminster:** These are rugs that look hand-tufted and have unlimited pattern complexity and color selection.

- **Velvet:** Cut-pile rugs that look like (but are less resilient than) Wilton rugs, Velvet rugs are usually woven in solid colors.

- **Wilton:** Woven on a *Jacquard* (a patterned weaving technique), tapestry-like loom that permits as many as eight colors, Wilton rugs are considered the best of the machine-made rugs.

Handmade rugs

Historic Western handmade rugs include

- **Aubusson:** Similar to a heavy tapestry, Aubusson rugs have distinctive floral patterns.

- **Savonnerie:** Made in France, Savonnerie rugs are constructed similarly to Oriental rugs, but with French patterns.

Oriental rugs come from the Near and Far East. The six most recognized types are Caucasian, Chinese, Indian, Persian, Turkish, and Turkoman. Each has distinctive traditional colors and patterns and comes in a variety of sizes. Knowledgeable salespeople are usually eager to point out the merits of a rug. But remember that, in general, better rugs have more knots, are heavier, have a more distinct pattern, and have finer (more distinct) lines.

Oriental rugs are a decorator's delight. Almost any color you could want is available, even though you may have to search a while. Patterns and colors range from formal to casual. Although Orientals go with any style, not every Oriental goes with just any style. Select your Oriental rug carefully. Like a beautiful jewel, it deserves the right setting. Ask whether you can try out your rug at home and, if it doesn't look just right, return it for another.

Homemade rugs

A number of rugs are either made at home (as they were years ago) or are commercially made with a homemade look. These affordable rugs — made in both wool and cotton — are highly decorative and make great floor and wall accessories. Homemade rugs include the following:

- **Chainstitch rugs:** Made in India, these rugs attach a chainstitch pattern onto a backing.

- **Dhurries:** These flat weave rugs, usually with floral designs, are made in India of wool or cotton — originally for use on summerhouse floors.

✔ **Hooked rugs:** These rugs are made by pulling and knotting yarns through a coarse, canvas burlap backing.

✔ **Kilims:** These flat weave rugs, made in the Near East, come in geometric designs and strong colors.

✔ **Navajo rugs:** These flat weave rugs also come in geometric patterns, but are woven by Navajo Indians in the American Southwest.

✔ **Needlepoint rugs:** These rugs are made in large quantities in such places as Portuguese convents.

Solving Problems with Flooring

If you're faced with an awkwardly shaped room, you can use floorings to reshape it (see Figure 14-5). Consider the following list of trouble areas and the way to incorporate all types of flooring materials, including carpeting, laminate, ceramic tile, stone, or wood. Draw on these suggestions when you're ready to redecorate — and reshape — rooms in your house.

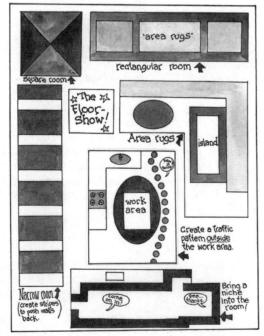

Figure 14-5: To reshape awkward spaces, use flooring materials to create designs.

✔ **Confusing traffic patterns:** Give busy rooms with confusing traffic patterns a green light by creating a "yellow brick road" pathway of stepping-stone-like inserts (circles, triangles, or rectangles) in different colors, textures, or patterns. This technique is a great way to create a pathway that keeps traffic outside a busy area (such as a kitchen).

✔ **Disappearing niches:** Niches can seem divorced from the rest of a room, so rein a niche in with the same decorative border that circles the rest of the room.

✔ **L-shaped kitchens:** These kitchens can seem disorganized. If you have an island, surround it with a strongly contrasting, decorative border. If not, create a strongly colored medallion (circular or oval) in the middle of the main work area. If the room is large, create a border around the perimeter in a color that matches either the border around an island or a central medallion. This technique creates lively, interesting interaction.

✔ **Narrow rooms:** Visually stretch the room's width with a series of broad stripes on the floor. The longer the room, the broader the stripes can be, and the more (and more dramatic) colors you can introduce. For shorter rooms, keep stripes narrow and palettes to two light colors. (Rough out your stripe design on graph paper and show it to the floorcovering dealer before you order material.)

✔ **Rectangular rooms:** Divide and conquer a rectangular room by using floorcovering inserts. Position them so that they look like *area rugs* surrounded by deep borders. The largest of these virtual area rugs should occupy the center two-thirds or so of the room and be flanked by smaller area rugs. Work out your design on graph paper until you get just the right area rug size.

✔ **Square rooms:** Make a stodgy square room appear dynamic by drawing an X from corner to corner and dividing the room into four triangles. Install one color in the top and bottom triangles and a complementary color of flooring in the remaining two triangles. Use this technique in any room that's intended for fun — a playroom, child's room, or garden room. For a sophisticated Contemporary room, use tints and neutral shades.

Chapter 15

Sprucing Up Ceilings

· ·

· ·

*V*ast, empty ceilings are wastelands — and great opportunities for creative decorating. Ceilings are as big as floors (that's a no-brainer), but most people decorate with fabulous floorcoverings and wallcoverings and leave this huge popcorned surface white.

This chapter helps you recognize and deal decoratively with potential problems. We explain the importance of keeping your ceiling's style consistent with the style of your house and the rest of the room. We also explain dozens of different techniques — from simple painting to serious rebuilding — that can change a room's mood for the better. Finally, we offer solutions for some common problems.

Considering Form and Function

Ceilings disguise whatever is directly above them, such as heat and air conditioning ducts, and they also anchor items such as lighting fixtures, smoke alarms, and sound equipment. Ceilings (and the insulation above them) affect a room's temperature and noise level.

In addition to paying attention to the practicalities, integrating your ceiling design into your overall room scheme will make your room look like a decorator showcase. (Mirrored ceilings, for example, are associated with Hollywood bedrooms. But beware: If you choose to use mirrors on a ceiling, be sure they're securely attached!)

Base your ceiling treatment on the architectural clues in your house. Do you see any Old World, Victorian, or Country elements? Or is your house strictly Contemporary? Most houses (and apartments) aren't one distinct style, but instead blend and mix many "vernacular" interpretations of architectural styles. For more information on styles, see Chapters 9 and 10.

If you're building or remodeling, ask the builder to hold off on the popcorn (a rough textured spray-on), shown in Figure 15-1. Ask for a plain, smooth surface that you can treat decoratively. Smooth ceilings not only appear higher than their popcorn counterparts, but they're also easier to paint or embellish. If you have a popcorn ceiling, ask your local paint dealer for the best way to remove it.

Figure 15-1:
If you can, choose a smooth ceiling instead of one with a popcorn surface.

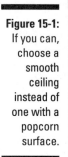

Painting Your Ceiling

Painting a ceiling a beautiful color is an easy way to change any room's appearance. Whether you want to create just a little interest or a work of art, this section gives you all the answers — and ideas — you need.

Getting it white

Okay, we admit it — a white ceiling reflects more light than any other color. So if you're looking for a sure bet, white may be for you. But you can add interest to a white ceiling by choosing the *right* white — that is, one of the many new whites with a smidgen of color that are a far cry from the old standard ceiling white.

Carry your wall color onto the white ceiling by creating a focal point of the same hue. Place a vibrant spot of color — in the form of an oval or circle painted on the ceiling — over a point of interest, such as a dining area, a conversation area, or a room's center.

Using color for unity

Unify the ceiling and walls by painting them the same color, or paint the ceiling a tint (lighter) or tone (darker) of the wall color. A tint makes a low ceiling seem to float away. A tone (also called a *shade*) makes a large room seem more intimate. Painting walls and ceilings in the same color family works especially well for lighter colors, particularly neutrals. This technique also works effectively for creating intimate rooms using deep or rich colors such as *eggplant* (a deep grayed purple).

Using color for contrast

Create drama by painting the walls and ceiling contrasting colors. This technique works wonders in large rooms with high ceilings.

In a small- or medium-sized room, paint the ceiling a contrast color lighter than the walls to help *open up* the room. An atmospheric pale gray-blue ceiling in an apricot room is a good example. In a room with an awkwardly high ceiling, you can lower the ceiling visually by painting it a dark color. A blacked-out ceiling, for example, can hide imperfections and make the ceiling disappear.

To make ceilings seem higher, keep molding the same color as walls. To make ceilings seem lower, paint molding the same color as the ceiling. If you're using the same or similar dark color as the walls, you can add a hint of drama by painting ceiling molding a gently contrasting color.

Designing your own pattern

Create your own modern art graphic design and paint away. If wallpaper covers the walls, use colors from the pattern for your ceiling design. This technique is inexpensive and adds a sense of fun and play. Graphics are especially cheerful in a child's room, bathroom, playroom, or laundry.

Painting a sky

Painting clouds on a ceiling is a popular technique for adding instant atmosphere. You don't need to be an artist to duplicate the effect of soft wisps of clouds. Plenty of faux painting books give step-by-step instructions and list all the materials and best colors. But, if you're no Monet, consider hiring an artist from a local art school (but be sure to see samples of the student's work first).

Gold stars and a moon on a midnight-blue sky may be just the cure for insomnia. A friend, who isn't an artist, painted a starry night scene on the ceiling of her young daughter's bedroom. Her daughter now counts stars, not sheep.

Stenciling

Stenciling is easy, even for an amateur. For inspiration, look at decorating magazines and art history books. They show designs as simple as trailing ivy borders that spill over onto the ceiling. Stencil a trellis pattern to raise a too-low ceiling. Stencil large flowers — cabbage roses or sunflowers — to lower a too-high ceiling. Stencil patterns, paints, and idea books are available in craft shops.

Creating a mural

Take a tip from Michelangelo — turn your ceiling into a giant mural (see Figure 15-2). If you're a rolling stone, make sure the mural is painted on a canvas and attached in such a way that it can be removed and carted off to your next home.

To make painting easier, use a projector to cast an enlarged image on the painting surface. You can use a slide projector or even your computer and an LCD projector. You can easily trace the image's major outlines on your canvas in pencil, and you may even use a paint-by-numbers approach to mark which colors go in which sections.

Figure 15-2:
A mural in the arched niche above a sink becomes a strong focal point in a kitchen by designer Barton Lidsky.

Photograph courtesy Rutt Kitchens from The Hammer & Nail, NJ

Disguising Your Ceiling

Painting isn't your only option. As this section explains, the sky's the limit when making your ceiling come alive. We give you ideas for using different materials — everything from fabric to straw matting — to cover your ceilings in an innovative, statement-making way.

Letting lattice work its charms

You can buy lattice at garden shops or home improvement stores. (Lattice may come in various sizes, but the most common is 4 x 8 feet.) Painted white and attached to a dark green or bright blue ceiling (and even to the walls), latticework creates a great garden room mood. If you know basic carpentry, you're on your way. If you're all thumbs with a hammer and nails, call a carpenter.

Extending wallcoverings

Wallcovering adds a finishing touch to a ceiling. You can decorate a small bathroom by covering the walls and ceiling in the same small, nondirectional print.

Don't hesitate to cover a small room's ceiling (and walls) in a wallpaper with a dark, even black, background. The dark background makes walls and ceiling fade away, and the pattern stands out. Wallpapering a room's ceiling in a lattice or trellis pattern makes the space seem more spacious.

In a larger room, use a small print for the ceiling that coordinates with a larger pattern for the walls. If you're using a large-scale floral pattern on walls in a not-so-big room, and the pattern is too big for the ceiling, cut out some of the flowers and glue them on the ceiling in a pattern that looks good to your critical eye. Want to know more about wallcoverings? Take a look at Chapter 13.

Tenting a ceiling with fabric

Tenting calls for yards and yards of fabric, but it creates a great sense of fun and fantasy. For the best method, yardage, and other vital information, check with your local upholsterer. In addition to looking wonderful, tenting absorbs sound, quieting a dining room, bedroom, bathroom, or garden room.

Tenting isn't necessarily a do-it-yourself project, unless you're very handy with fabric and you have assistance putting up the material. (Some how-to decorating books give instructions.) Use a fabric with an all-over, nondirectional pattern (no flowers with stems, book jackets with lettering, and so on), so you don't have a problem in matching the pattern. Only the pros work with stripes! Tenting is best installed by professionals.

Creating a ribbon trellis

Grosgrain ribbon (characterized by its large grain and thick fabric) glued on the ceiling in a trellis pattern creates a feeling similar to a wooden lattice. This technique is slightly less dimensional, but it's quick, easy, and inexpensive. We created a ribbon trellis in the tiny New York City kitchen of a celebrity client, matching ribbon color to the wall paint color. He loved it. We used a one-inch wide ribbon, but you can use any width you want.

Be sure to use grosgrain ribbon, because glue seeps through satin ribbon, marring it. Design, measure, and lightly mark where the ribbon goes before you start gluing. Plain ol' white school glue works well for applying the ribbon.

Applying straw matting

Straw matting adds an exotic touch to a garden room's ceiling and to an Africa-inspired decorating scheme. Mats come in a variety of sizes and shapes. Attach the matting with glue so that it doesn't sag. And don't use straw matting in a high moisture area. If you like the idea but prefer to use matchstick blinds, they work, too — especially if you don't have to cut them to fit between beams.

Installing ceramic tiles

Designers frequently use ceramic tile to cover bathrooms, garden rooms, decorative niches, and alcoves in kitchens and other rooms. Tile stores carry huge selections of distinctive tiles. Ask which ones are better suited for ceilings (some are thinner and work better than others). Also ask about techniques for securing tiles while the adhesive is drying. If you have any doubts about doing it yourself, don't hesitate in having a professional install them for the best results.

Reducing noise with acoustic tiles

Acoustic tile has its place — and that's wherever noise is a problem. A basement practice room for your rock-and-roll teenager's band may be one such place. More interesting designs and patterns are available every year, including painted plank looks. Ask at your favorite home center. If you already have acoustic tiles and want to spruce them up, don't hesitate to paint them (and those metal frames that support them). The loss of acoustic ability is negligible, and the results are well worth the paint!

Recently, a client asked us to beautify a room with a two-level ceiling. The dreaded popcorn covered the room's higher center, and the perimeter had a drop ceiling of acoustic tile. To make the too-low and really ugly acoustic tile disappear, we painted it the same garden green as the wall. We left the popcorn ceiling crisp Country white for strongest contrast, and it worked. Now, it's nearly impossible to see the dark green ceiling because the eye speeds to the higher bright white one.

Decoupaging your ceiling

You can apply favorite motifs on your ceiling using a technique called *decoupage,* which involves covering paper cutouts with several layers of lacquer or varnish. Try angels in your little cherub's bedroom, big cabbage roses above your bathtub, veggies in the kitchen, and so on. Look for a decoupage kit at your local craft shop — they come with easy-to-follow directions.

Before you decoupage, give the ceiling a fresh coat of paint (you won't be painting it after decoupaging). Base your new ceiling paint color on two considerations — your wall color and the dominant color of the motifs you're adding to the ceiling. You want your decoupaged motifs to stand out. Contrast is good — for dark prints, use a light background and for light prints, use a dark one. You may want to paint your ceiling a light tint of your wall color for greater unity and less chance of making a color mistake.

Building the Ceiling You Want

If you're thinking that big changes are in order, this section is for you. Read on to find more information on everything from raising and lowering your ceiling to other techniques, including adding beams or creating *coffers* (recessed areas defined by crossed beam-like architectural elements).

Constructing a false ceiling

Take the idea of a dropped or lowered ceiling to new heights by asking a carpenter to drop (lower) only the outside perimeter of a too-high ceiling. Then have the carpenter install a light in the center area and cover it with a stained glass (real or faux) or other translucent cover. (An alternative may be to install a prefabricated plastic dome that looks like stained glass. Ask your local lighting dealer for sources.)

Raising the ceiling

Liberate your room. Ripping out a too-low ceiling to the rafters creates a dramatic effect and expands the space. Raising a ceiling is definitely a job for professional carpenters or *highly skilled* do-it-yourselfers.

Including classical touches

Traditional interiors used fancy, carved plaster trims (called *anaglypta,* a classical Greek term for low-relief decoration) on ceilings, especially on ceiling areas above chandeliers. Many people now have a renewed interest in these ceiling-enhancing decorations. They're available in a lightweight, easy-to-install plastic that looks like the real thing. Ask to see them at your local home center or building supply store.

Adding beams

Beams add line, direction, and pattern to ceilings. Different kinds of beams are used traditionally in various styles of architecture. Heavy rough beams are characteristic of rustic Colonial American and certain Old World European interiors. Lighter, more refined box beams show up in fancier Early American homes. (For more information on styles, see Chapter 9.) In other interiors, beams are whitewashed, bleached, antiqued, or stenciled.

Painting the space between beams a light color and the beam itself a darker contrasting color heightens the illusion of depth. This trick is a neat space expander in a small- or medium-sized room. Another decorating trick is to paint a low ceiling and beams in a pale color. This trick tends to raise them both, making the ceiling seem higher.

Creating coffers

A *coffer* is a variation on a beamed ceiling. One difference is that, in beamed ceilings, beams run in one direction, creating repeating lines. When using coffers, you use fewer beams or beam-like architectural elements that cross at right angles, creating squares of empty space. Looking up at a coffered ceiling is like looking into the insides of many boxes. Take coffering one step further by decoratively painting or stenciling the *wells* (areas inside the coffers or beam-like structures).

Using planks

Planks — especially redwood and teak — add texture, rich color, and a subtle line to ceilings. If you use real-wood planks in a bathroom, make sure the room is well ventilated and ask your paint dealer about the best coating to protect the wood from moisture. Because planks create lines, make sure they run in the direction you want the eye to travel. Applied lengthwise in a rectangular room, planks make the room look even longer. To make the room seem wider and shorter in length, apply the planks crosswise. If you're handy, you can install the planks yourself. If not, contract a carpenter.

Chapter 16

Dressing Up Windows

With or without fancy treatments, windows provide a focal point (see Chapter 4) and a spot where everyone wants to sit — they're second only to a fireplace in winter. They open a room's interior to the views outside and flood it with natural sunlight. Practically speaking, windows provide views, ventilation, and security (especially if they're impact-resistant).

No sooner had windows been invented than some late sleeper discovered a need for simple shades and blinds. The first room-darkening shade was probably a boulder rolled across the cave door, but window blind design has come a long way since then.

In this chapter, we review different window styles, window coverings, and new concepts in shades and blinds. You'll discover conventional and unconventional window treatments to make all your windows wonderful.

Exposing Windows

Architecturally interesting windows — large or small — are things of beauty best appreciated when left without any sort of coverup. If such practical matters as light control and privacy aren't an issue, leave your windows bare or almost bare.

For example, a client's remodeled home had more than 100 windows. Covering them, even simply, was a major budget drain. For bare windows to be beautiful, they need beautifully designed trims. If your window is basically nice but just needs trim, add it. Note that windows in the same room have to be trimmed complementarily, but not necessarily identically.

If you decide to leave your window bare, consider using a window film that blocks harmful ultraviolet light, reduces interior heat, lowers utility costs, reduces glare, increases privacy, and adds some protection from storms (even hurricanes). Several companies make this film available. The Window and Door Manufacturers Association (WDMA) at www.nwwda.org has some basic information on window film.

Consider adding exterior awnings to your bare windows to shield your interior from direct sun rays. Exterior awnings are visible from inside your room, so consider them an extension of your interior design.

You can add softness by leaving the window mostly bare and adding a small valance (see Figure 16-1).

Figure 16-1:
A small, beautifully bare window, intriguingly trimmed, admits welcome light into an entry landing.

Photograph courtesy Blonder Wallcoverings

Naming your window

Knowing what type of windows you have allows you to discuss them with drapery makers, blind installers, and designers. (For information and illustrations, go to the window glossary at www.nwwda.org.) The rundown includes

- **Awning:** Awning windows sash-crank open from the bottom outward (like a patio awning). Awning-type windows called *hoppers* do just the reverse; they open from the top outward and are often used in

basements. They're also used below fixed-pane picture windows in Contemporary rooms.

- **Bay:** A bay window extends floor to ceiling and projects beyond the plane of the wall.

- **Bow:** A bow window is curved similar to a bay window in that it projects out from the facade, but it has more sashes and less angularity than the bay. It's also known as a *compass* or *radial bay* window.

✔ **Casement:** This window has sashes that crank open from the sides or outward from the center.

✔ **Double-hung:** Stacked windows open by sliding up or down past each other.

✔ **Fixed-pane or fixed-frame:** This window is immovable.

✔ **Garden:** A garden window is a small, high oriel window often installed at countertop height behind a kitchen sink.

✔ **Oriel:** An oriel window projects from the wall, but unlike a bay, the oriel doesn't go all the way to the ground. Instead, brackets, corbels, or a cantilever support it.

✔ **Palladian:** A particular configuration of two double-hung windows, a Palladian flanks a central same-height, double-hung window, topped with a semicircular fixed window.

✔ **Window walls or windowscapes:** They include collections of various windows and doors that make up a whole wall of glass.

Photograph courtesy Hunter Douglas

Looking at Shades, Blinds, and Shutters

Shades, blinds, and shutters are *hard* window treatments as opposed to curtains, which are soft treatments. When used alone, they provide crispness to a Contemporary room. For clarity's sake, we call the old-fashioned roller type (up and down) *shades,* and the newer verticals and horizontals (once called Venetians) *blinds.*

Shades, blinds, and shutters (solid, louvered, or novelty) do a great job of blocking out light. Traditionally, they were installed next to the window and then were topped with a glass or sash curtain, a draw curtain, and finally an overdrapery (more about curtains and draperies later in this chapter). The differences (and advantages) among shades, blinds, and shutters include the following:

- **Shades** are generally an inexpensive (but, surprisingly, not the least expensive) way to solve light and privacy issues. Now, they come in a wide assortment of materials, including novelty weaves and fashionable colors. They may come trimmed or decorated for custom looks. These shades can be installed to roll up from the bottom or down from the top, depending on your light control, viewing, and privacy concerns.

- **Blinds** have come a long way since simple wooden Venetian blinds, including wide-slat and thin-slat aluminum blinds. Clothlike materials in different weights and textures introduce a new softness that's more compatible with Traditional interiors. They offer protection from UV rays that damage textiles, woods, and art objects. Blinds may be set close to the window inside deep *reveals* (protruding frames with recessed areas that allow for inside mount), or on the same plane as the wall in an outside mount. Study your situation to be sure what effect you want and what your situation allows.

- **Shutters** come in conventional (2⅝-inch) width slats used in Traditional settings, as well as large-scale (4-inch or more) California or Plantation slats that are compatible with Contemporary and sophisticated Rustic interiors. Shutters add visual interest and a sense of drama to otherwise boring windows, rooms with bad views, and architecturally deficient rooms. Look for a variety of textures (plain, wood-grain, and so on), materials (wood and wood-look plastic), and colors (including unfinished that you can paint yourself). Whether natural wood or painted, shutters supply excellent energy efficiency.

Before you go shopping for blinds, consider the types. Many blinds manufacturers and catalogs offer several options, including decorative fabric trims and clatter controlling devices. Give the following blinds a good look (and don't get confused by their names or misnomers):

- **Matchstick blinds** (a kind of roll-up shade originally made of split bamboo or other tropical materials) add the spirit of the tropics, energy efficiency, and some privacy to a room. But they don't totally block out the sun or create a sense of privacy unless they're backed with light-absorbing material.

- **Venetian blinds** (usually horizontal) are made in vinyl, metal, and wood. You can control light and privacy by tilting the slats or vanes. Use them in almost any style interior from Traditional and formal to Contemporary and casual.

✔ **Vertical blinds,** a must for sliding doors, come in metal, vinyl (that can look like wood), and fabric and can be coordinated with other types of shades, throughout your home, for complete harmony.

Are you more interested in decorating your windows with shades? Don't think that all shades are alike. Remember, the words *blinds* and *shades* are used in various ways. Consider these types of shades:

✔ **Balloon or Austrian shades,** with extra volumes of material, are great choices for Romantic interiors. These kinds of shades are more than beautiful: They provide energy efficiency, light control, and sound absorption.

✔ **Cellular fabric shades** offer energy efficiency, UV light control (some styles *totally* block out light, but others don't, so check the manufacturer's light-control grading), sound control, and a unified look (the cords and controls are hidden).

✔ **Natural fiber shades** made from mesh add rusticity. Just like with matchstick blinds, back natural fiber shades if you want total privacy.

✔ **Roman shades** come in various degrees of fullness from almost flat to very full and are very decorative. Light control and privacy depend on how much you let them down. Roman shades work well with a wide range of styles but are tailored and more masculine.

Valances cover the hardware at the shade and add a decorative touch. If you need just a touch of decoration (for added pattern, color, or softness) consider using only a valance (see Figure 16-2).

Figure 16-2:
A barely-there valance adds a touch of dressing and softness to a window left beautifully bare.

Photograph courtesy Blonder Wallcoverings, Chesapeake collection

Taking your measurements

Measuring windows isn't brain surgery, but correct measurements are vital when you're ordering blinds and shades, particularly with inside-mount blinds. Follow these guidelines when measuring and estimating yardage and cost.

If you're the least bit uncomfortable with your measuring prowess, check with a professional before ordering.

✔ Use a steel measuring tape for accuracy. Rulers are less accurate, and cloth tape measures stretch and may not give precise results.

✔ Take exact measurements. Round up to the nearest ⅛ inch.

✔ Measure height and then width. Take note of which measurement is height and which is width, and measure all four sides because windows can be irregularly shaped.

✔ Measure every window. Just because windows appear the same to your eye doesn't mean they actually are.

✔ Decide whether you want mounting inside the frame or outside the frame and measure appropriately. Use inside mounting if you want a clean, Contemporary look — and determine if the frame space is deep enough

to hold the hardware. Use outside mounting if the window openings are small and you want them to look larger, or if the window is imperfect and you want to hide it.

✔ For measuring inside-mounting window treatments, make sure the opening has enough clear space for the mounting hardware. The manufacturer usually recommends a minimum depth possible for inside mounting.

✔ For inside-mounting treatments that are completely flush within the window opening, make sure you have the minimum depth for flush inside mounting.

✔ To allow for clearance of operating hardware on blinds and shades on inside mounts only, deduct the manufacturer's recommended amount for that model (commonly anywhere from ⅛ to ⅜ of an inch).

✔ To avoid the light-admitting strip beside blackout shades, measure for shades an inch or two wider than the window.

Various types of blinds and shades require unique measurements for hardware, operational equipment, or cornices. Check with your supplier for more detailed information before committing yourself.

Heeding the Curtain (and Drapery) Call

Curtains and draperies work hard at blocking light, sound, and temperature. In addition to these functions, they're also extraordinarily decorative, adding enormous personality to a room through color, pattern, and texture.

When choosing a patterned fabric for a curtain, especially an unlined curtain, scrunch the fabric in your hand. Doing so allows you to see how the pattern will look when gathered or pleated as it hangs at your window and how it will look with light streaming behind it. Don't wait until the fabric has been made into curtains and hung in your room to be surprised!

The new neutral colors — softened pastels like the faux yellow in a bedroom with a Morning Glory metal bed (top left) — are replacing the old whites, beiges, and grays. The new neutrals are foolproof backgrounds that create a sense of serenity. Warm reds and yellows enhance a sense of intimacy in any room and are especially appropriate for a bedroom. They are also great choices for inviting guestrooms, where cooler colors are less welcoming.

Pattern creates instant mood and continuing interest. Pattern mix is a great decorating trick that gets easier with practice in combining small-, medium-, and large-scale patterns. In the toile dining room (left), note the mix of a medium-scale scene in the toile wallcovering and matching fabric with a bold wide stripe on the chair seats and the small check in the chandelier shades. In the nautically themed sitting room, the designer mixes small-scale geometric and striped wallcovering with slip-covers and cushions in a medley of small-scale stripes, checks, and plaids in fun-loving red, white, and blue.

Photograph courtesy of Raymond Waites Collection for LaneVenture

Photograph courtesy of Michael Weiss Modernism by Vanguard Furniture Company

Decorating styles and periods begin with furniture designed to impart a particular message through line, texture, and color; and in materials and construction techniques. Designer Raymond Waites' Shangri-La chest for LaneVenture (top left) is inspired by historic European styles. Designer Michael Weiss finds inspiration for his contemporary Modernism group (top right) in the earlier Modern movement. Bernhardt Furniture looks back to the Arts and Crafts Movement for direction for the Arcadian Home collection (bottom), which extols simplicity.

Photograph courtesy of Bernhardt Furniture Company

Photograph courtesy of Storehouse, Inc.

Floors play a highly visible role, and character, determined by material and design, counts. Wooden flooring throughout an open floor plan is a sea of planks, in which a boldly colored and patterned area rug surrounded by a red modular Storehouse sofa creates an island of intimacy (top). Designer Sura Malaga, ASID, chooses variegated slate tile to integrate a large open great room and kitchen in a house on the New Jersey shore (bottom left). The floor also adds subtle pattern. Steve Tyrell's Palladian china cabinet is displayed on wooden floors painted in a diamond pattern that relates well to the trellis pattern on the wall (bottom right).

Photograph courtesy of Sura Malaga, ASID

Photograph courtesy of Pennsylvania House's "New Standards: The Steve Tyrell Collection"

Photograph courtesy of Blonder Wallcoverings

Like blank canvases, walls await the materials that will transform them into perfect backgrounds for living. Choices of materials and exciting examples abound, beginning with Bonjour Paris, an Artscapes/3 Pillars Design mural that recreates a street scene (right). Rutt/Atlanta's villa style kitchen (bottom) adds quoins on the wall surrounding the window and transforms a plain wall into a period wall.

Photograph courtesy of Rutt/Atlanta, Rutt Custom Cabinets

Photograph courtesy of Rutt Custom Cabinets

Photograph courtesy of Blonder Wallcoverings (Risky Business/York)

Photograph courtesy of Blonder Wallcoverings

Ceilings are large surfaces open to many interpretations, ranging from elaborate to simple. The exposed-beam ceiling in the Rutt kitchen (top left) is architecturally dramatic in scale and in the pattern play provided by beams and planks. More conventional-height ceilings gain interest with paint and paper.

Photograph courtesy of Blonder Wallcoverings, Americana Collection

Photograph courtesy of Sura Malaga, ASID

Windows — with or without a view beyond — are always on view. Designer Chris Madden uses matchstick blinds for light control and privacy in a Traditional living room (bottom). In an American Country style kitchen (top left), a simple swag softens the severe lines of a double-hung window. The window-walled game room of a Contemporary style shore-side home by Sura Malaga, ASID, is left undressed, the better to enjoy a spectacular ocean view (top right).

Photograph courtesy of Chris Madden Collection for Bassett Furniture

Photograph courtesy of Susan Huckvale Arann, ASID

Lighting options are unlimited. They range from a circular merry-go-round ceiling fixture and high hat lights (top) in the children's bedroom/playroom by Susan Huckvale Arann, ASID, to the tour de force in lighting in the villa style kitchen by Sura Malaga, ASID (bottom left). Here, the period French chandelier underscores the European flavor of the room. In *Southern Living* magazine's Idea House (bottom right), a variety of ceiling fixtures and handsome table lamps play up a den's sport-themed rug by Glen Eden.

Photograph courtesy of Sura Malaga, ASID

Photograph courtesy of Glen Eden Wool Carpets

No cookie-cutter kitchens, please! These rooms relish personal designs. Award-winning custom kitchen designer Rudy Santos (top left) incorporates mosaic stone countertops, cabinets, borders, murals, and hoods of his own design in Contemporary kitchens with Traditional overtones. Sura Malaga, ASID, opens a Contemporary kitchen with Modern origins to full view (top right). The urbane kitchen with a classical mood by Aristokraft Cabinetry (right) blends blond cabinets and stainless steel elements seamlessly in a timeless design that exudes serenity found in perfection.

Bathrooms are the most personal of rooms and an ideal place for expressing personal style. Designer Sura Malaga, ASID, does that in the high-style ultra-modern bath in bold yellow with black accents (top left). The Hammer & Nail, a noted New Jersey design-build firm, creates a villa style bath (top right) with classical architectural elements (columns, pilasters, and arches) and materials, including marble. MTI's neoclassical bath (right) places its whirlpool tub enclosed by columns in front of a modified Palladian window. The marble tile floor and barrel-vaulted ceiling underscore classical design origins of up-to-date luxury.

At-home offices, libraries, and studies can look any way you like — down home or uptown, Old World or New. Designer Patricia Hart McMillan's Cranbrook group for Hooker Furniture adapts to a loft-look Contemporary interior (top right). The warm wood exterior and gently softened lines of the PC armoire and matching bookshelves and display cabinet warm up the black and white color scheme. Hooker's corner PC cabinet fills the bill for an office in a small space. A wall of shelving (bottom) turns any room in castle or cottage into an at-home library. Just add a table for a handy read/work area and Maine Cottage sophisticated seating for utmost comfort!

There is room in the bedroom — a most intimate space — for a style that's one-hundred percent your own. Even a romantic style can be personally interpreted, as these bedrooms show. A delicate black wrought iron bed lends emphasis to the pretty-in-pink bedroom with walls covered in Toile de Jouy by Fairwinds Studio (top left). The clean lines of the pencil-post tester bed in a Traditional bedroom with white and yellow wallcoverings are softened by a romantic swag (top right). Designer Chris Madden's Chinese Chippendale tester bed serves as the romantic focal point of a high-ceilinged bedroom.

Photograph courtesy of Glen Eden Wool Carpets

Photograph courtesy of Sphinx Green Rug by Oriental Weavers

Large or small, grand or cozy, all living rooms are gracious when they're comfortable. Exposing the box beams and planks of a gambrel-roofed structure (top left) gives a combination living and dining room a sense of spacious grandeur. A custom Glen Eden wool area rug defines the living area. Informally arranged, well-cushioned upholstery and accessories that add a personal touch give this room with water views an inviting air. An equally grand space with a two-story-high window wall emphasizes elegance (top right), underscored by artfully draped lower windows and a Louis XVI style table that backs up to the sofa. A Sphinx area rug in a restful green echoes the green marble fireplace surround. In a cottage-sized living room (right), a medley of wallcoverings and fabric to match the Toile Impressions border used as a chair rail underscores the sense of warm and welcome Traditional style.

Photograph courtesy of Brewster Wallcovering Co. (Toile Impressions by International)

Elegance is an attitude, not a place! The trend today is to dine elegantly all through the house. This includes grand formal dining rooms, dressy but not-too-big dining rooms, and the kitchen and informal dining spaces just about anywhere. For example — momma mia — the Momma Gina Work Table from Storehouse (left). It's just the spot for whipping up a scrumptious meal to be eaten with elegant gusto at table. Deep storage drawers keep flatware and placemats at the ready. In a not-too-big room (bottom left), romantic Louis XVI chairs surround a draped table in a setting with red-and-white papered walls that rate an *oh là là*. If the menu calls for strictly formal dining, check out a splendid dining table surrounded by Chippendale chairs (bottom right). A glorious crystal chandelier shines overhead. A custom area carpet by Glen Eden underscores a sense of luxury.

Bonus areas — attics, basements, porches, and more — greatly expand living space. These areas also offer decorative opportunities. It seems very natural to call attention to attic nooks and crannies, whether quaint or sophisticated. In the Traditional bedroom attic (above), dark contrasting wallpaper by Bayside emphasizes the sloping ceiling, creating a canopy effect. Basements offer economical opportunities for expanded living, including dens and family rooms. Like the Kraftmaid cabinetry-filled room (bottom left), these areas can be quite elegant. Porches are ideal seasonal living space, and wicker, like seating by Maine Cottage (bottom right), is the traditional summer furniture.

The newest great room is the laundry! These new, expanded work centers combine all the elements of clothing care, including cleaning, washing, ironing, and repair. They also make room for hobbies and crafts. Here are examples of new "great laundries." Notice that appliances and fixtures in state-of-the-art technology determine function, while cabinetry establishes the style.

Traditionally, windows were treated to three types of *curtains:*

✔ A sash curtain (usually sheer, to filter light and provide some privacy)

✔ A draw curtain (to block out light)

✔ An overdrapery (which was purely decorative and stationary or unfunctional). Today, draperies usually open and close (or *draw*) and are called *draperies* (a noun) — never *drapes* (a verb).

In very formal rooms (with sufficiently high ceilings), all the layerings of window treatments were topped with a cornice or valance (to hide the hardware). This Traditional (expensive) multilayered treatment carries on today in period or very formal or dressy rooms.

Today, we think of *curtains* as sash curtains (often unlined and in a variety of lengths and tied or held back), and *draperies* as those that draw, completely closing off the window.

Readymade in the shade

Curtains and draperies are readily available as readymades in stock or standard lengths to conform to typical window sizes and ceiling heights. Finding readymades (generally less expensive than custom curtains) that work in your decorating project is possible. Perhaps they need only customizing with trim that's available from a drapery or fabric shop. Or, you can embellish them with appliques and ribbons with which you can embellish plain panels. Some need only to be hung — simply or creatively.

In her East Hampton bedroom, Liz Hart McMillan, former decorating editor at *Redbook* and a natural born decorator (probably because she's our sister and daughter, respectively), gets creative with readymades. On separate rods, she layers sheer silk saffron-gold and soft cinnabar red tab-top panels — imported from India and available from the Company Store catalog.

Customizing designed curtains

Custom curtains allow you to choose the exact fabric needed for your interior design. Check out curtain design books, which can help you in deciding how simple or how lavish to make your curtains. Before you begin your curtain search, know that curtain designs often are a matter of selecting a *heading* (pleats and other decorative devices for gathering fabric into the desired fullness when hung at the window). You can choose from many different headings, but these are the more familiar:

✔ **Brisby pleats:** What curtain makers call the technique of pinching pleats at the top, where rings are attached.

✔ **French pleats:** Narrow folds neatly stacked and attached together (usually in groups of three pulled together) — a classic solution — allowing for sewing rings on top or attaching pins for a traverse rod behind.

✔ **Pencil pleats:** Narrow columns of folds that are continuous across the top of the drapery panel. These pleats must be tied or held back because they don't fold, stack, and stay in place.

✔ **Smocked heading:** A *smocking tape* (a band of fabric with rows of cords that can be pulled, gathering material as the cords are pulled) creates a dressmaker's touch.

Top billing for your curtains and draperies

Curtains and draw draperies are often topped off by a separate item that essentially hides hardware, but may serve additional decorative purposes:

✔ **Cornice:** A cornice is an upholstered wood shape (usually architectural, but it may be entirely fanciful in design).

✔ **Lambrequin:** Think of a cornice that extends to the floor, creating a shadow box effect and adding a sense of architecture to both Traditional and Contemporary interiors. Use lambrequins over bare windows, blinds, or full curtains.

✔ **Pelmet:** A pelmet is an architecturally or artfully shaped fabric stiffened with *buckram* (a stiffly starched fabric that tailors and dressmakers use).

✔ **Valance:** A valance is a soft, shortened version of a bedhanging or curtain that may be more elaborately pleated, shirred, gathered, and trimmed than the curtain over which it hangs. A valance may match your curtains in the same fabric, or you can coordinate it with your curtains with pattern, color, and/or texture. You can also line your valance with a contrasting fabric for some added oomph.

A modern move is to drape fabric loosely over a decorative rod or pole or through brackets, in a nod to conventional valances and swags. Often, swags (sometimes called *scarves* because they resemble those sweeping women's accessories worn at the throat) serve no function, but they earn their keep by looking dramatic (see Figure 16-3).

Supporting roles

Hardware for curtains has always played a vital supporting role. Increasingly hardware vies for attention, if not stardom. Certainly, if the rod (and perhaps rings) and finials are to be visible, consider their style as an important part of the overall curtain design. The variety of styles related to historic styles and periods, as well as Contemporary design, is almost limitless. Finding the perfect curtain rod is only a matter of time. Because rods rest on movable brackets, they adjust easily to any height (and width) called for in your design.

Figure 16-3:
A simple swag of fabric adds a touch of softness to the hard lines of a plain window and a bit of color, pattern, and drama to a natural focal point.

Photography courtesy Blonder Wallcoverings, Americana Collection

Tiebacks (soft tassels, ribbons, and cords) and *holdbacks* (self-fabric cuffs, hooks, and knobs) keep curtains held back away from the view. Often, they're designed to match rods and finials. Make sure their design is compatible with the window treatment's overall design.

Trims, available in drapery and fabric shops, add great beauty and interest to both readymade and custom-made curtains. The assortment of *gimps* (pliable flat braids), cords (in varying thicknesses), tassels, and more can seem daunting. Allow time to consider all the possibilities, and don't rush to judgment.

Considering optional hang-ups

Don't spend too much time getting hung up on window treatment terminology. Instead, leave time to consider how many different things you can hang at your window:

✔ If privacy isn't a problem, but softness is, hang just curtains of lace, cotton, nylon, silk, or some other sheer fabric.

✔ Place a curtain — sheer, tieback, or draw — over a (Venetian) blind.

✔ Hang a sheer curtain beneath a chintz, silk, velvet, linen, or other draw drapery.

✔ Hang draw draperies over thin-slat blinds or an old-fashioned roller shade.

✔ Hang draw draperies alone on a decorative pole with fantastic finials.

✔ Top curtains — draw or tieback — with short, purely decorative over-draperies known as *swags* and *jabots*.

✔ Top a thin-slat blind or roller shade with swags, which drape over just the top of the window, and long or short jabots, which hang on the sides of windows.

✔ Top any or all these window treatments with a cornice or valance.

You can see that the variations are practically endless, especially when you combine these elements with more Contemporary window blinds and shades that look like accordion-pleated curtains.

If you're designing your own window treatments, don't hesitate to use Country-casual fabrics in a fancy, three-curtain and valance window treatment in a dressy or formal Country room. The surprise works magic.

And, just to be fair, don't be shy about using a lustrous silk fabric for simple, tieback curtains. This look is especially terrific when the silk is in a pink-and-white gingham check.

Going to great lengths

How long should curtains or draperies be? Generally, the longer the curtain or drapery, the more dignified, dressy, and formal the look. Shorter lengths always imply a casual, relaxed, and informal mood. The decision is yours. Take a look at Figure 16-4, and then read the following guidelines to find the style that's right for you.

✔ In formal or dressy rooms, curtains should just touch the floor.

✔ A romantic room deserves elegant, extra-long curtains that pool or puddle on the floor.

✔ Curtains to the sill, or to the bottom of the window trim (called the *apron*), look great and are practical in a kitchen.

Never hang curtains of any length near a stove.

✔ Dens or family rooms gain dignity from draw draperies or curtains that reach the floor.

✔ Curtains that stop short of the floor, ending at the top of floor moldings, look awkward. If curtains are hung too high, simply lower them (if possible) to solve the problem.

Figure 16-4:
Dressy or casual, curtain lengths add to the particular mood of any room.

Not all windows are beautiful. Fortunately, draperies can help hide flaws. Try these solutions for the following questions:

✔ **Window too short?** Attaching rods just below the ceiling molding and hanging long, to-the-floor curtains make the window look taller and more elegant.

✔ **Window awkwardly long?** Add a deep cornice or valance above draperies with a bold horizontal pattern. Create further distraction by adding a horizontal line in the form of a strongly contrasting louvered shutter.

✔ **Window too narrow?** Extend curtain rods beyond the window and hang draperies so that they barely cover the frame, leaving as much glass exposed as possible, all of which makes a narrow window seem wider.

✔ **Window too wide?** A huge window wall can overpower a room. Break up the space by hanging several panels across the window. They can hang straight, or be tied back in pairs. If draperies must be drawn for privacy, let the panels hang straight, and rig drawstrings so that the panels close as though they are separate pairs of draperies.

Creating Special Effects

If you want privacy, but you don't want to cover up your light source, consider the following alternatives to traditional window treatments:

- **Etched or frosted glass.** This solution provides a degree of privacy but lets in plenty of light.

- **Stained glass.** Stained glass provides a sense of privacy, hides ugly views, and gives you something beautiful to admire. If you've found a treasure at the flea market, for example, you can hang the panel over the original pane.

- **Glass block.** The Contemporary alternative to stained, etched, or frosted glass, glass block hides unsightly views and filters light beautifully, while providing a bit of privacy.

If privacy isn't a problem, simply hang a grapevine wreath or silk flower garland above the window.

Dressing up windows in a jiffy

Do you need window pizzazz in a hurry? Try some of the following ideas:

- Add silk flowered vines — especially roses. Artfully drape them across the top of a window. Just don't be stingy — buy several strands for lush fullness.

- Adorn a (clean) fishnet across a window by the sea.

- Craft a faux valance by cutting a plastic tablecloth to shape and then taping it (on the backside) to a rod.

- Create a faux valance by nailing crossed oars across the top of a window in a beach house.

- Dangle a strand of Mardi Gras beads, hippie style, across a small bathroom window.

- Drape a rectangular tablecloth (folded in half lengthwise) over a thick, decorated pole. Six or more inches from one side of the pole, hang a long folded length of ribbon across the pole with loose ends hanging below the cloth. Gather the ribbon ends and pull them up until the cloth begins to swag, and then tie the ribbon into a bow. Repeat on the opposite side. The result looks like a balloon shade.

- Flank a bathroom window with discarded mirrored bi-fold doors — they reflect the light and add sparkle and glamour.

✔ Fold butcher's paper (looks like a paper bag) into accordion pleats, punch holes through the pleats (on one end only), and push a curtain rod through, gathering it gracefully as you create a cafe curtain. (You need a length of paper two to three times the width of your window.)

✔ Fold colorful dinner-size napkins in half on the diagonal and drape them, pointed side down, over a thick, stained or painted, wooden pole. (Use enough napkins to cover the width of the pole.) This technique is great for a kitchen or breakfast nook.

✔ Glue seashells directly onto the window frame of a summer cottage.

✔ Hang a lace tablecloth, either running a narrow rod though the lacework or using pinch-clips.

✔ Hang a wooden plaque with an interesting painted scene or pattern across the top of the window.

✔ Hinge old doors to create standing shutters to flank a window. Choose plain or paneled doors to suit your scheme.

✔ Put *grommets* (donut-shaped pieces of metal) into one end of a wool plaid blanket. Run lengths of grosgrain ribbon (long enough to finish in a bow) through the grommets and tie them to a wooden pole or tree branch.

✔ Line your too-flat window with tall bookcases and hang tiny mirrors down the inside of the bookcases to reflect the sunlight.

✔ Make *sheet* curtains to match your bedding. Just buy extra flat sheets (two to serve as curtain panels) to *shirr* (gather) on a wooden rod and tie back at either side of a regular double-hung (not too wide) window. To create a curtain rod pocket with a narrow header, sew a seam ¾ inches from the top of the sheets' 4-inch hem, and then gather the panel over a wood rod. We plan on 100-percent fullness, so we buy sheets (twin, queen, or king) two times the width of the window.

✔ Open your window to the season by stripping off all treatments and adding a few glass shelves to hold colorful glass bottles.

✔ Paint window trims in a dashing, contrasting color. Leave well enough alone, or take this treatment one step further by painting a few flat baskets in the same or even wilder colors and arranging them over the top of the window for added impact.

✔ Pierce a fascinating pattern into a sheet of tin, and fit over your window and frame (if desired) for a window that isn't an egress and has no redeeming view. This idea is great with lodge-look and other rustic interiors.

✔ Prop a salvaged iron gate across your window for a beautiful pattern that doesn't obstruct light or view.

✔ Put those antique *antimacassars* (crocheted and knitted arm covers) to work as a valance. Drape them over your rod, or clip them on with pinch clips that come in white and various metal colors to match your rod.

Chapter 17

Lively Lighting

. . . .

In This Chapter

▶ Decorating with lighting

▶ Understanding general, task, and accent lighting

▶ Designing lighting for every room

▶ Using professional help

▶ Picking stylish fixtures, shades, and controls

. . . .

You don't have to know everything about lighting or spend tons of money in order to make rooms look light and lively. You do need to know the basics about functional and decorative lighting — and how to get help for planning and buying lighting.

In this chapter, you find all the information you need to design your lighting on a room-by-room basis. In addition, we help you figure out which types of fixtures to use, and which kinds of controls you need for the lights. Whatever your lighting needs, you can find answers to your questions here.

Understanding Lighting Basics

When Thomas Edison invented the first light bulb in 1879, function was what he had in mind. Today, though, we use lighting for practical and decorative purposes, but also as a form of decoration.

Lighting is complicated by a number of factors including:

✔ The colors of walls and furnishings

✔ The size of the space

✔ Your decorating goals

You may want to consult a lighting consultant certified by the American Lighting Association (ALA). ALA (800-274-4484) has a Web site at www. americanlightingassoc.com that offers up-to-the-minute information, locations of certified showrooms, and a free booklet.

Functional lighting

Functional lighting provides illumination to keep you out of the dark, indicate where activities take place, and control the flow of people. For example, chandeliers signify where major events like dining take place.

Lighting needs vary from room to room. A kitchen needs different lighting from a living room, for example. The level, type, and *color temperature* of light (how warm or cold it is — specified on lightbulb labels), as well as how the light is delivered, all play an important role in a lighting scheme.

Demands change from room to room, as Figure 17-1 demonstrates. In Figure 17-1A, functional, flexible light consists of a recessed halogen (1), accent lights (2, 3), a ceiling fixture (4), and a task light (5). In 17-1B, halogen lights (1) balance fluorescents (2) and under-counter strips produce task light (3). In 17-1C, glamorous grooming is made possible by recessed lights (1), Hollywood-style vanity lights (2), and vapor-proof shower/tub fixtures (3).

Figure 17-1:
Lighting
demands
change
from room
to room.

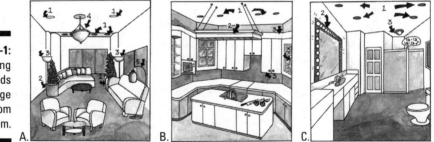

Decorative lighting

Decorative lighting creates *mood* (an overall feeling of serenity or playfulness) and *meaning* (communication; sometimes this includes signage, such as EXIT). Flat, functional lighting (such as the kind in your office) puts people on the alert. Decorative lighting, on the other hand, brings out the shape of objects, the "feel" of texture, and important keynotes.

Choosing light levels and locations

A decorative lighting scheme has variation in light levels and sources that indicate what rooms are for (dim lights in rooms for sleeping, bright lights in playrooms) or what a room's focal point is.

Create focal points with chandeliers and pendants. In a dining room, for example, a chandelier placed over a table draws attention with its soft upward-cast light. (Chandeliers are Traditional.) A pendant light used over a table, how-ever, casts a more concentrated light downward and out. (Pendants are Contemporary.)

Designing decorative lighting

To create a plan, consider what, where, and when activities take place. Lighting needs to vary its intensity to accommodate multiple activities that occur in a single room. For example, your kitchen may be your favorite place to cook, read, do your hobbies, watch TV, and entertain. Would you want the same level of light for a party that you want for mopping the floor?

Lighting stores and home remodeling centers have trained personnel who can steer you toward your best possible lighting choices. Bring your floor plans and other decorating notes with you when you consult a lighting expert.

Lighting Up Your Life

Start planning your lighting with a floor plan (see Chapter 3). Include win-dows, doors, furniture placement, locations of electrical outlets and switches, and any installed fixtures. Record your activities and special needs. Having this information all spelled out helps, whether you're working alone or with a lighting specialist.

A lighting fixture should be conveniently close, and so should its on/off switches! Take full advantage of multiple locations for on/off switches, and consider remote control devices when they're called for.

Illuminating logically

Your room's architecture and design, its uses, and its users determine your lighting needs. Every room should have enough fixtures to cast adequate light, leaving no large areas of dark shadow or glaring hot spots. Consider a few basic questions:

- ✔ Where do you need overall light?
- ✔ Where do you need stronger light?
- ✔ How many fixtures do you need?
- ✔ What types of lighting fixtures do you require?
- ✔ Where do you want the light coming from — down from the ceiling, up from a lamp, or both?
- ✔ What can you afford?

Focusing on aesthetics

Lighting design involves choosing fixtures that are good-looking, throw light in the most desirable fashion, and have the right kind of bulb for the job (halogens, fluorescents, or incandescents). For tips on picking the right fixture, see "Picking Perfect Fixtures" later in this chapter. Ask yourself the following questions:

- ✔ Do I want to highlight my walls' texture?
- ✔ Do I want to spotlight certain objects?
- ✔ Do I want to focus on a specific location in the room?
- ✔ Do I want to raise, lower, or create flexible lighting patterns?

Note all your ideas on your floor plan. The more information you have, the better job a salesperson can do in helping you.

Lighting 101

Lighting design is broken down into three kinds of illumination: general lighting, task lighting, and accent lighting. Mix all three types to achieve *decorative* lighting. Figure 17-2 shows you some of the many lighting choices.

General lighting

General, or *ambient,* lighting illuminates an entire space for visibility and safety. Light bounces off walls and ceilings to cover as much area as possible. General lighting can come from up-lights or down-lights:

- ✔ Up-lights point illumination toward the ceiling. Up-light fixtures include torchiers and wall sconces.
- ✔ Down-lights cast light down from the ceiling or wall. Popular down-lights include recessed lights *(cans)* and track lights.
- ✔ Some lights, such as table and floor lamps, are both up- and down-lights because they cast light toward both the ceiling and the floor.

See the upcoming section "Planning General Lighting" for more information about how to successfully illuminate an entire room or space.

Figure 17-2:
Types of lighting fixtures include (a) traditional table lamps, (b) wall sconces, (c) pendants, (d) floor lamps, (e) torchiers, (f) chandeliers, (g) theme table lamps, (h) swing-arm lamps, and (i) desk lamps.

Task lighting

Task, or *work,* lighting illuminates smaller areas where more intense light is needed. Task light should be three times as bright as general lighting. Overly bright work lamps won't make up for a dimly lit room (instead, you may develop eyestrain). Using higher light per watt (LPW) bulbs in other fixtures or increasing the number of fixtures to boost general lighting fixes this problem.

Good task lighting fixture choices are well-positioned recessed lights, track lighting, pendants, table or floor lamps, and under-cabinet lighting strips.

Accent lighting

Accent lighting adds brilliant shimmer to make your precious objects, paintings, sculptures, and outstanding architectural features stand out. Use a bulb that's no more than three times as bright as the surrounding general light. Position the fixture so that the light doesn't block your line of sight so that no glaring reflections bounce back.

If you're using track lighting for *wall washing* (lighting a nontextured wall) or *wall grazing* (lighting a textured wall), aim the beam of light at a 30-degree angle from the vertical to prevent glare and hot spots.

Halogen makes the best accent light because of its intensity and brilliance. (See the section on "Buying the Right Bulbs," later in this chapter, for information about halogen lights.)

Planning General Lighting

Figure out general lighting first, because all other lighting (task and accent) must be in balance with it. Some rooms, such as kitchens, require stronger lighting than others. Larger rooms need more light fixtures than smaller ones. Don't rely on a couple of strong lights to illuminate a big room — you'll end up with uneven, stress-inducing lighting.

Creating contrast

The contrast of light and shadow is the key to lighting. Reasonable contrast is desirable for two reasons:

- ✔ Contrasting of light creates visual interest and mood.
- ✔ Differing levels of light let the eye rest as it moves from bright to dark.

Plan for two to three areas of stronger light to generate a focal point in a room. (The larger the room, the larger these areas will be, and the greater number of fixtures you need.)

Avoiding glare

Direct glare is more than ugly; it can cause accidents. Keep lights from shining directly into eyes.

Two types of glare cause aesthetic problems. A *hot spot* is a bright spot of light reflected onto an object. *Veiled glare* happens when a light is placed above a flat, glossy horizontal surface (such as a table) and the light bounces up. Replace your old bulbs with coated or antiglare bulbs to fix the problem.

Balancing light

The chief problem created by windows is a misbalance of light. Some people believe that they don't need lighting in a sunny room because the sunlight will distribute itself. Wrong! Instead they find that one area is too bright while the other is downright dark. Because the eye needs time to adjust to lower light levels, you may feel confused when moving from one area to the next. Control excess sunlight with shades (see Chapter 16).

Mixing incandescent, halogen, and fluorescent bulbs may best simulate sunlight. (See the next section for details about each type.) Avoid using fluorescents alone, because they tend to emit narrower spectrums of light than incandescents and halogens; colors may not be true, skin tones may look dull, and the room may look unnatural. When picking fluorescent bulbs, make sure the Color Rendering Index (CRI) is between 80 and 100. (The closer a bulb's CRI is to 100, the more it appears like sunlight.)

Buying the Right Bulbs

How well your lighting fixture performs depends on the light source — the bulb. Different types of bulbs produce different lighting effects and different electric bills.

Light is measured in terms of wattage, lumens, and foot-candles. *Wattage* is the amount of electricity used, *lumens,* the amount of light produced, and *foot-candles,* the amount of light that reaches your subject.

You're probably already familiar with the three main categories of bulbs:

- **Incandescent:** Incandescent bulbs are the most widely used in homes. They produce a pleasant, yellow-tinged white light. They come in an array of wattages and shapes such as *general* (A; standard bulb), *globe* (small, round), and *decorative* (flame, teardrop).

  If you like a more controlled beam of light, use a reflectorized bulb that has a mirror-like coating that aims that light forward. Reflector (R) and parabolic reflector (PAR) bulbs cast two and four times the amount of light on the subject as a general service (A) bulb does, respectively.

✔ **Fluorescent.** Used in rooms that demand lots of light, these are the most energy-efficient and least expensive source of lighting available. They use only 20 to 35 percent as much electricity as incandescent bulbs and last up to 20 times longer.

You can get Compact Fluorescent Bulbs (CFBs) that screw into regular lamp sockets so that you can turn any fixture into a more economical light source. CFBs are small lengths of fluorescent tubes that are usually doubled over to fit into lamps.

✔ **Halogen.** Halogens produce a brilliant white light (with more lumens per watt than incandescents), and the bulbs tend to last longer. They also maintain maximum efficiency over their lifetime (they don't grow dim like incandescents). They're used in track and recessed lighting fixtures because of their superior beam control compared to PAR-type bulbs. They're also used in wall sconces, torchiers, mini-cans, and pendants (see "Picking Perfect Fixtures" later in this chapter).

Figure 17-3 illustrates the many different types of bulbs available. Many light stores have the various types of bulbs on display so that you can see before you buy.

Don't let light bulbs come in close proximity to fabrics or flammable surfaces. The heat of halogen or incandescent bulbs can set some materials used in furnishings (such as foam rubber) on fire.

Table 17-1 provides direction for choosing the right kind of light bulb.

Table 17-1	Picking the Right Bulb		
Bulb Type	*Emits Light That Is*	*Brightens*	*Mutes*
Incandescent	Yellow-white	Warm colors	Cool colors
Halogen	Brilliant white	All colors	None
Cool White Fluorescent	Blue-white	Cool colors	Warm colors
Cool White Deluxe Fluorescent	White	Most colors	Almost none
Warm White Fluorescent	Light amber	Skin tones	Red, blue
Warm White Deluxe Fluorescent	White	Warm colors	Blue, green

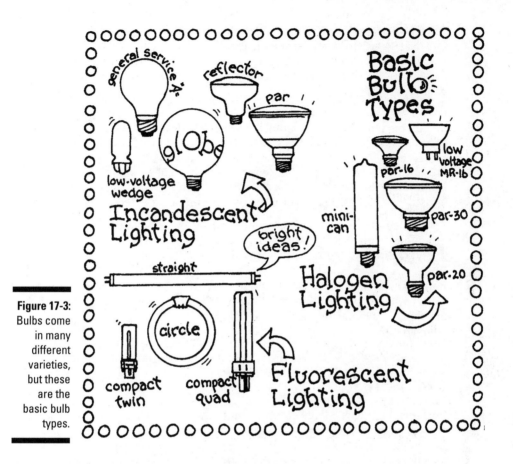

Figure 17-3: Bulbs come in many different varieties, but these are the basic bulb types.

Picking Perfect Fixtures

Fixtures throw light up, down, to the sides, in focused spots, or in diffused areas. Some lights function only as general, task, or accent lighting. Others are more flexible depending on the bulb's wattage.

Most light fixture types are available in incandescent, fluorescent, compact fluorescent, or halogen. Many fixtures can be adapted to use an alternate bulb. Replacement halogen bulbs (available at retail and lighting stores) are designed to go right into a lamp that normally uses an incandescent bulb.

Ceiling fixtures

Ceiling fixtures throw light down toward the walls and floor. Some fixtures let light bounce up toward the ceiling as well. Practical for illuminating wide areas of space efficiently, these general lighting fixtures are available in incandescent, halogen, fluorescent, and compact fluorescent models.

Chandeliers

Chandeliers, a type of pendant light, generally direct light upward to bounce off the ceiling. Traditionally used in dining rooms, living rooms, and entry areas, they look as though they're holding candles, but they're wired and fitted with flame-shaped lights (either incandescent or halogen). We put a beautiful, small chandelier in a gem-like kitchen in a Chicago high-rise. Consider hanging one in your bathroom for an unexpected pleasure.

Pendants

A pendant light — a light fixture suspended from the ceiling over a table or work area — casts light downward. It can provide either general or task lighting. Pendants come in a wide variety of styles and can vary from a single halogen bulb to a multi-bulb creation.

Portables

Portable lighting is a large category that encompasses anything that can be carried, such as table lamps, floor lamps, clamp-on lights, and torchiers. Depending on the bulb's type, portable lamps can furnish general, task, or accent light. Upright cans, mini-reflector spotlights, desk lights, piano lights, and painting lights provide only accent or task lighting.

Recessed lighting

Recessed fixtures can provide general, task, or accent lighting. The actual light is set into the ceiling and is virtually inconspicuous, because only the trim shows at the surface. If you have a low-ceiling area, recessed lighting is a better choice than a ceiling fixture. The fixtures are sometimes referred to as *can lights* because they look like tin cans. They're available as down-lights, adjustable accent lights, and wall washers. If you're using them for accent lighting, make sure that the bulb position is adjustable.

Tracks

Track lighting provides general, task, and, accent lighting. It can even serve all three functions at the same time, if you have enough lights with high enough wattage. Incandescent, halogen, and compact fluorescent models are available. Very flexible and modern, these lights can be moved, swiveled, rotated, and aimed at individual points along the track. Need more light? Hang pendants or chandeliers from the track. Newer track lighting designs allow multicolored and shaped lamps on the same track.

Under-cabinet and under-shelf fixtures

Use under-cabinet and under-shelf fixtures as task and accent lighting. They're great under kitchen cabinets to light the countertop or work area. They're also good for curio cabinets, bookshelves, or any other spot that needs a highlight. These lights are available in incandescent, halogen, and fluorescent; in miniature track; and in strips of low-voltage minilights.

Vanity lighting strips

Vanity lighting strips with gently glowing incandescent globes provide task lighting for grooming. Great for applying makeup, they create a professional Hollywood makeup studio look.

TIP

Staying on track

Track lighting is ideal as accent lighting. Any time you change artwork or want to make a new lighting statement, you can reposition the fixtures along the track. Track lighting can illuminate art, wash non-textured surfaces with light (called *wall washing*), or enhance dramatic textured walls (called *wall grazing*).

Consider these rules and tips for getting the most out of track lighting:

- Affix the track in the right place. For ceilings up to 9 feet high, mount the track 2 to 3 feet from the point where the wall and ceiling meet. For ceiling heights between 9 and 11 feet, place the track lighting 4 feet away from the wall.

- Consider flexible track with which you can create curves that follow or repeat a pattern on the floor or in furniture (a curving kitchen island, for example).

- Consider using flexible track lighting with beautifully colored lamps in lieu of a chandelier.

- Mount the track closer to the wall (at a distance of 6 to 12 inches) for wall grazing than you would for wall washing, and aim the lights downward. Wall grazing brings out the best in brick or stone.

- Use one fixture per object to light art. Place fixtures at an equal distance from each other, if possible. Aim fixtures at a 30-degree angle to prevent hot spots and glare.

Wall-mounted fixtures

Use wall-mounted fixtures to furnish general, task, or accent lighting. They come in a variety of designs and range from swinging arm lamps to wall sconces. Wall-mounted lights are terrific when floor or table space is too limited for lamps. They can also emphasize pretty wall surfaces with up- or down-light and de-emphasize an uninteresting ceiling.

Lighting Your Home, Room by Room

Think of lighting your entire house adequately: Plan room by room. As you move through the house, you should see no dark places — especially in hallways and stairwells.

Station the light controls at all entry and exit points, particularly in hallways, so that you can turn lights on or off as you move into a new area. (Alternately, use motion-sensitive lights that turn themselves on and off as you move from space to space.) Think safety first! Most areas have updated building codes that require a switch for every entry or exit area.

Hallways

Safe hallway lighting should be a happy medium between the most softly and brightly lit rooms in the house. Hallway and entryway lighting may simply consist of some up-lights that cast indirect light. If an up-light isn't enough, use a stronger bulb or install extra lights. A nice chandelier isn't a bad option. If you opt for a higher-watt ceiling light, install a dimmer switch so that you don't blind yourself when you get up in the middle of the night.

If a hallway is long, space lighting evenly. Wall sconces placed at regular intervals look dramatic, create a pleasant sense of rhythm, and seem to furnish the space. (For more info on rhythm, see Chapter 4.)

Stairways

To safely light stairways, avoid *flat light* (light that falls straight from above). At the foot of the stairs, use a strong directional light to increase the contrast between risers and treads. At the top of the stairwell, use a down-light. You can also place strip lights at each riser for 24-hour illumination. Concealing lighting at the handrail is another way to keep stairs safe. Position controls at the foot and head of the stairs.

Bathrooms

Two key issues for lighting bathrooms are safety and function. Keep general lighting bright, as well as task lighting (for grooming). Balance overhead down-lights with up-lights. Don't position fixtures and bulbs to interfere with splashing water or wet hands.

Small bathrooms may only need up-lights positioned over a mirror or strip lights around the mirror. Mount decorative wall brackets at both sides of the mirror, and add one at the top if you need additional light. Position wall brackets 60 inches off the floor. Use warm white fluorescents for energy-efficient lighting. Install theatrical globe lights around the mirror.

Larger bathrooms may require ceiling fixtures — use warm white fluorescent or incandescent bulbs. Don't forget to include a night-light that you can leave on 24 hours a day for maximum safety. (The most common cause of broken foot bones is stumbling into the toilet. Ouch!)

Use mirrors freely to help bounce light around the room. For applying makeup and grooming, use vanity lights (globes) around the mirror to create a shadow-free grooming environment.

Tub and shower enclosures need enclosed, damp-location, recessed down-lights in the ceiling. (A shower light is a must, to prevent everything from shaving nicks to stumbles.) For added heat, install an infrared heat lamp.

Bedrooms

Bedrooms need general lighting that's not overly bright. Task and accent lights can do more of the lighting work. Lamps placed on tables or nightstands cast ample light, but make sure the lamps are tall enough to keep light from glaring directly at the level of your eye. If glare is a problem, place a stack of coffee table books under the light or buy a taller shade.

For a bedroom shared by a couple, plan for separate task lighting with separate controls. Position controls on either side of the bed to make it possible for one person to read while the other sleeps. Turning lights on and off is also easier when you have more than one control panel.

Swivel-arm wall lamps used on each side of the bed save valuable nightstand space, and some are conveniently touch-controlled. If space is at a premium, use recessed lights or pendant lights fitted with a diffuser that prevents glare.

Light the interior of closets with recessed or surface-mounted lighting to make early morning and nighttime dressing easier. Door-activated on/off switches are most convenient.

Adding pizazz with decorative lamps

Selecting the right lamp that adds to your overall decorating mood can be tricky. Keep these points in mind:

✔ **Check the lamp's height and scale.** Relate the lamp's height and scale to that of the furniture that it will set on (such as a table) and near (such as a sofa). If you already own a lamp that's a bit too short for your table/sofa combination, do what the pros do — place the lamp on a stack of attractive hardback books. If you're shopping for a new lamp, measure first and avoid that problem!

✔ **Decide whether your table lamp should attract attention or go unnoticed.** The answer depends on the surroundings. For a sofa covered in strongly colored and patterned upholstery, select a plain (but beautifully colored) lamp. For a plain sofa, consider a lamp with strong pattern or personality. For strongly thematic rooms (Western lodge, for example), your lamp can underscore that theme.

✔ **If you're buying a new lampshade, take the lamp to the store.** Trying the shade on is the tried-and-true technique for knowing whether a lampshade is just right or not.

✔ **If a lampshade doesn't seem to look right on your lamp, check the harp.** If it's the right width but hangs too low or too high, the *harp* (the metal piece that the shade rests on) may be the wrong size. The right size harp makes all the difference in the world. If in doubt, try several size harps and shades until you have the right combination.

✔ **Lamps flanking a sofa don't have to be identical, but they should have same- or similar-colored bases, and same or similar shades.**

✔ **Lamps don't have to be identical throughout the room.** How boring would that be? Sizes should vary from mini (on a secretary or bookshelf), to medium (on a sofa-library table), to tall (on low end tables). But, they should relate in some way, such as by reflecting the same style or period (especially if they're different colors and materials).

✔ **Lamps should be carefully placed throughout the room so as not to create a sense of jumble and confusion.**

✔ **Don't let lamps block important views and vistas, indoors or out.**

Children's bedrooms

When lighting young children's bedrooms, decorate for fun, but think safety first. Here are some tips:

✔ Include lamps and other lighting fixtures that are playful and fun. Just make sure that they're not breakable.

✔ Install track lights, which are great sources of light for task and accent lighting, with a dimmer switch.

✔ Install light bulbs with a built-in backup filament. If the main filament burns out, the second filament lights up. Specialty light bulb stores carry these bulbs.

✔ Keep a wall-mounted flashlight that your child can reach for in emergencies.

✔ Make sure lighting is adequate, but not so bright that there is glare, for children who work at computers.

✔ Place individual lamps with independent switches for bunk beds.

✔ Provide a nightlight with a built-in sensor that turns on when light levels are low. Place these lights in hallways and bathrooms as well.

✔ Simplify turning on overhead lights by placing controls at kids' reach level — about 30 inches from the floor — and by using easy-to-operate rocker or slide controls.

✔ Take extra precautions with wires throughout the room. Make sure that lamp cords are neat and out of the traffic flow (but, for safety reasons, don't tuck them under carpeting).

✔ Use only bulbs recommended by the fixture's manufacturer. Make sure halogen fixtures, which get hot to the touch, are surrounded by a guard.

✔ Use smart light bulbs with programmable microchips that gradually dim the bulb over a period of time. Check your specialty light bulb store.

Dining rooms

You'd think those fast-food places would catch on — nothing kills the appetite like a too-bright light. On the other hand, have you ever been afraid to taste food because you couldn't see it? Try these ideas for adding just the right lighting to your dining room:

✔ Accent artwork. Put a soft focus on it with recessed adjustable fixtures or halogen track lights.

✔ Create a focal point and add glamour to the dining room. Hang a chandelier in the center of the room. If the dining table is in the center of the room, hang the fixture 30 inches above the tabletop (allow a clearance on each side of 6 inches).

✔ Focus on the china cabinet. Install strips of halogen minilights under the shelves in a china cabinet or hutch to highlight your china and collectibles.

✔ Play up your buffet. Hang wall sconces on either side and then place recessed lights 24 to 36 inches apart from the ceiling above it.

✔ Tout any table, whether in the center of the room or not, by suspending a pendant light that is 12 inches narrower than the table top 30 inches above the table. Or position a ring of four track lights or recessed halogen lights over a table to make table settings sparkle.

Kitchens

With all those knives, open flames, and hot pots, kitchens are dangerous places. Let there be tons of light where you need it. Consider these pointers for picking lights and placing them where they'll do the best job:

- ✔ Center halogen pendants over bars and counters.

- ✔ Install individual recessed down-lights as task lighting at the sink and range. (Use compact fluorescent bulbs for energy efficiency.)

- ✔ Make sure the fluorescent light in dimmer areas (far away from windows and natural light) equals the brighter sunlight areas of the kitchen.

- ✔ Mount fluorescent strips (12 to 48 inches long) close to the front edge of cabinetry to avoid glare. Under-cabinet lighting is a must for food prep. Lighting should cover two-thirds the length of the counter.

- ✔ Place additional strips of mini-incandescent lights in soffits and other concealed locations to highlight cabinetry and add a warm atmosphere to the kitchen.

- ✔ Position low-voltage minilights over, under, or inside kitchen cabinets that have glass panes.

- ✔ Remember that overhead general lighting — with energy-efficient fluorescent tubes — is the easiest way to supply diffused light.

- ✔ Suspend pendant lighting 30 inches above an island's surface.

Home offices

Home offices are workplaces, and effective lighting is a must. First, think of glare-free lighting strategies. Next, be careful to eliminate harsh contrast. Consider these tips:

- ✔ Illuminate credenzas that have a cabinet above them with under-cabinet lighting. Use fluorescent bulbs and place them close to the front of the cabinet to prevent glare. If your credenza has no cabinet above it, add a pair of table lamps. If your credenza is a heavy work area, augment table lamps with wall sconces or flanking torchiers.

- ✔ Place two or more large, energy-efficient fluorescents to the front and back of the desk area for well-diffused general lighting that eliminates shadows.

- ✔ Position adjustable portable lamps to the side and rear of computer screens to reduce glare.

- ✔ Use accent lighting to create pleasant, homey areas in the office.

Living rooms

If you have a live-in living room, make lighting a decorating priority. In this section, we provide some ways to help your lighting make big differences in the way you see and are seen in this important space:

✔ Accent handsome houseplants with an up-light can fixture. Place the fixture between the wall and the plant to create a dramatic silhouette. Don't let the fixture come in contact with the plant.

✔ Add interest to a long, boring wall by creating a scalloped effect of light, with wall-washing lights placed so that their arcs of light gently overlap.

✔ Bring out the beautiful textures in stone or brick fireplaces or walls in your living room with recessed lights.

✔ Highlight a pretty painting with halogen track lighting.

✔ Place a reading lamp behind every reader's shoulder (40 to 42 inches above the floor). To avoid glare, the bottom of the shade should be a little lower than eye level.

Part V

Tackling the Three Tough Rooms: Kitchen, Bath, and Home Office

The 5th Wave   By Rich Tennant

"Douglas, I don't recall beer taps being a part of our bathroom decorating motif."

In this part . . .

The kitchen, bath, and home office are perhaps the most challenging spaces to decorate because they demand technical knowledge concerning fixtures, appliances, and the mechanics (such as plumbing and wiring) to support them. They also involve sizable budgets — so you want to get these spaces right the first time! Here's help.

Chapter 18

Cooking Up Your Dream Kitchen

Whether your kitchen is a chef's haven (designed for gourmet cooking) or Central Command (where you do a bit of everything), it needs to work well and look great. To accomplish that, you must be intimately involved in its design and decorating.

In this chapter, you find great pointers for specialized design help (from the National Kitchen & Bath Association). If remodeling is in order, we help you consider some key questions before you seek design help. If redecorating your kitchen will bring it up to speed, we offer ideas to get you on your way.

Considering Your Wallet

Making architectural changes is more costly than making decorative changes. Sometimes you don't have a choice but to make major changes. For example, if your stove and refrigerator are more than eight feet from the sink, remodeling is mandatory. Check out *Home Remodeling For Dummies* by Morris and James Carey and *Kitchen Remodeling For Dummies* by Donald Prestly (both from Wiley Publishing, Inc.) for help.

Luckily, most kitchen decorating doesn't require applying for a building permit. Most projects involve only light remodeling, such as changing floor-coverings, cabinets and countertops, wallcovering, and so on. Do these changes before you buy new furniture, curtains, and accessories.

Your budget and priorities are key factors in deciding how to decorate your kitchen. The following sections contain guidelines for helping you make the most of your budget.

Spending the dough

Figure the cost for lightly remodeling a 10-foot by 12-foot kitchen at up to $10,000 depending on the cabinets you select. (Industry experts say you'll get back 80 to 87 percent of what you spend if you sell within a year.) See Table 18-1 for estimates of cost breakdowns, determined by the National Kitchen & Bath Association (NKBA).

Table 18-1 Estimated Allocations for a Kitchen Decorating Project	
Specific Project	*Percentage Allocated*
Cabinets	48 percent
Labor	16 percent
Countertops	13 percent
Appliances	8 percent
Interior design	6 percent
Fixtures	4 percent
Flooring	4 percent
Lighting	1 percent

Cutting corners

You can reduce some budget allocations so that you can spend more on other things. For example, sweat equity (doing the labor yourself) can mean sizable savings.

Consider ways to save on kitchen cabinets, which make up almost half of a budget. If you're buying new cabinets, don't buy two if one works. (Two 24-inch cabinets cost more than a 48-inch one.) Choose less expensive veneered, flat-center paneled doors instead of more costly solid wood, raised panel doors. Forego luxury items, such as glass doors, decorative plate racks, and fancy trims and moldings.

Consider using your existing cabinets, especially if they supply adequate storage but simply need a facelift (see the sidebar "Giving your cabinets an extreme makeover"). Apply this same approach to all the items on your kitchen design list. Don't be shy; ask the experts to show you more ways to stretch your budget. Saving where you can allows for luxuries (TV and audio systems, for example) where they count.

Reviewing Design Guidelines

Comfort ranks ahead of style and is neck-and-neck with efficiency (which contributes to physical and emotional comfort). Consider the following NKBA guidelines. (For a complete list, log on to www.NKBA.org.)

- ✔ **Appliance placement**
  - Place your dishwasher within 36 inches of the sink.
  - Locate your main sink between or across from the cooking surface, food preparation area, or refrigerator.

- ✔ **Cabinets (in kitchens smaller than 150 square feet)**
  - Use 144 inches of wall cabinet frontage with 12-inch-deep cabinets, 20 to 30 inches high with adjustable shelving.
  - Use 156-inch base cabinet frontage with 21-inch-deep cabinets.
  - Use 120 inches or more drawer or rollout shelf frontage.

- ✔ **Cabinets (in kitchens larger than 150 square feet)**
  - Use 186 inches of wall-hung cabinet frontage. Cabinets should be least 20 inches high (30 inches or more if ceiling height allows) with adjustable shelving.
  - Use 192-inch base cabinet frontage, with at least 21-inch-deep cabinets.
  - Use a minimum of 165 inches of drawer or roll-out shelf frontage.

- ✔ **Counter surface and landing space for containers**
  - In kitchens smaller than150 square feet, create a minimum of 132 inches of usable countertop frontage.
  - In kitchens larger than 150 square feet, create a minimum of 198 inches of usable countertop frontage.
  - In an open-ended kitchen, keep a minimum of 9 inches of counter space on one side and 15 inches on the other of a cooking surface (for those hot pots).
  - Make at least 15 inches of landing space (16 inches deep) near a microwave oven.
  - Create a 36-inch continuous countertop (16 inches deep) for a food preparation center (next to a water source).
  - Leave at least a 15 x 16-inch landing space next to an oven.

Determining Your Dimensions

Before you get into your decorating, create a floor plan (see Chapter 3 for tips). Make sure you show the following items:

- ✔ All electrical outlets, wall switches, and lighting fixtures
- ✔ Dimensions of appliances (stove, refrigerator, freezer, microwave oven, dishwasher, and so on) and fixtures (sinks, and washer and dryer, if they're a part of your kitchen)
- ✔ Ducts, vents, and radiators (things that may remain or may need moving in order to make room for cabinetry)
- ✔ Plumbing and gas connections

Photocopy several copies so that you can experiment with layouts. After doing more research, you may want to revisit your initial layout and draw a different one. Continue to update your layout until you're satisfied.

Finding the Right Furnishings

Making choices for walls, floors, and ceilings is tough enough. Now throw in cabinets, countertops, appliances, furniture, and dishes, and the decorating process can be overwhelming. To keep up with the parade of new products and designs, log on www.kitchens.com. The following sections pinpoint the key elements for the perfect kitchen.

Characterizing cabinets

Many designers suggest starting your kitchen design by selecting cabinets because they determine style direction. What cabinets are right for you? Consider two types of cabinet construction: *face frame* and *frameless.*

The face-frame type has a solid wood frame between doors and a structural support. The frame, which is exposed around doors and drawers, has mounted exterior hinges. This type of construction is most commonly used for Traditional designs.

The frameless cabinet is commonly associated with Contemporary design. In frameless cabinets, the doors are hinged directly to the sides of the cabinet box, leaving little or no reveal.

Not all cabinet construction is equal. Sturdily built cabinets, called *boxes,* have mortise-and-tendon joints (where one portion of the joint slides into the other), which is the strongest joinery. Look also for cross rails or corner braces that hold cabinets square and tight.

Drawers

Materials affect appearance, performance, and price. High-quality cabinetry may have ¾-inch solid wood drawer boxes with solid wood drawer fronts, while medium- and lower-priced drawer boxes are made of ¾-inch solid wood with veneered drawer fronts.

Aren't sure about quality? Carefully inspect a drawer. A well-made drawer contains solid hardwood sides and a plywood bottom — it feels smooth and well sanded. Check for heavy-duty slides that don't produce side-to-side movement. Drawers should allow full extension. If drawers are well made, you can usually rest assured that the cabinets are also.

Finishes tell a quality tale, too. Fine wood cabinets have no rough spots (even on undersides of drawers), no blemishes in the finish, beautiful (non-plastic) patina, and appealing color. Laminates should be bubble-free. Painted finishes should be smooth and ripple-free. Some varnishes protect like a urethane coating. Another durable kind of coating — synthetic resin — is heat-cured. Not even nail-polish remover affects that finish.

Cabinets

When selecting cabinets, keep function in mind. Plan your kitchen layout around particular activities. For greater efficiency, select cabinets designed for each activity and group them in work-designated areas.

Work centers include surface areas for food prep and cabinet space for storage. Position your work center near a sink for easy clean up. Portable work centers have big casters so they can be rolled anywhere for use. To display items stored inside, use glass front doors if you like.

Aren't sure about how much storage space and what cabinet sizes you need? Count and measure the items you store in your kitchen. One easy way is to line up your pots and pans and measure how many linear inches you need. Simply sum up all your measurements to get a rough answer. Remember that home improvement centers have experts to help you plan.

In kitchens with high ceilings, add drama and storage by stacking cabinets — especially cabinets with display glass doors. Place these cabinets opposite a high Palladian window for balance. (A *Palladian* is a large window topped by a semicircular window and flanked by two smaller, rectangular windows. See Chapters 9 and 13 for more information.) In other areas, use a variety of cabinet heights for added interest and storage.

Escaping to your own special island

Islands and peninsulas are a great way to make the best use of limited or unorthodox space. They're easy to build, using stock cabinets as the base. If can't match your new island to your old cabinets, don't worry; paint the island cabinets a contrasting color. (Butcher block or work tables can act like an island. Many are on casters and move about with ease. What you'll miss is below-worktop storage.) A new trend in larger kitchens is two smaller islands. They offer more efficient walk-around space than one large island. Countertops on one or more islands can match function, but need not match one another or existing countertops.

Islands and peninsulas are usually 36 inches high — the same as a kitchen counter. If you prefer, build yours at table height and use an ordinary kitchen chair instead of a high stool for working or eating at the counter. Or make it taller (for a tall cook) or multilevel (if space allows) to suit several cooks' needs. If your peninsula is lower or higher than the kitchen counter, use a different surface for visual contrast.

The minimum width for any countertop is 15 to 18 inches, but manufacturers make 24-inch-wide countertops that extend the kitchen counter. A table-like peninsula can be 30 to 42 inches wide (the same as a standard table) or as wide as space permits.

Consider unique geometric shapes that utilize your space, including circles, triangles, ovals, Ls, and Ts. If your island isn't plumbed or wired, consider placing the island on casters so it can be moved to sinks or electrical outlets.

Free-standing or *unfitted* cabinetry lets you add antique or storage units to kitchens with standard built-in cabinets. Baker's racks, old medical cabinets from dentists' and doctors' offices, gym lockers — anything goes as long as it goes well.

After finalizing your kitchen plan, take it to a home center with NKBA-certified kitchen designers to review your layout and suggest any necessary improvements. They'll help you select the right cabinet for the right task, and print out a materials list.

Countering your top

Switching that outdated countertop for a stylish one may be just the thing to make your kitchen stunning. To make a decorating statement, choose from the following materials:

✔ **Butcher block:** This surface is generally used for small chopping areas because it requires care and wears down. Use it in areas such as work centers or wherever you do your slicing and dicing. It isn't the most sanitary surface available; use bleach regularly to keep it clean and sand it down to renew the surface.

✔ **Ceramic tile:** Ceramic tile is decorative and heat-resistant, but it can chip, making it into an uneven work surface. However, replacing a damaged tile is more affordable than replacing a stone countertop. The surface is somewhat difficult to keep clean, but manufacturers are continually making it more stain-resistant. Over time, you may have to replace the grout.

✔ **Concrete:** This cutting-edge material is a finer grade of concrete than that used for sidewalks. Use it in its natural state (perfect for lofts and Contemporary interiors) or let chemical stains, coloring pigments, aggregates, and epoxy coatings add the look, texture, and feel of quarry stones (perfect for Traditional interiors). It can also be stamped into patterns, including leaves and handprints, or inlayed with mosaics, fossils, pebbles, or faux jewels. For more about concrete, log on www.concretenetwork.com.

✔ **Glass:** You're probably thinking, *Glass? On my countertop?* Well, fabricated glass from Curvet and others is now the cutting-edge material. You may not want to consider a glass countertop for main work areas or wherever little children eat or play. However, you may find a place for glass in a decorative bar area — and there's furniture to match! For more information, go to www.curvetusa.com.

✔ **Laminate (Formica, Wilsonart, and others):** Laminate, a man-made material that can look like natural stone, wood, or almost anything, comes in more colors and finishes than any other countertop material. It's also affordable. Different edge treatments and profiles (curved, right-angle) provide style options that complement cabinet styles. Some laminates have color all through that eliminates the old (undesirable) black-line edge. A beveled edge takes advantage of the black line by incorporating it into the design.

✔ **Solid surface materials:** Usually a blend of acrylic and other materials, these countertops are a popular choice because they wear well, resist staining and germs, and clean up easily. Solid surfaces are available in many colors (check out Samsung's Staron at www.staron.com) and patterns (check out Corian's *Bas Relief* at www.corian.com). For a surface with natural stone character, take a look at DuPont's Zodiaq (www.zodiaq.com), which combines quartz crystals with man-made materials.

✔ **Stainless steel:** If you like the idea of a countertop to match high-tech stainless steel appliances, ask your countertop dealer to recommend a source. Or, contact a custom fabricator, such as Julien (www.julien.ca). Don't expect these customized countertops to be cheap, but you may find more affordable stock sizes.

✔ **Stone:** Granite and marble are increasingly popular countertop surfaces. Granite is all but indestructible and costs about the same as solid surface materials. Marble is softer than granite and not as durable; therefore, it's usually used for pastry-making areas only. Soapstone, an old favorite for countertops and sinks, feels soapy to the touch, has a warm matte look, and develops wear flaws that many find endearing.

✔ **Stone stand-ins:** Called *lavastone* or *enameled lavastone,* this new material is a glasslike stone look-alike that comes in 20 vivid stock colors (custom colors are available). Glazing at high temperatures makes the enameled surface nonporous and resistant to water, oils, and acids, but it does scratch. You can purchase it from Pyrolave USA (`www.pyrolave.com`) at about $210 per square foot.

✔ **Teak:** Teak is a viable option for countertops because it stands up to water and is hard and long wearing. Ask your countertop fabricator about its availability in your area and for advice regarding whether to finish teak or leave it in its natural state.

Stretch your countertop budget by mixing expensive with less-expensive countertop materials. For example, use marble for your bake center countertop and teak for other areas, stainless steel near the cooktop, stone on the island, butcher block near the food prep center, and ceramic tile elsewhere.

Make a place for sipping and snacking — whether it's an island, peninsula, countertop, or table (see Figure 18-1). A welcoming kitchen — small or large — has a comfortable place to sit down for a cup of morning coffee, afternoon tea, or a late-night snack.

Figure 18-1: Adding a few inches to the width of an island countertop provides a comfortable place to perch for a cup of coffee.

Walking on fabulous floors

No matter what the style, kitchen floors have to stand up to hard wear and tear (see Figure 18-2). They should also be easy to clean and skidproof (and kid-proof doesn't hurt either). Popular flooring options include relatively inexpensive carpeting (made especially for kitchens), synthetic (vinyl or other) sheet or rolled flooring, and vinyl tiles. Hard flooring includes brick, ceramic tile, laminates, wood, and stone.

Figure 18-2:
Choices for flooring in a Country or Western themed kitchen are wide open, including wood, tile, stone, or laminates or synthetics that mimic them.

Photograph courtesy Blonder Wallcoverings,
Chesapeake's Home & Heritage Collection

All these substances are reasonably durable. However, you may expect hard surfaces to wear longer than soft flooring. Keep in mind that:

- Brick and stone need renewable protective finishes (sealants) to prevent them from absorbing grease and stains and to make them easier to clean.

- Top glazes may wear away from ceramic tile. If you're concerned, consider porcelain tile, which has color throughout that won't wear off.

- Laminate, once a wood look-alike, now also looks convincingly like stone or ceramic tile. Laminate floors are constructed for quick and easy installation (see Chapter 14). A do-it-yourselfer can install a laminate floor in a 10-foot by 12-foot kitchen for approximately $350, according to Lowe's. For how-to information, go to www.lowes.com.

- To increase the life of a wood floor, especially if it has a painted surface, protect it with several topcoats of polyurethane. Expect to renew it every three to five years.

In addition to old woods — cherry, maple, oak, and pine — newer woods are showing up in trendsetting kitchens. Teak and bamboo are gaining popularity. Bamboo's unique appearance makes it a stylish and durable alternative.

Counter intelligence

Countertop work surfaces have a big effect on a kitchen's appearance and function. If you're updating your kitchen by changing the counter, consider these tips:

✔ Give yourself a break. Lower the counter's height so that you can sit down to do jobs that don't require standing.

✔ Install a good-looking grab bar at the countertop edge or end for people with special needs. A matching grab bar can make an interesting and unusual towel rack.

✔ Make the countertop edge obvious by adding a contrasting edge.

✔ Round or dog-ear (cut on a slant) countertop edges. Eliminating sharp corners reduces the chance of injury.

Don't be shy about using more than one type of countertop material (marble for the bake center and laminate elsewhere, for example). On long islands in big kitchens, separate counter sections intended for different functions by changing the height, interrupting them with an appliance, or using a contrasting material on the island base. In small kitchens, blend colors and patterns for greater unity and a sense of expanded space.

Countertops may or may not, depending on your preference, match the backsplash. Matching provides greater unity; contrasting materials adds visual interest. If you're ordering stone for the countertop and want the backsplash to match, be sure your stone dealer can provide the thinner backsplash stone. (Not all granite, for example, is available in both countertop and backsplash thicknesses.) If you're using contrasting materials (stone countertop and ceramic tile backsplash, for example), plan on using materials of similar quality for greatest appeal.

Enjoying wonderful walls

The kitchen is the number one place for spills and splatters. So even if you're not obsessed with cleanliness, cover your kitchen walls with something washable, because they're going to need washing. The following sections provide some options for kitchen wall materials. Think creatively — you may want to mix two or more of these materials.

Ceramic tile

Ceramic tile isn't your ordinary material for complete kitchen walls, but it's very popular when used as a backsplash for countertops, stoves, and hoods. An endless variety of styles, colors, shapes, patterns, and textures is available. Ceramic tile is, of course, synonymous with Old World charm, but nothing says Contemporary more than new large-format Italian tiles.

Don't use heavily textured tiles directly behind a stove, where hard-to-remove grease may accumulate, or anywhere where dirt and dust accumulate. These labor-intensive materials demand tender loving care.

Turning on fantastic faucets

Faucets come in a mind-boggling number of styles (ranging from Vintage to Contemporary), and finishes (brushed chrome, brass, ceramic) to match or contrast with appliances. They're available in a wide range of prices that depend on quality of materials and workmanship.

Compare an expensive faucet with a less expensive one to see differences in finish. Some differences include smooth versus rough surfaces, solid brass versus plating, and multiprotective coatings for platings versus one or two.

Glass tiles

Glass tiles are rapidly becoming hot decorating items. They come in an infinite number of brilliant colors, patterns, and textures. Most importantly to a sun- and light-loving generation, they're translucent. Use them as backsplashes, focal wall areas, or whole walls in mini-mosaic, 3 x 5-inch brick tiles, and standard and large format tile sizes.

Paint

Use a washable semigloss or high gloss paint. Decorative paint techniques that add pattern, texture, and depth are great, especially if you're just using paint alone. Don't hesitate to paint ceilings a contrasting color. High ceilings can show off rich, deep, strong colors without making a room seem claustrophobic. Use tints for lower ceilings. (To get the lowdown on painting techniques, go to Chapter 13.)

Paneling and planks

Wood is a very comforting surface and shows up in kitchens in various guises, including knotty pine, barnboard, bead board, and paneling of all kinds. Choose the one that underscores your decorating theme or style and a finish that can be cleaned.

Wallcoverings

Wallcoverings (vinyl, paper, and other materials) establish a decorating theme. The added color, pattern, and texture from wallcoverings add interest to rooms where so many surfaces — cabinets, appliances, and ceiling — are plain solids. If you choose wallcoverings (see Chapter 13 for how to estimate rollage), follow these guidelines:

- Choose a pattern that hides fingerprints, especially if small children and messy adults are around.

- Use big patterns if you have large expanses of uninterrupted wall space.

> ✔ If architectural features (such as doors or windows) or kitchen cabinets and appliances break up the space, stick to a small, all-over pattern that doesn't require much matching.
>
> ✔ Use bold, distinctive patterns in bright colors as room identifiers for young children and people with poor vision.

Don't think that you have to stick to typical kitchen patterns if they're not your style. Check out bedroom, living room, dining room, and texture sections of wallcovering books.

Decorating Do's

After you've decided on your furnishings and backgrounds, stop wasting time and get down to the nitty gritty!

Selecting a style or theme

After all the budgeting, measuring, plotting, and planning, now the fun begins. Try to answer this question in 25 words or less: "What do I want my kitchen to look like?" Read on to find out how to get the look you want.

Determining your style

If you think that you may prefer a period style, rip photographs from decorating magazines, brochures, and kitchen style books (scan or copy if you don't want to destroy the book). Don't be surprised to discover that you've collected lots of different looks. Put them on your inspiration wall so you can compare the pictures. Are there any common denominators among the photos? Are they all white? Do they have lots of natural woods or use stainless steel appliances? Do they have painted cabinets, loads of big windows, big islands? Are they mostly Contemporary (or Country)?

Make a list of your likes (and dislikes) about photos. By mixing a little of one and a lot of another, you craft your own personal style.

Decorative themes are another way to go. You'll be surprised how many wallcovering patterns and accessories have themes such as hearth-and-home, hunting dogs, and the beach. Magazines feature examples of decorating with themes that are very helpful because they focus on details.

Letting cabinets be your guide

Cabinets are a kitchen's main furniture. If you must replace old cabinets, buy a style and color that will be the basis for your new scheme (French, English, Country, Victorian, Euro-Modern, and so on).

If possible, reuse existing cabinets. Using your old cabinets saves a bundle of money and tons of time. Ask yourself the following questions:

- ✔ Are my cabinets sturdy and in good working condition?
- ✔ Do they provide adequate storage?
- ✔ Is the color of the cabinets okay? If not, can it be easily changed?
- ✔ Are the cabinets simple square boxes that can be resurfaced?
- ✔ Can old doors be exchanged for new?
- ✔ Can outdated hardware be exchanged for a new style?

If your answers to these questions are "yes," cosmetic changes will save the day. See the sidebar "Giving your kitchen cabinets an extreme makeover" for ideas on how to redeem your old cabinets.

Creating the background

Cabinets star against a background chosen to show them off. The key is contrast. For fancy cabinets, backgrounds (walls, floors, and ceilings) should be plainer. Choose a simple paint, paneling, or a small-patterned wallcovering for walls. Paint the ceiling in a light color that coordinates with the cabinets. Flooring should be darker value than the walls, but shouldn't be too colorful or patterned.

If you want cabinets to recede into a unified background, reduce the contrast. Keep cabinets and wall, floor, and ceiling treatments related. The less contrast you use, the quieter and more serene your room. A calm background paves the way for something else to become the focal point.

 Don't overlook your kitchen's ceiling. Most ceilings get short shrift in decorating. Kitchens are great places for beams, coffers, beautiful paint colors, wall coverings, stenciling, and trellises. The larger the kitchen, the more obvious the ceiling and the more it demands that some visual interest be added. (For great tips on stunning ceiling treatments, see Chapter 15.)

Spotlighting a hood

In kitchens today, the hood is the design prima donna. Hanging on carved *corbels* (supporting brackets) above a fully integrated backsplash and stove, the hood is a focal point. Consider creating your own focal point in any number of styles.

Giving your kitchen cabinets an extreme makeover

If your cabinets need a facelift, think of the following tips as botox for old boxes.

✔ **Clean your cabinets.** A good cleaning may bring new luster to tired but handsome wood.

✔ **Change the hardware.** Try something zippy, like bent twig fork handles, hand-painted ceramic knobs, clear glass handles and knobs, or metal pharmacy pulls. For unity, match cabinet hardware and faucet finishes (all brass, copper, steel, iron, or so on).

✔ **Paint them.** A little paint goes a long way. Are you going Contemporary? Paint simple cabinets with a high gloss lacquer-look finish in a zingy new color or colors. For example, paint base cabinets one color and wall-hung cabinets another. Antiqued cabinets in off white, buttery yellow, mellow rose, watermelon red, and apple green add an Old World charm that's especially comforting. Paint cabinets high-gloss white

for an instant Country look. Or stain them a natural, wood color in the Victorian style.

✔ **Add bead board as a backsplash and paint it a crisp white.** Paint your cabinets' outsides white and the insides a nautical blue for a seaside effect.

✔ **Relaminate all cabinets in one solid color.** Or, for a more Contemporary or Eclectic look, mix and match colors and interesting patterns. For example, keep the cabinet boxes plain and add different colored or patterned doors (or vice versa).

✔ **Exchange old doors on plain cabinets.** Try new fancy doors in the style of your choice.

✔ **Add classic architectural trims to plain cases.** You can include fluted pilasters at the corners, pediments and crown moldings on top, or deep base moldings at the bottom.

Underneath this show horse is a workhorse — the ducted ventilation fan. Make sure that you have the right number of CFMs (cubic feet of air moved per second) to clear your kitchen of cooking odors. You can plan to spend a thousand or more dollars for a large, truly decorative hood (in addition to the cost of the fan).

Furnishing a great kitchen

Kitchens are getting bigger, breaking down walls between living areas (formerly known as *dens* or *family rooms*), hallways, laundry areas, butler's pantries, breakfast rooms, and more. These *great kitchens* include full-blown seating areas (living rooms without walls), including a sofa and lounge and accent chairs.

If your kitchen incorporates a seating area, decide whether you want your furniture fabrics to play a starring role or second fiddle to an exotic floor or wall pattern. If upholstery's the star, patterns can be as big and bold as suitable scale allows. If your upholstery plays second fiddle, choose a pattern that's on the small side (such as a small woven check, plaid, or stripe). Coordinate seating-area fabrics with fabrics on kitchen chairs. Make fabric chair pads or cushions in coordinating patterns, colors, and texture.

Choose easily cleaned upholstery and other fabrics. Consider using washable slipcovers over any upholstery.

If your decorating style is Eclectic, don't hesitate to pit antique-style chairs against a Contemporary table or vice versa. This sort of visual opposition can be fun.

Treating windows

Usually, the kitchen needs all the light it can get. The kitchen is one place where a handsome window with no treatment at all is most desirable. In most cases, less is better — unless your style calls for dressy draperies, especially in an upholstered seating area. Thick-slat blinds, wooden shutters, matchstick, and old-fashioned window blinds are great simple solutions to providing light control and privacy. But dozens of alternative style draperies, curtains, swags, and *jabots* (arrangements of looped material) are available (see Chapter 16).

Accessorizing to add eye appeal

Larger kitchens make room for china cabinets, bookshelves, and displays of favorite family photographs, antique plate collections, pitchers, a clutch of colored candlesticks, and more. Arrange your collectibles on open shelves with care; the better the items relate to one another and to the space, the more attractive they look.

Paint the wall behind an open shelf a snappy color to show off displayed items better.

Almost anything used in the kitchen can double as an accessory (see Figure 18-3), especially when you've got a collection of items, such as wooden bowls, spoons, or rolling pins, interesting pottery or porcelain, colorful trays, woven baskets, old painted tins, cookie cutters, copper pots, and *tole ware* (decoratively painted tin objects). Just arrange them artfully for the world to see. (To light up your kitchen like a pro, see Chapter 17.)

Figure 18-3:
In a friend's New England kitchen, a collection of baskets doubles as a window treatment.

Two accessories you can't forget are those that aid in fire prevention. Keep a fire extinguisher near the cooktop (under the sink or mounted on the wall) and a smoke alarm just outside the kitchen.

Chapter 19

Beautifying Your Bathroom

Bathrooms are bigger and more beautiful than ever. They've gone beyond the basics to include expanded dressing areas, handy laundry facilities, exercise space, and more. The most recent trend is toward *bath as spa* — an almost sacred place for enjoying the recuperative powers of water.

In this chapter, we share tried-and-true decorating secrets that can transform a plainly pragmatic place into a beautiful, highly functional bathroom. We provide ideas for adding zest to the primary areas of walls, floors, and ceilings, and give great tips on accessorizing. Finally, we turn our attention to master baths, small bath, guest baths, and children's baths.

Budgeting Matters

Establishing a workable budget is step one for your bath beautiful project. If you're redecorating more than one bath — most homes have at least two — you need to make every cent work for you. By redoing more than one bath at the same time, you can save time and money — beginning with the plumbing and wiring savings involved in relocating fixtures and lighting.

Before you spend a dollar, get information. The best source is the National Kitchen and Bath Association (NKBA; go to www.NKBA.com or call 877-NKBA-PRO). Most home centers have NKBA-certified designers on staff.

Measuring your facility

To estimate how much paint to buy or how much space you have for extras, you need to measure and make a floor plan. For details, see Chapter 3.

Measuring a bathroom for fixtures requires special considerations. You need at least a foot and a half in front of your toilet for leg space. Remember to allow at least the door width's area for opening and closing — you'll need extra space on the pull side. For other bath design guidelines, go to www.NKBA.com.

While a major overhaul of your bathroom could cost thousands of dollars, simple redecorating can run as low as the cost of a gallon of paint. A dated-looking bathroom can get quick and easy spruce-up with new showerheads, faucets, and hardware for less than $100. Relaminating countertops and cabinets saves a bundle. New shower curtains, towels, rugs, and window treatments can cost as little as $50 to $100. A gallon of paint ($12–20), a new border (under $5), and fancier (but not high priced) light fixtures are all relatively inexpensive stylemakers.

Consider these budget-stretching ideas:

- ✔ **Accept others' rejects.** Shop showrooms for custom-order items that a client refused.

- ✔ **Choose classic white fixtures.** They never go out of style — and they're less expensive than colored ones.

- ✔ **Consider solid surfaces that look like stone.** Less costly than real marble or granite, solid surface countertops are easy to clean and never go out of style.

- ✔ **Create a timeless background with white or neutrals.** Jazz them up with a few decorative tiles in exotic colors and patterns.

- ✔ **Forego real stone, and use a vinyl look-alike.** Vinyl looks great for less, is easy on the feet, and is simple to maintain.

- ✔ **Think big.** Use large ceramic tiles for walls and floors. They look good and cost less to install than smaller tiles.

- ✔ **Use chrome faucets, fittings, and accessories.** They look classy but cost less — and, in wet climates, hold up better — than brass.

Strategizing for Resale

Thinking of selling your place within two years or less? Shift into neutrals — white, almond, and other classics that prospective buyers prefer. If you don't know what's hot and what's not in bathrooms, ask a local real estate agent.

Incorporate these simple tips as you redecorate:

✔ Add glass handles, classic silver or pewter pulls, or hand-painted ceramic knobs to your cabinets.

✔ Find sink and faucet designs that suit your home's style — people notice them first. (To determine if your home is Traditional or Contemporary, see Chapters 9 and 10.) Also, stick with the same metals and finishes throughout.

✔ Look for a new tub faucet to match the new sink faucet, give the shower a new glass door, and replace floor tiles.

✔ Give your bathroom an instant facelift with a coat of light (white or some pale antique color) paint.

✔ Select durable cabinetry. Cabinets are often part of the background — they should be nice, but they don't have to be total knockouts. Keep cabinets light for small spaces.

Your decorating goal is to create an attractive and functional bath that any buyer could love. Neutral colors, paint, and simple fixtures fit the bill. Avoid wallpaper — the pattern might not suit everyone. Keeping it simple is the best policy. Look for:

✔ A few important, not-too-busy, functional accessories such as towel bars, a paper holder, and a soap dish

✔ Classically colored (white, beige, cream) ceramic tile for the floor and walls (a *must* for a quality tub/shower area)

✔ Decorative but not-too-fussy lighting fixtures

✔ Decorative narrow, open shelves to display perfume bottles and pretty items that take up space in cabinets

✔ Good lighting near the vanity mirror

✔ Large three-way mirrored medicine cabinets (for seeing your hairdo from the back)

✔ Light-penetrating — but privacy-guarding — window treatments (stained, frosted, etched, or opaque glass)

✔ Storage space for necessities — especially important with a pedestal sink — such as a small cabinet with a door

Customizing Your Bathroom

Planning on sticking around for a long while? Then customize your bathroom to meet your needs. Customization isn't so much a matter of money as of thoughtfulness and the desire to have it *your* way. The truly personal bathroom works the way you need it to work.

Gathering information

Take stock of your and your family's needs and wishes. Think function first, then style. For example, are you or your family members short, tall, or physically challenged? If so, you need to consider your vanity's height and ease of usage. For more on *universal design* (designs that meet the needs of the physically and mentally challenged), go to www.NKBA.com.

Make a list of physical comforts you're looking for (including height of the lavatory, toilet, tub, showerheads, and so on), and then consider purely decorative desires (colors, textures, style of cabinetry, and so forth). With this information gathered, you're ready to proceed.

Sprucing up surfaces

Ceilings, floors, walls, and windows join forces to create the perfect background for your cabinets, faucets, fixtures, and accessories. Your bathroom's heat, humidity, and sanitation facilities call for specialized walls, floors, ceilings, and windows. Keep in mind the considerations discussed in the following sections.

Walls

Choose easy-to-clean, moisture-resistant surface materials, such as ceramic tile and vinyl, for walls in and near tubs and showers. Of the two, the more expensive ceramic tile is more durable. In Traditional rooms, extend the tile around the remaining walls to at least chair rail height (about 30 inches).

In Contemporary baths, especially in smaller city apartments, tiling all walls, the ceiling, and the floor with ceramic or stone tiles is fairly standard. Depend on other furnishings — towels, artwork, and accessories — to add interesting color, pattern, and texture.

Give your bathroom a big bang for the buck by finding decorative tiles to intersperse with the plain vanilla ones. You can also create themes by cutting tiles and creating star patterns, for example.

Stone surfaces, including marble and granite, are more expensive than ceramic tile, but many designers choose them because they look beautiful, are easy to maintain, and last forever. New luxury stones include onyx, a translucent natural stone.

Don't rule out wallcoverings for bathroom walls (see Figure 19-1). Be sure to install washable vinyl or vinyl-coated wallcoverings that stand up to moisture. For unity's sake, choose a background color that blends with other wall surfaces and those in nearby rooms.

Strong motifs in a wallcovering can establish a distinct theme. Figure 19-1 shows a wallcovering with architectural domes that add a sense of history. The wallcovering in Figure 19-2 is unique because it creates a timeless sense of unique, purely personal style.

Make sure that your bathroom has ample ventilation to prevent moisture damage. Install a combination heat lamp and ducted fan. Use the heat lamp to dry out excess moisture and prevent mold, mildew, and peeling wallcovering.

Figure 19-1:
A wallcovering can transform your bathroom by creating a mood or, like this one, a historic theme.

Photograph courtesy Blonder Wallcoverings,
Signature Series/Grand Impressions

Photography courtesy Blonder Wallcoverings, "Tile Tricks/IdeaStix"

Floors

Bathroom floors must stand up to continual wear, water, and cleaning. (For info on flooring, see Chapter 14.) Best choices include stone, tile, and vinyl.

Natural stone is an upscale choice. Add an Oriental rug for some texture and softness. (Get the look for less by using laminate.)

Ceramic tile looks and performs well, and that's what makes it so popular. Tile sizes range from 1 inch to 24 inches. Using large tiles and fewer grout lines makes typical 5-x-9-foot bathrooms look larger, especially if the tile is set on the diagonal. Use light-colored large tile with matching grouting.

Vinyl floorcovering costs less than ceramic tile and is also softer — dropped jars are less likely to break, and it's gentle on legs and feet. But it won't last as long.

We don't generally recommend wood flooring for the bathroom. However, engineered hardwoods and hardwoods covered in protective polyurethane can stand up to the wear and tear. Don't let water stand for too long.

A simple solution to a really ugly floor is washable, wall-to-wall bathroom carpeting that you can cut with shears (to fit around fixtures) and lay in place. Secure the carpeting with double-faced tape. You can pull it up and toss it in the washing machine whenever you like. Relatively inexpensive, it comes in 5-x-9-foot bundles and is sold in bed and bath shops.

You can add extra color and pattern with washable throw rugs with nonskid backing. Inexpensive machine-made area rugs that look like Orientals may also be a good bet.

Ceilings

Bathroom ceilings are usually white to reflect the most light. But white can be boring and too visible. (For a bevy of ceiling spruce-ups, check out Chapter 15.) Here are some tried-and-true tips for decorating this surface:

- ✔ In a large bathroom with a high ceiling, use a strongly contrasting color or pattern to create interest and intimacy.

- ✔ In small bathrooms and in low-ceilinged large bathrooms, keep contrast to a low level.

- ✔ In a wall-covered small powder room (where moisture isn't a problem), treat the ceiling to either the same or a coordinating wallcovering. (If you're using a directional patterned wallcovering, use a small-scaled coordinate on the ceiling.)

- ✔ Your bathroom's ceiling can be wood plank (especially if it's in a mountain cabin). Just make sure the wood is properly treated to withstand moisture and that your room is adequately ventilated.

If you like the look of Victorian pressed tin ceilings, you can get it at a fraction of the price by using anaglyptic-style vinyl wallcovering. Find it at home improvement stores. (We found ours on sale!) After hanging it, spray-paint it with a metallic gold or silver for a rich look that costs almost nothing.

Windows

Most of us want the bathroom to allow daylight to stream through, but we also want privacy. Following are tips on how you can accomplish both:

- ✔ Consider installing frosted glass windows, which allow light to filter through while also providing some privacy.

- ✔ Install blinds that roll from the bottom up to allow the sunlight in and still provide some privacy.

- ✔ Install roll shades on windows. If you like the look of undecorated, no-nonsense windows, roll up these shades out of sight when not needed.

- ✔ Other types of blinds are also available if you want semi-privacy. For example, matchstick bamboo shades come lined for privacy or unlined for semi-privacy.

Light cotton curtains work well in most bathrooms where a light and airy mood is desired. Figure 19-3 gives a good example of how you can use various combinations of curtains and valances in the bathroom. For more information on window coverings, skip back to Chapter 16.

Figure 19-3:
Gingham checked curtains frame the tub and a tab-topped valance softens the rear window in this cheerful bath.

Photograph courtesy Brewster Wallcoverings, "Kindred Spirits"

Accessorizing Your Bathroom

Accessorizing is the fun part of decorating. Consider the following tips:

- ✔ **Add a fireplace mantel to your dressed up, formal-looking bath (with space enough for a comfy chair).** Electric logs are okay to use in a well-ventilated space with due caution. But, working or not, the effect of a fireplace in this haven is out of this world!

- ✔ **Build your color scheme around a decorative sink with mosaic detailing and a matching mirror.** It makes a major statement.

- ✔ **Consider live plants as accessories.** Make sure to place them out of harm's way (where they can't fall into the tub or cause someone to stumble). If you use fake plants, pretend they're real: Place them near a window.

- ✔ **Don't try to match your towels and shower curtain to your walls.** Paint stores can custom-match paint to your towels. You can also buy white towels and a white shower curtain and monogram them in a matching beige thread.

✔ **Keep accessories related but not repetitious.** If you want a personalized bathroom, avoid ensembles that came straight from a bed/bath shop. Instead, take some time to select or make your own grouping of things that especially appeal to you (see Figure 19-4).

✔ **Match, don't mix, metals.** If the faucets are brass, keep towel bars and rings, curtain rods, and other metal surfaces brass as well. If the faucets in your home mix metals — brass trim with chrome faucets, for example — match all other metals to the faucet body, not its trim.

✔ **Protect pictures on the wall by keeping them away from splashing water.** The bath isn't the place for watercolors and fine art — the humidity destroys them. Think posters and acrylic paintings. Keep gilded picture frames away from direct water sources, which damage the finish. (We discovered the hard way!)

Figure 19-4: Accessories — especially those suggested by but not replicating wallpaper patterns — add flair to a bathroom.

Photograph courtesy Blonder Wallcoverings, "Chesapeake/Quiet Water"

Meeting a Bathroom's Needs

Certain bathrooms require special decorating tactics. Master bathrooms, small bathrooms, guest bathrooms, and children's bathrooms have different needs. The following sections can get you on the right track.

Mastering your bathroom

For convenience and efficiency during the morning rush hour, consider functional and decorative touches. Two of (almost) everything comes in handy when two share a bathroom, for example. And don't forget luxury touches. Even a tight budget can allow for a few luxuries to enhance the bath's ritual. Consider these tips for creating magic in your master bath:

✔ Add a standing screen (made by hinging louvered shutters together) to create privacy for the toilet, if you have enough room.

✔ Create comfort with furnishings for the bath: a terry-covered chaise lounge for him, a comfy chair for her. They're useful for relaxing after a bath or blow-drying your hair. Inexpensive white plastic chairs covered in white terrycloth make a handy spot for a stack of folded towels, too.

✔ Customize cabinets with compartments for drawers and pullout shelves for optimal storage and greater convenience for each partner.

✔ Design a glass-enclosed bath/shower with glass etching — perhaps your initials to match your monogrammed towels and terrycloth robe.

✔ For visual comfort, include a television/DVD (either wall-mounted or concealed in a cabinet on a pull-out shelf). Store the unit in a special holder that sticks to the tub or wall to keep it out of the water.

✔ If you have the room, expand the uses of your master bath by creating a mini-gym area with exercise equipment.

✔ Include a telephone. Be careful not to use a wired phone while soaking!

✔ Incorporate a heated towel rack that serves up several warm towels on cold days and adds heat to a chilly bathroom.

✔ Two lavatories (perhaps at custom heights) or, better yet, two vanities add convenience to a shared bathroom. Mount adjustable magnifying mirrors for each.

✔ Let the light in with skylights, windows, or glass block walls that illuminate the lavatory area(s).

✔ What's luxury without soothing sounds? Add a compact audio system so that you can listen to your favorite music as you soak in the tub.

✔ Include pretty washable area rugs for color, pattern, and warmth for cool feet. Treat yourself and your room to several in different patterns — and change them when your mood changes.

✔ And don't forget the little things — scented candles, potpourri, fresh flowers from your own garden, sachet packets for drawers, and a display of pretty bottles (perhaps with different fragrances).

Making the most of small bathrooms

Want to make your small bathroom seem larger? First, combine smart layouts and small-scale fixtures. Next, consider these suggestions:

- ✔ Add mirrors. They're great space (and light) expanders when used on opposite walls and even on all four walls.

- ✔ Cover a window in sparkling, colorful glass mosaic for a continuous light show.

- ✔ Increase storage by building recessed shelves between wall studs, so that shelves don't intrude into the space.

- ✔ Keep accessories to a minimum to avoid clutter and confusion.

- ✔ Keep window treatments simple, and blend blind and fabric colors with the walls' background color.

- ✔ Make a bathroom appear larger and lighter by using panels of space-expanding transparent glass between fixtures.

- ✔ Replace a hinged door with a *pocket door* (one that slides back into the wall), which requires no swing space.

- ✔ Store only the essentials in a tiny bathroom. Keep refills and replacements handy in an adjoining room or hallway closet.

- ✔ Use glass tub or shower doors.

Gussying up guest bathrooms

Consider these points to make your guest bathroom a great one:

- ✔ Keep bath and bedroom color schemes strongly related to create continuity. Consider a positive/negative color scheme (see Chapter 5): Use dark walls and light accent colors in one space, light walls and dark accents in the other.

- ✔ Store paper, linens, a new toothbrush, and other necessary supplies inside the bathroom, for easy access.

- ✔ Use a glass or light-colored shelf over the toilet if the bathroom is small. Don't make the shelf wider than the top of the tank.

If you don't have room for a wall-hung shelf, you can store rolled towels in a wicker basket, and perhaps add in some bathing sponges and shower gels. Provide a magazine rack, pretty soaps, and maybe even an audio system or TV.

Styling your children's bathroom

When you think of children's bathrooms, primary colors, clown motifs, and other tried-and-true themes may come to mind. If that's what your child likes, that's fine, but ask before you decorate.

In a child's bathroom, safety takes center stage. Following are some suggestions that spring from real-life experiences:

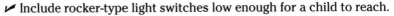

- ✔ Avert scalding by installing hot stop valves that prevent a child from turning water on to the highest, hottest temperature.

- ✔ Avoid using slippery area rugs, make sure the tub and floors are skid-proofed, and consider adding child-height grab bars.

- ✔ Check that the glass for the shower or tub doors is tempered so that it doesn't shatter. Make sure it's properly installed.

- ✔ Include rocker-type light switches low enough for a child to reach.

- ✔ Install easy-to-maneuver lever faucet handles. Mount them on one side of the sink, near the front edge of the counter, so that a child can reach them without having to climb on top of the vanity.

- ✔ Keep a nightlight on at all times.

- ✔ Lock medicine and cleaning supply cabinet doors.

- ✔ Make sure the shower door opens out so that no child (or adult) can become wedged in. (Make sure doors can swing freely.)

- ✔ Place lever handles on all doors at a child's height.

- ✔ Prevent a child from locking himself in the bathroom; make sure that you can unlock the exterior door from the outside.

- ✔ Provide a stool that doesn't tip over for small children to use at the sink.

- ✔ Remove electrically powered radios, hairdryers, and any other small appliances that could be dropped into the tub or sink. Substitute battery-operated products if desired or necessary.

- ✔ Round corners on countertops to prevent injury to tots whose heads may be near the same height.

- ✔ Screw freestanding storage cabinets to the wall so that they don't tip.

- ✔ Verify that your Ground Fault Circuit Interrupter (GFCI) works. It shuts off electrical current when an appliance comes in contact with water.

When it comes to decorating, if you're thinking of resale any time in the near future, take a moment before adding, applying, or installing anything that will cost time, effort, and dollars. Consider some temporary ways to bring special colors into your child's bath — with accessories.

Colorful accents and fun motifs in towels, bath mats, framed art, soaps, the shower curtain, and so on add fun. Perhaps use some of the new peel-and-stick ceramic tiles to create a border on the sink wall or cabinets. Peel-and-stick wall-covering borders add interest, too, and they're easy to remove when you're ready to move.

Transforming Tacky into Terrific

Using your imagination and elbow grease to transform an ugly bath into a beautiful bath saves money — and it's fun. Consider suggestions in the following sections for sprucing up bathrooms in older houses.

Spicing up your vanity

Bathroom vanity cabinets (the cabinets that hold bathroom sinks or lavatories) are sometimes less than beautiful, even when they're brand-new. Age certainly doesn't improve them. Before you give yours the old heave-ho, consider these possibilities:

- ✔ **Add pizzazz.** Create an Old World look by outlining cabinet doors with a row of decorative brass upholsterer's nail heads. They're available from an upholsterer, home center, hardware store, or craft shop. (Before you nail, remove the door and place it on a firm surface.)

- ✔ **Antique a carved and fancy cabinet.** Use a paint kit to highlight raised carvings, fancy moldings, and trims.

- ✔ **Change the hardware.** Upgrading the hardware to new brass or ceramic handles and knobs may be all that you need.

- ✔ **Cover a simple vanity base with wallcovering.** Use the same pattern that's on the walls to blend in the old eyesore.

- ✔ **Paint it.** Pick a great color and the right paint and painting techniques.

- ✔ **Relaminate.** Countertop specialty shops can relaminate any cabinet. Look for those who can relaminate on-site so you don't have to unplumb your sink (a costly deal).

- ✔ **Stencil on a motif.** Paint hearts and flowers, geometrics, or whatever. You don't have anything to lose but a little time and a dab of paint.

Making the best of old tile

Tile is expensive to replace. If you've inherited an unappealing color scheme, don't despair. We have the following remedies for you:

 ✓ **Apply wallcovering above the tile.** Search for a pattern that incorporates several colors, including that of the old tiles.

 ✓ **Dress up ceramic tile with stick-on accents.** They come in plenty of themes, styles, and colors, and are easy to apply.

 ✓ **Faux paint.** Paint the wall above the tile, using layers of color that relate to the old tile.

 ✓ **Throw down an area rug.** Rugs are great for covering offending flooring. Choose one that picks up and plays back the colors in your wall treatments.

Not sure what colors to use? Look to wallcoverings, fabrics, and even gift-wrap for inspiration.

Chapter 20

Setting Up Your Home Office

· ·

· ·

Do you work out of your home, or do you need a place to manage your finances, showcase books, or do some serious studying? Professionally equipped home offices are becoming the norm.

The first challenge is finding the right location. The next challenge is creating a balanced environment of professionalism and personal expression. Forget about Spartanism — the perfect office, library, or study places major emphasis on comfort (see Figure 20-1). Comfort and function are no accident — you accomplish them with design.

Figure 20-1:
Combine all the comforts of home with the efficiencies of a profes-sional office.

Photography courtesy Blonder Wallcovering

In this chapter, we guide you through the process of achieving this balance and more. We show you what you need to make your office, library, or study work well. We then discuss space, functional floor plans, power and lighting, and those little extras that mean a lot — accessories.

Locating Your Work/Study Space

Location, location, and location — it's just as important for a home office as it is for real estate. The ideal location provides easy access for users, privacy, and enough space for equipment, furnishings, storage, and comfort. These factors all affect productivity.

Pick the best location the first time around, because relocating your workspace can be a serious (and somewhat expensive) business. Seeking a great location means answering some key questions:

- ✔ **Who will use your home office?** A converted garage makes a great space, and it's a short commute! (A furniture designer we know converted a two-car garage into an office that she and her assistant use.) However, if others use your computer or equipment, you may want your office in the house. If you need to keep an eye on small children while you work, claim a room that's near them, perhaps installing French doors to control sound but allow views. In some cases, you may need to set up an office in a bedroom — for example, if your child needs an "office" of his or her own (see Figure 20-2).

- ✔ **What kind of work will you do in your office?** What you do affects what you need. Researchers, students, and writers need bookshelves and tabletop space for spacing out their research materials. Accountants and consultants need filing cabinets for storing records. List your requirements, plus any special equipment you need, in order to figure out necessary floor and wall space.

- ✔ **Will you see clients or colleagues in your home office?** Having clients or colleagues walk through private living areas is awkward — it's more comfortable (and professional) to have a separate entry. You also need an adequately large conference area with a table and seating.

- ✔ **What kind of environment do you prefer working in?** Do you need privacy and total silence? Or do you like flux and flow and background noise? Find a location for your home office that comes as close to your perfect environment as possible.

When your home office is a separate room, you can close the door during working hours and keep outside distractions at a distance. For a particularly small office, substitute a glass French door that shuts out sound but makes the room seem larger. We did this for a client in a Chicago high-rise so that she could see the rest of her apartment.

Figure 20-2:
Increasingly,
kids need
"home
offices,"
too —
usually as
part of their
bedrooms.

*Photography courtesy Blonder Wallcoverings,
Kids World Collection*

If you prefer being in the fray, or you don't have a separate room for an office, a computer armoire or work center is a great solution. When you finish working, simply close its doors, and the office disappears.

Measuring Your Space

Put your furniture and equipment in its place. Actual square footage is the most vital consideration. Measure the space you're considering to be sure that you can fit in all the furniture and equipment you need.

The first step in designing your home office is drawing your room's floor plan (see Chapter 3). Measure each piece of furniture and equipment (including your computer, printer, fax machine, desk, and chair) so that you can experiment with different layouts. Note on your floor plan the location of windows, doors, and electrical outlets. Imagine yourself walking through a typical workday — reaching for one item, filing another — until you find the plan that best suits you.

If you have a beautiful view from the windows in your home office, don't block the view with furniture. Instead, build cabinets, shelves, or window-seat storage below and around the windows.

Lighting Up

Offices need three kinds of lighting: general, task, and accent. (For the lowdown on lighting, see Chapter 17.) Take a critical look at a room's natural light sources. Does the room have plenty of windows? If not, can you add them before you set up shop?

Natural light needs balancing with artificial lighting, even in the daytime. Shadowy areas need lighting, and not every day is sunny. Use blinds to control sunlight; for tips on window treatments, see Chapter 16. Place computers and other equipment at right angles to the sunlight to prevent glare. Don't position your computer in front of a window — constantly adjusting your eyes to two different light sources causes eyestrain.

Make sure that task lights for reading and working are adjustable so that you can change the angles and heights when you need to. Check out halogen lights, which produce as much light as an incandescent bulb ten times larger in size. Consider the new long-life fluorescent task lights that use at least 60 percent less energy than a standard bulb and last ten times longer.

Before settling on lighting, check with a certified lighting consultant at your lighting or home improvement store. Be prepared to install a variety of light sources, including general and task lights.

Equipping Your Office

Your work and how you do it influences the kind, quantity, and arrangement of your home office equipment and furniture. The following sections deal with your special needs for high performance equipment and furniture.

Electronic equipment

Computers have become the focal point of most home offices. Buy the best computer you can afford — consider its performance and looks. Flat monitors, for example, save space and look elegant. Consider a laptop (which goes where you go) and desktop conversion extras (big monitor, keyboard, and mouse) if you travel. If children and other family members plan to use your computer, look into adding workstations (which keep your own desk area off-limits.) Most computer makers and retailers have great deals — be sure to comparison shop before plunking down your dough. If you plan to use more than one PC, plan for extra outlets and desk room.

Staying connected is essential. Some offices require two telephone lines, especially if there are two people working in the same space. Phone and cable companies offer high-speed access for Internet users that will leave your phone line free for talking. To save space and phone line connections, consider phone, fax, and answering machines that are also printers. Cordless phones that let you move around while you talk and headsets that keep hands free for other uses are must-haves. Invest in the highest quality you can afford. Up-to-date, efficient equipment keeps you competitive in the marketplace — and it lasts longer, too.

Furniture

Forget about using a quaint kitchen table and a straight-back chair as your office furniture. You won't find carpal tunnel syndrome, a stiff neck, or other discomforts very quaint when they keep you from doing your job. Ergonomically designed work surfaces and chairs, which support your body, are available in many affordable price ranges, and are scaled for children and adults (see Figure 20-3).

Ready To Assemble (RTA) furniture available from such places as Office Max and Office Depot offers real savings. Many different styles and materials are in stock and ready to roll out of the store and into your office. Furniture stores show only a relatively few styles of higher-priced finished furniture but have catalogs galore for special orders. Keep in mind that custom ordering from a store catalog may require weeks (or months!) for deliveries.

Figure 20-3:
Ergonomically correct furniture may cost more, but it pays back in comfort and productivity.

Ergonomically Incorrect   Ergonomically Correct !

Desks

A desk is usually the most important piece of furniture in a home office, so spend some time looking at the options and finding the one that's right for you. To determine how big a desk you need, choose a position for your computer (dead center, on the right, or on the left of the desk). Then figure in enough extra work surface to accommodate the different jobs you do.

Any desk should be at least 24 inches deep. The standard height of desks is 29 inches. A computer keyboard should be between 24½ and 28 inches off the floor. (You can install an adjustable, retractable keyboard tray under the work surface if you want to leave your desk space free.)

L-shaped and U-shaped desks provide a wraparound work surface that's easy to use. A P-shaped desk (which is a variation of the L-shaped desk) flares out into a wider semicircle at one end, and it allows for comfortable desktop conferencing. Work surfaces of between 32 and 36 inches wide, flaring to 42- to 48-inch-wide conference table ends, are very popular. Either end of the desk can be attached to a matching, standard 6-foot-long wall unit comprising a desk with a file-drawer pedestal and optional bookcase hutch. These units are available in all price ranges and come in a wide variety of materials, including fancy wood veneers and easily cleaned laminates.

Allow a 5-foot square floor space for a P-shaped, U-shaped, or L-shaped desk. Add another two feet to each side of the square if you augment these work surfaces with a freestanding credenza.

Whenever you draw a desk on your floor plan, add a minimum of two feet for your office chair, plus another two feet in which to push back your chair when you stand up.

Custom-built and built-in furniture is generally more expensive, but it often makes the most efficient use of space. If space is tight, try building an adequate desktop that's less than the standard 32 inches wide. Or you can even build a desk with a space-saving breakfront shape (which is wider in the middle and narrower on the sides) or banjo shape (wide on one side and much narrower on the other). Some rooms have such odd-shaped nooks and crannies that custom furniture is the only way to make use of the space efficiently. So, although custom costs, consider the possibilities.

You may need a second desk in a different location, just for your own use. If you spend a lot of time conceptualizing, treat this desk and yourself to a view.

Chairs

Forget using a straight-backed chair — they're killers. Do your back, bottom, and mental health a favor. Your best bet is an upholstered swivel chair with five legs for stability and casters for mobility. Choose an adjustable model — one that you can raise and lower, tilt forward and backward. Be sure that the seat is well padded and firm for comfortable support — some of us stay in our chairs for days at a time!

Upholstery fabric should be leather (which is cool in the summer and warm in the winter), a high-quality vinyl, a tightly woven fabric, or see-through mesh that takes up no visual space. The fabric should be easy to clean (especially if you drink coffee and snack at your desk like the rest of us do). Your chair should have open, not confining, adjustable armrests. And before you buy it, try it!

The kinds of guest chairs you need depends upon the number of visitors you have and whether they'll be examining papers (which requires a table) or just chatting while they're in your office. You want to impress a visiting client, but if you don't see many clients at home, your standards may be lower. Guest chairs can be anything you like, as long as they're comfortable and meet your quality code. Wing chairs (add an ottoman if you're going to read) and rocking chairs provide comfortable seating. Place guest chairs beside your desk and at small tables.

Storage

Don't forget bookshelves (freestanding or wall-hung), filing cabinets (4- or 2-drawer or some of each), and other storage areas. But if you can't find space for storage in the room, consider taking over a nearby hall closet. You can put filing cabinets in the closet and add shelving above them. You can create shelving in many ways; armoires, baker's racks, gym lockers, and many other pieces can double as storage units.

Not all ready-to-assemble bookshelves are quick and easy! We had to pay a carpenter to assemble one set of particularly complicated shelves, and that ended up doubling their cost. Ask to see assembly directions before you buy.

Save decorating dollars by painting inexpensive white laminate bookshelves a richer, more dramatic color. To paint a bookshelf, follow these easy steps:

1. **Cover the bookshelf with primer and let it dry.**

2. **Lightly sand the bookshelf and gently wipe away excess debris.**

3. **Coat the shelf again with primer and let it dry.**

4. **Cover the bookshelf with two coats of an oil-based, semigloss, enamel paint, sanding it well between each coat of paint.**

    Use a sponge brush, which leaves no brush strokes. Add Penetrol, (which improves your paint and is available at your local supply store) to the paint to make a smoother surface. (You can substitute latex enamel paint for the oil-based paint if you want, but the oil-based version makes the laminate look more like real wood.)

Let the paint cure for 10 days before you stack anything on your bookshelves.

Wiring Up

Do you have enough outlets? Some older homes have poorly placed and too few outlets. Building codes require newer homes to have a certain number of outlets per feet, but even then, you may need more. Also check your wiring's type and condition, especially if you own an older home. Some wiring can't handle the load of all the equipment you need. Other homes don't have adequate electricity running into the house (Double-check with your electric company.)

Experts recommend 20-amp dedicated circuits for computers, printers, and fax machines. If your space needs a portable air conditioner, it needs its own circuit. If your home was built prior to the 1990s, you may want to call in an electrician to determine your needs. Nothing is more frustrating than having your work disrupted by a total blackout. You should safely be able to run your microwave oven in the kitchen at the same time you're running Windows in your office — without a power crash.

Keep the following tips regarding electricity in mind as you create your office plan:

✔ Add wall-hung, strip outlets above the height (and within reach) of your desk. These outlets are easily accessible for your computer, printer, and other equipment.

✔ Upgrade telephone wiring from the normal CAT 3 wire to faster CAT 4 or 5, especially if you plan on using the Internet. (Check with your phone company for details.)

✔ Use surge-protector extension cords to protect all your electrical equipment.

Color Scheming for Productivity

Color your office productive. Put color's power — its ability to profoundly affect and effect mood — to work. We're not saying that you can't have fun with color in your office; we're saying that even fun colors should receive due deliberation. Don't just pick out a pretty color. Pick out a color that's going to earn its keep — or at least enable you to earn yours.

Do you need a jumpstart in the morning? A sunny yellow or a tone of orange does the trick. (You probably don't want a drop-dead red, which would be overkill.) Perhaps you enter your office with your mind going at least a mile a minute, and you don't stop all day. A soft blue can slow you down a wee bit. Are you having trouble concentrating, thanks to ringing phones, beeping faxes, and flashing PCs? Perhaps a reflective pale green can help. The idea is to look before you leap for a particular paint. But after figuring out all there is to know about color (see Chapter 5), doing due diligence, and duly deliberating, you'll have to be the judge.

Start color scheming by selecting your furniture. Let it be your guide, because furniture largely determines your room's style. If you're having trouble deciding whether your office furniture should be dark or light, take into consideration the following guidelines:

✔ Dark furniture (such as cherry, fruitwood, or mahogany) appears Traditional and more formal and serious than light furniture.

✔ Light woods (such as birch, maple, or oak) look Contemporary and more casual and lighthearted than dark finishes.

✔ Light laminates (such as white, beige, or gray) work well in Contemporary styles.

Furniture color and style influence your choice of a color scheme for your office, so before you make a final decision regarding furniture color, think about the colors you're considering for walls. ***Remember:*** Light cool colors recede (great for small spaces), and dark cool or warm colors advance, eating up space (not good for small spaces but just fine for large ones). Strong contrasts make spaces seem smaller, too.

Keep in mind the following guidelines:

✔ To make a room appear smaller, heighten contrast by using dark furniture in a light-colored room or light furniture in a dark-colored room.

✔ To make a room appear larger, reduce contrast. Use light furniture in light-colored rooms or dark furniture in dark-colored rooms.

Accessorizing for Productivity and Fun

When you work at home, you can decorate the way *you* want, keeping the degree of professionalism or non-professionalism where you want it. (You won't have to worry about corporate taste police!) Start by making the most of attractive desk accessories in a style compatible with your furniture. Then, take a look at the following ideas to get your creativity going:

✔ Add a big blackboard or dry-erase board for notes and messages on a work-and-plan wall.

✔ Bring order to open shelves with basket trays that can hold magazines, brochures, or papers.

✔ Check home centers for cork tiles that you can glue to a wall, creating a corkboard for page and photo review or memos.

✔ Don't forget home fragrance products.

✔ Drape a throw over the wingchair for those long read-through sessions.

✔ Hang a decorative mirror on the inside of a cabinet door or somewhere handy so that you can check your appearance before you answer the door.

✔ Include a TV, so you can monitor the news and that must-see program. An audio system can provide pleasant background music, too.

✔ Let grouped diplomas, certificates, awards, photos of family and friends, old maps from favorite vacations, framed book dust jackets, framed magazine covers, or other favorite things do duty as wall decor.

✔ Place rolled architectural drawings or rolls of colorful wallpaper in a decorative umbrella stand, nail keg, or covered cardboard box.

✔ Put a large, decorative, easy-to-read calendar within sight.

✔ Stencil inspirational quotes on one or more of the walls just below the cove molding or on a focal wall.

Part VI
Fixing Up Four Easy Rooms

"I've tried thought remedies, meditation and breathing techniques, but nothing seems to work. I'm still feeling anxious and disoriented all day long."

In this part . . .

Living rooms, bedrooms, and dining rooms are considered easy to decorate because they involve few, if any, technical considerations. They're mostly a matter of choosing wonderful furnishings that speak to you. The chapter on decorating what we call *bonus areas* (attics, basements, and porches) is a bonus, since these are extra-fun places to decorate.

Chapter 21

Styling Serene Bedrooms

*T*o sleep, perchance to dream . . . and so much more. The bedroom serves many functions — catching alone time, dressing, exercising, reading, sharing intimacy, watching TV, and more. Meeting all these functions within a room's limited space — most bedrooms average a modest 10 by 12 feet — and making it dreamy can be a tough challenge.

In this chapter, we help you figure out all the functions your bedroom serves and how to personalize your bedroom to suit your preferences. You find out how to make the most of the space you have, and how to select a bed, bed coverings, a mattress, and pillows. You also discover ways to maximize your storage space. Finally, this chapter provides great suggestions for ways to tailor a bedroom for the people who will be using it.

Considering Function First

Bedroom basics include the right size and style of bed, storage space for clothing, a nightstand, and task lighting. Beyond the basics, you may want to include other conveniences of contemporary life, such as a TV and DVD/VCR; a stereo; storage space for videos, DVDs, or CDs; a desk for reading and writing; and a chair or two for lounging.

A good first step is to take an inventory of your activities. Answer the following questions to determine your needs and wants:

✔ Who occupies this bedroom?

✔ What is the personal style of its occupant? (See Chapter 11 for help answering this question.)

✔ What will you and your family (or guests) use the bedroom for? (Some possibilities include nighttime and daytime sleeping, reading, studying, watching TV, listening to music, using the computer, grooming, dressing, and exercising.)

✔ What size (and how many) beds will you have in the room?

- Twin

- Full/double

- Queen

- King

- California king

- Custom

✔ What style or type of bed will you have?

✔ What additional furnishings do you need in the room?

- Armoire

- Bureau

- Chaise lounge

- Convertible sofa bed

- Desk and chair

- Dresser

- Easy chair

- Footlocker

- Hope chest

- Media cabinet

- Mirrors

- Nightstand

- Reclining chair

- Sofa or love seat

- Table
- Vanity table

✔ Where do you need task lighting?

- Bedsides
- Desk
- Tables
- Vanity table

✔ What equipment do you need for the room?

- Answering machine
- Computer
- DVD/VCR
- Fax machine
- Intercom
- Stereo
- Telephone
- Television

Keeping your answers to the preceding questions in mind, take a look at the sections in this chapter that pertain to your specific decorating needs.

Selecting the Right Bed Type

To figure out which bed suits your decorating needs, think about the bed you currently have: its size, its style (which may be the starting point for your room's style), and the comfort of the mattress. Are you satisfied with what you have? Or are you looking to purchase something new? If a new bed is within your budget, keep reading for tips on selecting the best option for your space.

Fitting your room (and your body)

Before you go shopping for a bed, figure out the maximum amount of space your bed can take up. A too-big bed makes it nearly impossible to move around. You need adequate space to walk through the room, open closet doors and drawers, and place other furnishings. (For help calculating your available space, see Chapter 3.)

Making your own headboard

You don't need to spend a lot of money to get a great look. Check out the following suggestions for quick, easy, and inexpensive headboards:

✔ **Antique shutters:** Attach shutters to the wall at the head of your bed. (Antique ones from the local salvage yard add a true cottage flavor.)

✔ **Demi-canopy:** Attach a curtain rod shaped like a semicircle on the wall near the ceiling, leaving a space of about two to three inches for the top of the curtain (sometimes called a *curtain heading*). These special rods are available at craft stores, decorating shops, and drapery makers. Then hang readymade curtains long enough to reach the floor.

✔ **Pillowcases:** Above the bed, firmly install a drapery rod that extends the bed's width. Add grosgrain ribbon tabs at intervals along one side of the pillowcases. Insert pillows into the pillowcases, and hang them on the rod as a headboard.

✔ **Standing screen:** Place a standing screen between your bed and the wall. If the screen is in need of stability, you can secure it to the wall.

✔ **Tapestry or quilt:** Hang a tapestry or quilt on the wall behind your bed. Make sure it's fastened securely by drilling hooks into the wall or by installing a rod supported by brackets. Make sure that your hanging isn't so fragile that rubbing against it will damage the tapestry.

✔ **Wagon wheel:** An old wagon wheel makes a natural headboard for a boy's twin bed. Fasten a wheel securely at the height that you like.

✔ **Wrought iron gate:** Check out the salvage yard for an old iron gate that you can secure to the wall for a headboard. These gates add plenty of Old World charm to any bedroom.

Turning the bed sideways along a wall is one option because it gives you plenty of floor space — a perfect solution for small rooms or rooms with beautiful flooring. To dress it up, install a *corona* (a crown-shaped piece) and drape fabric from it over the sides of the bed. Or, use a king-size headboard — it will work for any size bed. Add stacks of pillows to complete the look.

You have to be able to get the bed through the bedroom door. Measure all the door openings and hallways. You may have to take the doors off the frames in order to squeeze the bed through.

The mattress you choose should be at least 3 inches longer than the height of the tallest person sleeping on it. The standard mattress sizes are as follows:

✔ **Twin:** 39 inches wide by 75 inches long

   If you plan to use two twin beds, allow a minimum of 24 inches between them or place a nightstand between them.

✔ **Extra-long twin:** 38 inches wide by 80 inches long

✔ **Double:** 54 inches wide by 75 inches long

✔ **Queen:** 60 inches wide by 80 inches long

✔ **King:** 76 to 78 inches wide by 80 inches long

✔ **California king:** 72 inches wide by 84 inches long

To find out how much floor space a bed will take up, consider the following elements of a bed and add the appropriate measurements to the basic mattress size:

✔ **Bed covering:** Add 3 inches to both the bed's width and length.

✔ **Changing the bed covering:** In order to comfortably change the bed coverings, add 15 inches of clear space around the bed.

✔ **Footboard:** Add 3 to 4 inches to the bed's length.

✔ **Headboard:** Add another 3 to 4 inches to the bed's length.

Also keep in mind the bed's height. You may want a higher or lower bed for decorative reasons or for physical comfort. Here are some tips:

✔ Adding an extra box spring to a bed set can raise a bed high enough for you to have a better view out of your window.

✔ A simple low metal frame may be all that's needed to raise a bed to the exact height of a windowsill, so that the window and the view out of it aren't obstructed.

Getting comfortable

No objective industry standards exist for labeling mattresses, which means that the quality of firmness and support varies from maker to maker. When you go mattress shopping, wear comfortable clothing. Test out the mattresses by getting into the positions you actually sleep in — and expect to take a few minutes to fully relax. Getting a feel — literally — for a mattress is the best way to tell if it's right for you.

Read the labels for specific information on the number and kinds of layers, the number, type, and construction of the coils, and any special features. Look carefully at the cutaway sample that demonstrates the mattress's construction.

The most common type of mattress is the innerspring, which features tempered spring coils covered by layers of upholstery. The more coils, the better — the minimum is 400 and the recommended is 600 or more. Buy the best mattress you can afford.

When you buy a mattress, always buy the matching box spring — they're designed to work together as a system. Don't combine a new mattress with old box springs, because your mattress won't get the support it needs.

If you need a hypoallergenic mattress, a good alternative is a foam mattress made of natural latex rubber. The foam density should measure at least two pounds per cubic foot. The higher the density, the better the foam. But remember: You still need a box spring or foundation to support a foam mattress.

Finding great style

Add personal style instantly with a dramatic bed. Because your bed is the dominant furnishing in your bedroom, choose a style that suits your taste.

You spend one-third of your life sleeping (or at least you *should!*), so spend it sleeping in beauty. Beds come in a variety of styles, so you can always find one that complements your decorating scheme. We list some of the most common styles of beds here:

- ✔ **Captain's bed:** Inspired by the beds made for ships, captain's beds feature a drawer beneath the mattress for storage — a plus when you need more storage. They're often used in children's and teenagers' rooms because they hold tons of stuff. They're available in a range of sizes and styles. The frame's top edge should be lower than the mattress top to prevent banging your knees when you crawl into bed.

- ✔ **Daybed:** These beds (see Figure 21-1) are intended for napping — or even sitting — during the day. They're usually more compactly sized than standard beds and typically are placed sideways along a wall to save space. (Some double as sofas.)

- ✔ **Four-poster bed:** This bed features four vertical posts and usually a headboard and footboard. Four-poster beds come in a variety of styles, from Traditional to Contemporary (see Chapters 9 and 10 for more about these styles). Four-posters are good choices for rooms with high ceilings or large rooms where anything else would seem proportionately too small.

- ✔ **Hollywood bed:** A Hollywood bed is a very low bed, with or without a headboard. Sleek and contemporary, this style doesn't take up much space visually. A Hollywood bed's headboard is very tailored, with straight lines.

✔ **Platform bed:** A platform bed is a mattress "floating" on a stage-like box that raises the bed one to two (or more) feet off the floor. The platform bed adds a streamlined sense of drama and is especially good for large, open spaces.

If the platform is more than one step high, include a handrail and allow an 8-inch toe kick (like those beneath kitchen cabinets) to prevent stubbed toes.

✔ **Sleigh bed:** Sleigh beds are usually very high, with slightly curved headboards and somewhat lower, curved footboards, drawing on the design of 19th-century sleighs. Sleigh beds may feature heavy carving or simple, plain wood surfaces. Sleigh beds generally aren't for very small spaces, because they're heavy in appearance.

✔ **Tester (canopy) bed:** A tester (or canopy) bed is a draped four-poster bed. Originally designed for warmth and comfort, a canopy bed has draped fabric covering the top and sides. Most people choose canopy beds today for a romantic sense of luxury and privacy, especially in spacious rooms. Testers come in Traditional and Contemporary designs.

Figure 21-1:
A daybed, or a larger bed set alongside a wall and piled high with pillows, offers a place to cat-nap during the day.

Photograph courtesy Garcia Imports' Sun Country Style
by Patricia Hart McMillan

Creating a bed fit for a king or queen

Alfredo Brito, of Miami-based Brito Interiors, created marvelous bed hangings from crown molding and drapes for his own Renaissance style bedroom. You can adapt his technique to suit any style.

Select thick crown molding and run the molding all around the room and over door openings until you get to the bed area. You'll need two extra one-foot lengths of molding to create side-pieces for the canopy effect. Attach these two sidepieces to a length of molding that is a few inches wider than your bed.

For drapes, pick any sort of drape you prefer. If you're on a budget, you can even use four (or more) queen- or king-size sheets. Other possibilities include thick, plushy velvet for a royal touch (it's great for colder climates, too) or sheer, gauzy drapes for a summery mood. The amount and type of pleating you use influences the total. Alfredo says for ultra romantic looks, use plenty of pleats, and for a masculine look use fewer. You need at least twice the total length of the sides and backs of the molding for a luxurious look. Attach the fabric to a soft valance. For extra glam, affix fringe to the top edge and sides of drapes. Attach the soft valance to the inside edge of the crown molding and across the back wall.

For lighting that's functional and decorative, Brito suggests installing a pair of wall sconces or swing arm lamps about midway between the top of the bed and the crown molding. The light provides a dramatic focal point and illumination for reading at night.

Storing Your Stuff

Although storage space — for clothing, shoes, accessories, and myriad other things — is a necessity in any bedroom, space is usually at a premium given the limited space of most bedrooms and closets. The first step in tackling the storage issue is to analyze what you already have and compare it to what you need. Then you can figure out how to make the most of your bedroom space. With just a few simple steps, your bedroom can accommodate virtually all your storage needs (see Figure 21-2).

Taking stock of your storage needs

Before tackling the storage space in your bedroom, determine how much space you have and how much space you need. The following questions help you do just that:

✔ How many of the following storage facilities do you need?

- Armoire
- Cabinets
- Closets

- Drawers

- Media center

- Shelves

- Walk-in closets

✔ How much hanging storage do you need for coats, dresses, pants, shirts/blouses, skirts, and suits? (Measure in linear feet.)

✔ How much shelving space do you need? (Measure the height and width of folded garments.)

✔ How many shallow drawers (2 inches deep) and deep drawers (4 or more inches deep) do you need?

✔ How many pairs of boots, sandals, shoes, and sneakers do you need room for?

Figure 21-2: A child's bedroom, usually multifunctional, has special storage needs.

Photograph courtesy Brewster Wallcoverings, Jack & Jill Collection

Maximizing storage space

After you've determined your storage needs, you can start thinking about ways to get the most out of the space you have. Try these few suggestions for maximizing storage space:

✔ You wear only about 20 percent of all the clothing and shoes you own. The other 80 percent takes up space. Periodically weed out the out-of-date items. Charities are happy to have the power suits you wore back in the '90s.

✔ Use wire-shelving systems, rods hung at various heights, hooks, and shoe racks in your closets to use the space efficiently.

✔ Use an oversized armoire or glass-fronted bookcase as a media cabinet. The drawers and shelves allow you to store clothing and other things, and your TV is out of the way and at an optimum height for viewing.

✔ Stack a smaller chest of drawers on top of a larger chest of drawers or two. Make them look spiffy by painting them the same color and adding decorative stenciling. (Fasten the units together in the back with simple hardware and secure to the wall or floor to prevent them from tipping over, especially if you have small children.) This technique allows you to store a large amount in a small space — and it looks great, too!

Placing Nightstands and Tables

Nightstands, tables, and task lighting aren't just simple accessories — they're necessities. They provide surface space for accessories, lamps, and necessities.

Nightstands also have drawers that let you keep medicines, personal items, and supplies out of sight. Place nightstands on each side of the bed for storage. Place a lamp — any kind you prefer — for reading in bed. (If you're short on surface space, hang pendant lamps or swing arms lamps. For more on lighting, see Chapter 17.)

You can inventively use tables of various heights for function and decoration. Place an armless slipper chair next to a low table for a cozy reading spot. Nestle two wing chairs around a higher table for an intimate coffee and conversation spot. For a touch of personal style, drape a round table (you can buy very inexpensive ready-to-assemble ones) with a favorite sheet or coverlet.

Beautifying Your Bed

Dressing a bed beautifully is an art. Your sheets, pillows, and bedspread reflect your style, and they're every bit as important as the furniture you choose. The way your bed looks and feels plays a huge part in your comfort, so spend some time thinking about what you want, and have fun planning! Give thought to thread count (the higher the count, the silkier the texture), care, and instructions (washable is less expensive than dry-cleaning).

Dressing your bed

Start by picking out sheets that coordinate with your color scheme and personal style. Pick solids, patterns, or prints that match your bedroom's mood. If you enjoy variety, select three sheet sets that work with each other, and then mix and match. Floral patterns can easily mix with both solids and stripes to create interesting, varied effects.

When you buy sheets, read the label for information about what they're made of and how they're made. Check the sheet's feel, or *hand,* to make sure. Printing can stiffen sheets.

Buy at least one white or ivory set of sheets. Have on hand a minimum of three sets of sheets — one for on the bed, one in the closet, and one in the laundry, at any given time.

A dust ruffle or bed skirt is great for hiding the ugly box spring and the frame legs. If you don't like dust ruffles or more tailored bed skirts, cover the box spring with a flat sheet tucked to fit — an inexpensive and tasteful solution (as long as the bed's legs don't show).

An inexpensive and easy way to freshen up your bedroom or furnish your spare bedroom is with a "bed in a box" — a coordinated set of a comforter, dust ruffle, pillowcases, and sheets for around $50.

You can also dress a bed with a floor-length bedspread or a coverlet, comforter, or duvet that simply tops the bed area. A *coverlet* is thin like a bedspread (both are Traditional ways to cover a bed). A comforter or quilt is generally decorative and is a more Contemporary bed dressing. A *duvet* is a European, down-filled comforter that comes in a plain casing and is designed to be inserted into a duvet cover, which is like a giant pillowcase. A duvet cover can also go over a comforter for a quick change.

The Traditional bedspread generally covers the pillows to create a seamless top. But if you like more romance, add decorative little pillows, pile on your favorite dolls or stuffed animals, or drape throws or extra quilts over the top.

Draping a bed adds plenty of drama, pattern, texture, and interest. If you have high ceilings, a tester (canopy) bed fits the space well. For Traditional bedrooms, use traditional fabrics (toile, chintz, and classic florals are good choices) and pick a Traditional style bed. Use simpler draperies with tailored pleats to drape a Contemporary bed frame. Mosquito netting adds sheer mystery. Attach netting to the ceiling with simple hoops, or buy netting already attached to a frame.

Making pillow talk

You can never have enough decorative pillows on your bed. For more Contemporary appeal, arrange pillows on the top of the bed, propping them artfully against the headboard. For a stylish mix, use two or more European-sized pillows, which are large, square shapes that show nicely behind a rectangular pillow. Stack a mix of regular pillows and pillows covered with dramatic shams.

Add drama to the entire look by choosing shams with flanges and deep edges that are either tailored or ruffled. You can add dimension with round neck pillows or bolsters and small accent pillows. Or add texture by mixing weaves, finishes, laces, and tapestry.

Arranging Your Furniture

Any bedroom's focal point is the bed, and other furnishings play a supporting role. Bedroom furniture is traditionally arranged according to a few general rules. Follow these guidelines:

- ✔ **Traditionally, people tend to place a double, queen, or king size bed against the center of the wall opposite the main door to the room.** With this arrangement, the headboard is the center of attention as you enter the room.

    If your room's dimensions prevent you from positioning your bed on the wall across from the door, other possible choices depend on which walls are long enough to accommodate the bed. Diagonal placement works well when you have the space.

- ✔ **Don't place a bed under a window, if the window will frequently be open.** Open windows can create uncomfortable drafts. Positioning a bed between two windows, however, works well.

    If your home is air-conditioned or heated year-round and the windows are seldom open, you may be able to ignore this rule.

- ✔ **Don't place the bed where it obstructs a door into the room or a walkway through the room.**

- ✔ **Consider nontraditional furniture arrangements if doing so will free up space or use space in a more interesting way.** For example, a bed may look dramatic placed in front of a secure window; on a diagonal, which takes up extra space; sideways along a wall, to maximize floor space; or in an alcove (a technique called *lit clos*).

- ✔ **If your closet is large enough and you want to free up floor space, put your chest of drawers inside a walk-in closet.** Doing this lets you add additional furniture, such as a writing desk, a seating group, or a big screen TV, to transform any bedroom into a luxury suite.

Decorating for Your Bedrooms' Needs

Bedrooms must meet the needs of their users, and all types of users have unique needs. Whether you're decorating a master bedroom, a guestroom, or a child's room, the following sections provide you with great tips.

Master bedrooms

A master bedroom doesn't have to be huge, but it does need to offer certain amenities. If your space is less masterful than you want, take a look at some of the following suggestions for decorating your bedroom:

- ✔ **Make the bedroom look larger by eliminating clutter.** Take out any excess accessories and store necessities in drawers or closets.

- ✔ **Use only necessary furniture.** If you can, push a chest of drawers into a walk-in closet to free up floor space.

- ✔ **Keep the bed visually low.** Use a headboard, but don't use a footboard. Avoid four-poster beds because they tend to take up space visually, and that makes the room seem smaller.

- ✔ **Keep all your furniture — like the rest of your color scheme — light.** Light-colored furniture, walls, floors, window treatments, and bedding make a room seem bigger.

Regardless of your master bedroom's size, the following tips can help you to make it as comfortable as possible:

- ✔ **Add bedside tables that are as big as the space allows.** If you read or watch TV in bed, you'll find these tables helpful. You can buy restaurant cafe tables for very little money and drape them with quilts.

- ✔ **Try to make room for at least one comfortable chair.** Chairs are great for company on a sick day, for daytime resting, or for reading.

- ✔ **Consider carpeting all bedroom floors to reduce noise.** Carpeting is soft and warm for the feet.

- ✔ **Add a lady's desk — a small, delicately proportioned furnishing for writing letters — if you have room.**

Teen bedrooms

Teenagers usually know what they want in a bedroom. They need storage for their books, music, and collections of just about anything you can name. They also have firm ideas about style and colors, so ask! And when your son or daughter requests a wild color, do your best to persuade him or her to use it as an accent. Choose neutral furnishings that can adapt to a new color scheme just in case your teen's taste changes overnight.

More and more activities, from surfing the Internet to entertaining, take place in a teen's room. Extra seating and small tables provide space for visitors. Keep furnishings practical and easy to care for.

Children's bedrooms

Plan a nursery with your child's future years in mind. But from the beginning, make room for a changing table near the crib. As always, keep safety in mind. The following tips can help you:

- ✔ **Choose chests and cabinets that can't be tipped over (even when drawers are opened and a child crawls up and into them).** This may call for fastening them to the wall for security.

- ✔ **Double-check that cribs and bunk beds meet federal safety standards.** Check to see that mattresses fit snugly against the crib's sides. Slats, spindles, rods, and corner posts should be no more than 2⅜ inches apart from each other. Make sure a child can't release the drop side of a crib.

- ✔ **Eliminate any small throw rugs on slippery floors.** Little ones can trip over these hazards.

- ✔ **Equip all electrical outlets with plastic safeguard plugs.** Young children love to stick their fingers where they don't belong.

- ✔ **Find hardware that's rounded, sanded, and has no sharp edges.** The smoother the hardware, the less the chance of cuts.

- ✔ **Keep cribs away from windows and window blind cords.** Keep your little ones from falling out of windows or getting wrapped in cords by placing them a safe distance away.

- ✔ **Make sure all flooring is skidproof.**

- ✔ **Select bunk beds with sturdy ladders, handrails, and safety rails.**

Make sure you have a guest bed for sleepovers. A trundle bed, which stores a second bed beneath a regular one, is ideal for children's rooms.

Guestrooms

Setting aside a room for guests makes their stay more comfortable not only for them, but also for you. Furnish the guestroom with a marvelous bed and all the necessary furnishings. Check out the following suggestions for ways to make your guestroom comfortable:

- **Buy a handsome, space-saving daybed or sofa bed that fits smartly against the wall and out of the way.** The versatility of these beds makes them a delightful option in a home office or other double-duty room. A Murphy bed that hides away in a closet is another option.

- **Consider fitting your guestroom with a telephone, a TV, a connection for getting online, and a mini-fridge filled with water, juices, and snacks.** Be warned — your guests may never leave.

- **Dedicate two sets of sheets, a comforter, a duvet cover, and pillows and pillow shams to your guestroom.** Store them in the guest closet or guest bathroom in case your guests need anything during the night.

- **Make sure that your guest has plenty of closet space for hanging and drawer space for putting away personal items.** Place sachets in drawers and padded hangers in the closet for a posh touch.

- **Use a queen bed.** Couples will appreciate the comfort. If you have two guestrooms, fit the second one with twin beds.

Chapter 22

Creating Your Living Room

· ·

· ·

*W*hether your living room is lived in a lot or is used only on special occasions, designing and decorating this space allows you to express yourself. So, have fun doing just that, beginning with the planning stage.

In this chapter, we show you how to identify the many functions your living room serves. We then explain how to pick pieces of furniture that meet your needs and look stylish, too. We tell you how to arrange your furniture for maximum aesthetics and function. We discuss floors, walls, ceilings, and window dressings. Lastly, we reveal our decorating magic — ways to accessorize your living room to express your personal style.

Thinking about Function

What activities take place within your living room? (Hey, being a couch potato a very important activity!) A living room — even a formal one — should be flexible enough to handle multiple activities. If your living room also serves as a den (or family room), you probably expect more of the room, perhaps more seating or entertainment space. If you have a family room in addition to your dressy living room, you can probably leave the dressy room for more formal occasions — and finer furniture, fabrics, and accessories.

Fresh points of view

Seasons, fashion, and you change — you see things in fresh, new ways and with renewed appreciation. Art galleries, store-window displays, and grocery shelves get moved around, so why not your living room? Try these good ideas for giving your living room a fresh point of view — and perhaps your furnishings and you a new lease on life.

- ✔ **A new season.** Winter is over! The fireplace is cold and black. Suddenly, the sofa that faced a once-roaring fire — a very satisfying focal point — seems out of place. What could be better? Try turning the sofa to face the big windows with the view of the flower garden beyond! Place a loveseat or two lounge chairs opposite to complete your new focal grouping.

- ✔ **New furniture.** You've had your eye on a fabulous armoire at your favorite furniture store, and it's on sale. Buy it; it's yours! Now, where do you place it in the living room? Stand it opposite tall windows, so that one tall object balances the other. A few attention-getting accessories, and the armoire is your new focal point.

- ✔ **New paint job.** You want to be daring and paint one wall in your pale yellow room a fire-engine red — a perfect backdrop for your red-and-yellow floral chintz sofa. Good reason for moving that sofa, and for hanging a smashing landscape above it.

- ✔ **New slipcovers.** You've finally slipcovered the three inherited but previously incompatible sofas. Now you can create the U-shaped seating arrangement that will make your too-big lobby-like living room seem cozy as a country cottage.

Start your plan by listing all the activities that may take place in your living room. Ask yourself if you'll use the room for any of the following purposes:

- ✔ Gathering with friends and family
- ✔ Knitting or sewing
- ✔ Listening to music
- ✔ Playing board games or card games
- ✔ Playing the piano
- ✔ Reading
- ✔ Spending time on your computer
- ✔ Watching television
- ✔ Writing letters

Leave out no activity, no matter how trivial it seems. Next, list the furniture and electrical equipment you need to make each function possible. Determine which of the following items you need:

- Coffee table
- Computer
- Desk
- DVD player
- End table
- Entertainment center
- Floor lamps
- Lounge chair
- Love seat
- Occasional chairs
- Ottomans
- Piano
- Sofa or couch
- Stereo system
- TV/VCR

As you figure out your activities, you may think of places where activities take place. For example, the piano could (and should) fit on an inside wall, the sofa may work well near the fireplace, your rocking chair may be perfect near the window, and the reclining chair could face the TV. If you're not quite sure where each piece of furniture works best, read the next section to find plenty of great suggestions.

Putting your furniture in its place

Furniture arrangement is the art of establishing working relationships among individual pieces of furniture — all within a room's context. You may think of only one way that the furniture fits because that's the way you arranged it years ago. You may have many unexplored options for arranging furnishings. Or you may have the opposite problem: You simply can't choose the one best arrangement because of all the tempting possibilities.

To see the many arrangement possibilities in *any* room, lay out various floor plans on paper (see Chapter 3). This technique is much easier than shoving a grand piano around a room! Use layout kits, with graph paper and to-scale furniture templates. Don't be afraid to experiment with different locations.

For some rooms, because of the location of architectural elements (such as windows, doors, and a fireplace), finding the perfect layout doesn't come easily. Difficulties arise when a room has two *focal points,* areas where attention lingers. For instance, trying to situate seating in rooms with a television and a fireplace or picture window is frustrating — how can you focus on two points? Occasionally, you may figure out a way to take advantage of both focal points, but sometimes you just have to choose one over the other. Take a look at the upcoming section "Focusing on a focal point" for more information.

Checking out different layouts

To demonstrate that you can arrange a room in more than one way, we prepared four different layouts for a client's living room. The one the client chose was not the one *we* would have chosen, but that's the point of drawing several layouts — you can choose *your* personal favorite.

The first two arrangements take into consideration many functions. Each layout provides seating areas for big gatherings, small and large conversation groups, television viewing, reading and writing, scenery watching, piano playing, and group sing-alongs.

In the first layout (see Figure 22-1), we arranged seating Traditionally, with the large fireplace as the center of attention. The baby grand piano and chaise lounge make the bay window a second strong focal point, while the television, placed in front of picture windows, is incidental.

In another plan (see Figure 22-2), back-to-back love seats create two living areas. The imposing fireplace draws the most attention, while the bay window and the grand piano play a supporting role. Your guests and you can see the television from the love seat and lounge chairs placed at an angle.

In the third layout (see Figure 22-3), a Contemporary, L-shaped couch on a diagonal faces away from the windows. The fireplace is the strong focal point of the room, but this layout makes the television more important. A necessary traffic path to the couch creates a separation between it and the lounge chairs. The grand piano sits in front of the bay window.

Finally, in the fourth layout (see Figure 22-4), two separate seating areas create a sharp distinction between indoor and outdoor focus, allowing room for both. The main seating area focuses on the fireplace, but has a clear view of the television. The secondary seating area makes the most of the bay window and outdoor scenery. And the grand piano, tucked behind the sofa, fits nicely with both seating areas.

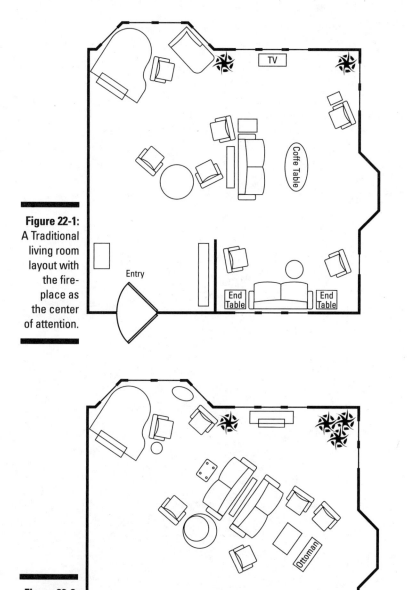

Figure 22-1:
A Traditional living room layout with the fire-place as the center of attention.

Entry

TV

Coffe Table

End Table   End Table

Figure 22-2:
Two living areas, with the help of back-to-back seating.

Entry

TV

Ottoman

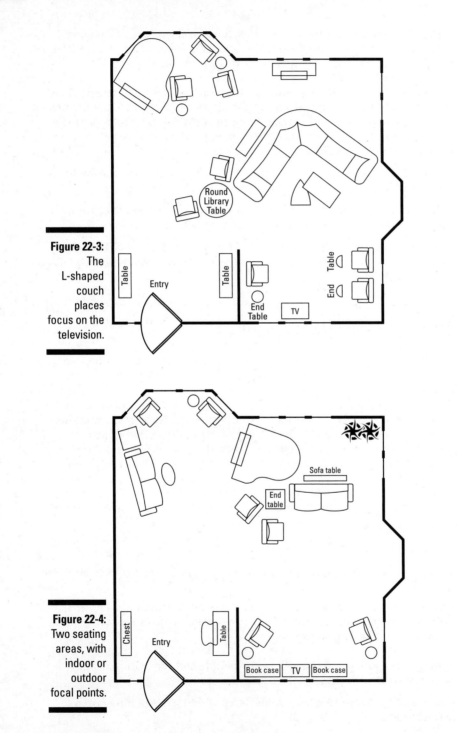

Figure 22-3:
The
L-shaped
couch
places
focus on the
television.

Figure 22-4:
Two seating
areas, with
indoor or
outdoor
focal points.

When arranging your furniture, consider architectural features. We followed some basic guidelines when we created the layouts in Figures 22-1 through 22-4. Check out the following suggestions for devising your own layout:

✔ **Keep a piano in the background, so it doesn't obstruct the traffic flow.** If you have both a piano and a fireplace, place the piano opposite the fireplace wall, to balance the room. Serious musicians insist that a piano be on an interior wall, away from direct heating and cooling vents, because heat and cold changes affect pianos and their sound.

✔ **Let the fireplace, a prominent element in any room, be the natural focal point that it is.** Create major seating areas around the fireplace.

✔ **Nestle some furniture near the windows that have a beautiful view.** This technique balances the seating in the room's primary area.

✔ **Place plenty of seating around the television set, if you want it to be another focal point.** More seating adds function and visual weight (and importance).

Focusing on a focal point

Like any artistic composition, a well-designed room needs a *focal point* — a point of reference, a space that seems whole or complete and, for that reason, provides visual relief and rest. But what do you do with a room that doesn't have a natural attention-grabber like a fireplace or a large window? You can create a focal point with an imposing piece of furniture. Secretaries, armoires, wall units, and media centers fill the bill. So do big buffets and handsome dressers and chests (who said they have to remain in the dining room or bedroom?). Make a dresser or chest even more important by hanging a big mirror or painting above it. Underscore this arrangement with a pair of decorative lamps and a super floral or fruit arrangement. Go even further, if you want, by adding small, decorative items in a *tablescape,* an artful arrangement of objects.

Discovering furniture-arranging basics

Some general guidelines exist to help you narrow down the almost endless possibilities of arrangement. Before trying to decide how to arrange your room, keep in mind the following suggestions:

✔ Arrange for traffic *not* to pass between people and the television set if at all possible.

✔ Avoid placing furniture where it interferes with the operation of doors and windows.

✔ To create a greater sense of unity, place furniture so its lines are parallel to the wall. Furniture placed on the diagonal, sometimes called the *dynamic diagonal,* creates excitement and contrast.

✔ Experiment by leaving a wall free of furniture (especially when the wall flanks a walkway).

✔ Keep conversations going by grouping chairs a comfortable three to four feet apart. A foolproof and very comfortable seating arrangement is a sofa or love seat flanked by two comfortable, upholstered chairs.

✔ Make the most of unusual space by building furniture (shelves, consoles, and so on) into the room. The only potentially negative aspect of built-ins is that you can't take them with you if you move. (Then again, that's not necessarily bad.)

✔ Place a table near each chair for holding refreshments, reading glasses, a book, and so on.

✔ Shield your living room for more privacy by placing a standing, folding screen at right angles to the wall if the front door to your house opens directly into your living room.

✔ Large rooms can seem alienating. Cut a too-large room down to size. Treat it as though it were several small spaces by creating more than one intimate seating and activity area.

Creating a Great Backdrop

Walls, floors, ceilings, and windows form a background not only for your furniture, but also for *you.* Choosing the materials to use for each of these elements involves practical, aesthetic, and budget considerations. Make a clear distinction between what you want and what you need, especially if you don't necessarily *need* everything you *want.* For example, if your house is home to small children and pets, you need something more practical than a white rug.

For unity, plan adjoining rooms that are openly visible to each other as though they were one space. Treat them both positively (with the same backgrounds) or as negatives and positives (using a dark background and light furnishings in one and a light background and dark furnishings in the other). Use contrasting colors in adjoining spaces only if you want to create a sense of activity and movement.

Settling on wall materials

Walls, the greatest background area of any room, determine a room's mood. You can choose from many different materials to cover your walls. Some popular choices include paint in plain or faux finishes, wall covering, and paneling (see Chapter 13 for more information on each).

If you're having trouble choosing between these popular materials, remember that combining the materials (paint and wall covering, wall covering and paneling) is possible to provide the best solution and help you achieve your goals (see Chapters 5 through 7).

Your house has many rooms, several walls, and great opportunities to use plenty of different materials. Consider two factors first: the room's architectural style and its actual architecture. Is the room Traditional? Use Traditionally patterned wallpaper, faux paint, paneling, or fabric. Or, update a Traditional house with Contemporary materials to create an eclectic and personal style. Is the room Contemporary? Play it up by using *textured* materials on the walls, such as plain wood paneling, textured papers, mirror, metal paneling, or fabrics such as solid-colored linen.

With any style, period, or mood, keep in mind that texture — plain or patterned and in any material — not only adds tactile interest, it affects space in the following ways:

✔ The lighter, smoother, and silkier the texture of all surfaces (walls, floors, and ceiling), the airier the space.

✔ The rougher, coarser, and furrier the background textures, the smaller (and perhaps cozier) the room.

Texture is particularly important to neutral-color schemes, popular in Contemporary spaces and in conservative living rooms. If neutrals are your cup of tea, add excitement by adding rich texture.

Paint

Paint is an inexpensive source of color, a powerful mood maker. Use it as a versatile decorating tool to visually reshape an architecturally deficient room (one that's too long, short, square; Chapter 5 includes some great tips). Other colorful materials — wall coverings, ceramic tile, and fabrics — may do the same job as paint, but at a higher cost for materials and labor. Painting a room has the following advantages:

✔ **Painting is cheap.** The cost of a bucket of paint compared to other wall coverings is much lower.

✔ **Painting is easy.** Even amateurs can paint a room.

✔ **Painting is fast.** A freshly painted room doesn't take weeks to do like a more complex project; it's readymade for instant gratification.

✔ **Painting is impermanent.** You can easily change and repaint your wall's colors as your mood changes.

Paint allows anyone to be daring with color! For example, a friend's house has a burnt-orange dining room, an apple-green living room, one bedroom in light yellow, and another bedroom in baby blue. Why not make your rooms pop and come to life? You can even take this advice in open floor plans — just take extra care in selecting colors that look great together!

Paint can provide pattern, too. Think of stenciling to create a wallcovering-like pattern over the entire wall. You can create your own stencil or use a stencil kit. You can form a trellis pattern with the stencils, which makes a small space seem larger and a square room more dynamic.

Wallcoverings

Wallcoverings are minor miracles of color and pattern (see Chapter 13). Don't overlook textured textiles, skins (suede and other leathers), and other wallcoverings for neutral living room walls. Textured wallcoverings, such as suede, brocade, velvet, linen, burlap, and metallic, add richness and depth. Take a look at the following tips for decorating your living room with wallcoverings:

- Marry Traditional colors and patterns (such as stripes) with Traditional furniture.

- Try a small amount of handscreened wallcovering as an accent, if your budget doesn't allow for an entire room done in this expensive material:

    - Consider adding the wallcovering as a border just above a *wainscot* (paneling below a chair rail molding).

    - Create small panels of paper and border them with decorative wood moldings.

    - Cover just one short wall.

- Use textured wallcoverings with Contemporary furnishings — the more distinctively textured, the more dramatic the contrast and thus, the more powerful your decorating statement.

Paneling

Today's wood paneling is a far cry from the older luan paneling that made itself at home all across the country. Paneling adds a certain richness to walls. And, while initial costs make paneling more expensive than paint or wallcoverings, in the long run, it proves a savvy solution for repairing damaged walls. You can nail paneling directly to the studs, saving time and labor. If you haven't seen new paneling, take a look.

If your living room has that old luan paneling, don't despair — paint it! Ask your paint dealer to show you the right products to use.

Dealing with your ceilings

As a guideline, the more obvious the ceiling, the more it needs decorating. If the ceiling is unobtrusive (out of sight and out of mind), you may want to save time, money, and effort by just painting it a pleasant white to reflect maximum light. If you want your ceiling to stand out, take a look at Chapter 15 for a variety of options for creating a sensational living room ceiling.

Adding drama to the floor

With floors, the options are numerous (see Chapter 14). Choose warm and friendly floorings, such as wood, carpeting, or rugs, for casual living. Choose cooler, more distant floorings, such as marble or ceramic tile, for formal rooms. For rooms that fall somewhere in the middle, consider options like wood, carpeting, ceramic tile, and resilient and laminate floorings. You may even want to combine some of these different floorings — especially in large rooms. This adds dramatic interest and greater function.

The following are some guidelines for decorating your living room floor:

✔ Consider a new material, such as bamboo, leather, mosaic, or stone.

✔ Let upholstery play second fiddle to an extravagant rug. The gentler the wall (in a soft color with little or no pattern), the louder the rug pattern and color can be.

✔ In a Traditional room, the flooring is usually the darkest of three color values (dark floor, medium walls, light ceiling).

✔ In a Contemporary room, the floor is usually the lightest color in the room (turning the tables on Traditional color distribution).

✔ Match the scale of a patterned floor to that of the room. In a small room, choose a small pattern; in a big room, select a big pattern.

✔ Quiet a marble, ceramic tile, or wood floor with a well-padded room-size rug.

If you combine two different flooring materials (carpeting and wood, for example), make sure that the finished surfaces are the same height, in order to prevent someone from tripping or stubbing a toe.

Doing up the windows

Decide early on whether the window treatment is to play a starring or supporting role. Certain windows — such as picture and bay windows — are architecturally significant and need very little dressing up for their roles as focal points. Keep them simple — the better to show them off. Plain double-hung windows need a thoughtful window treatment (beautiful drapery and handsome curtain rod, interesting shutters, attractive blinds, or perhaps combinations of these elements) to make them scene stealers. See Chapter 16 for details.

Start your planning by determining whether your window treatment will carry on the particular style of the room (Traditional or Contemporary) or offer an eclectic contrast.

Traditional window treatment designs abound. Decorating magazines offer a feast of window treatments that you're free to copy. Pattern books of beautiful designs of *over-draperies* (a draw drapery over sheers over window blinds, valances, and cornices) are plentiful. Drapery shops can create custom designs (or perhaps you're talented and can make your own). Many stores offer both custom and readymade window treatments.

Contemporary treatments run the gamut from no treatment to simple blinds or shades to draw draperies in an interesting textured fabric. Romantic Contemporary — a relatively new style — uses colored sheer fabrics as curtains in rooms full of clean-lined furniture.

Go eclectic by using a Contemporary treatment in a Traditional room or vice versa. Dramatic juxtapositions create tremendous excitement.

Handling Accessories

Accessories add the final touch. Consider them a way to further express your personal style. Chapters 25 and 26 offer more information on art and accessories, so check them out.

The following are some general tips for adding accessories to your living room:

✔ **Accessorize according to the season, helping yourself to budding blossoms or turning leaves.** Pussy willow and forsythia branches that signal spring time, fresh-from-the-garden floral bouquets that spell summer, and a mound of pumpkins on a great plank table that speak fall all tell your decorating secret — you love your home.

✔ **Add accents to break up large expanses of overbearing solid color, such as big sofas and large upholstered chairs.** Include pillows, an afghan, or a quilt for relief and for physical and emotional comfort — a big part of what home is about.

✔ **Add flowers, but not fruit, to a formal living room.** Keep edibles in the den, great room, kitchen, or dining room.

✔ **Avoid lavish tablescaping.** Accessories should delight but not get in your way. Put accessories on an easily moved tray.

✔ **Choose unbreakable accessories for living rooms where children are welcome.** Put china and crystal items in a china cabinet. Substitute items that children can touch, handle, and play with safely! Children's toys — books, truck collections, and wooden blocks — are very decorative!

✔ **Edit your accessory displays.** No matter how much you love a particular vase or painting, if it doesn't add to the room, subtract it. (If in doubt, take it out!)

✔ **Hang an ancestor oil portrait over the mantel in your dressy or formal living room.** Placing casual photographs of family and friends in a hallway or bedroom and not in the living room makes the living room a little more formal.

✔ **Hang any artwork at eye level; that is, not too high, nor too low.** Your guests can enjoy it at eye level with the least effort.

✔ **Keep lamps flanking a sofa similar in size, shape, and color, though not necessarily identical.** If lamps are different, make sure the shades are the same or similar.

✔ **Less is more.** Use very few good quality accessories in formal and Contemporary living rooms.

✔ **Place a stack of colorful books beneath the base of a lamp that's too short.** This technique looks great, works well, and is a budget stretcher.

✔ **Shun the idea of a lot of little lamps.** Vary lamp shapes and sizes, and reserve mini-lamps for secretaries, china closets, and etageres.

✔ **Stay away from any clutter.** Even in a Country-style room, too much clutter can be unnerving.

✔ **Steer clear of loading a sofa with so many pillows that there's no space for sitting.** Make extra pillows available by piling them into a handy basket. Vary pillow sizes and shape for comfort's sake.

✔ **Use lamps and light fixtures as accessories.** In addition to providing lighting for specific tasks and contributing to overall ambient lighting, they're great sources of added color, pattern, and texture.

✔ **Vary the lamps throughout a room.** Include torchiers for style and soft, indirect light. Using the identical lamp repeatedly is unimaginative.

Chapter 23

Designing for Dining

. . . .

In This Chapter

▶ Figuring out your dining room's style

▶ Decorating your formal dining area for special occasions

▶ Dining all through the house

▶ Decorating quickly with on-hand accessories

. . . .

Dining takes place almost anywhere in your house — kitchen, family room, and even the bedroom. Casual dining — eating here, there, and everywhere — is a fact of the American lifestyle. Meanwhile, the formal dining room is growing in importance. New home builders tell us it's one of the most asked-for features.

Decorating needs differ for informal (casual) dining and formal (dressy) dining. Informal dining can take place on almost any surface, from coffee tables to TV trays. The formal dining room, on the other hand, features a table (often a large one) and chairs that are especially for family rituals, formal meal service, and holidays.

In this chapter, we show you how to figure out how many people your formal dining table seats (comfortably) and help you decide on an overall — personal — style for your dressed-up dining room. We show you how to make other rooms work for pleasant dining. We also give you tips on making small spaces more dining friendly. Lastly, we show you how to decorate your dining room quickly with accessories you have right there in your home.

Preparing a Comfortable Table

Although you want family and friends to admire your beautifully set table, you also care that they're comfortably seated when they gather around your table. If you're not sure how much space you need for each place setting or how many guests your table can seat, take a look at the following guidelines:

- **Plan a minimum of 24 inches for each place setting.** If you have the room, 30 inches is ideal and much more comfortable.

- **Make sure the table doesn't have a low *apron*.** A low apron (the wood panel below the tabletop) may prevent your guests from crossing their legs. If you have a low apron, find chairs that seat at a comfortable height.

- **If you use a sofa (or bench) for seating at a long table, choose one with a high enough seat.** Add casters to sofa legs if you need to raise the seat height.

- **Be sure that the chairs arms are low enough to slide beneath, and not bump into, the table.** Too-low tables can be raised with casters or devices that elevate (which are available at home stores).

- **Provide at least 24 inches of space behind each chair when someone is sitting in it.** This is the minimum space needed for people to pass by when serving or leaving the table.

You're better off setting up an additional table in another room than crowding a dining room with a too-big table and too much furniture.

If you're in the market for a new dining room table, or you're just not sure how many people the table you have can comfortably seat, check out Table 23-1 for the lowdown on table shapes, sizes, and seating capacity.

Table 23-1	Table Sizes and Seating Capacities	
Shape	*Dimensions*	*Seating Capacity*
Round	36-inch diameter	Four for drinks, two for dining
Round	40-inch diameter	Four
Round	56-inch diameter	Eight
Square	38-inch square	Four
Rectangular	60 x 36 inches	Six
Rectangular	72 x 36 inches	Six to eight

Shape	Dimensions	Seating Capacity
Rectangular	84 x 36 inches	Six to eight
Rectangular	96 x 48 inches	Eight to ten
Rectangular	132 x 48 inches	Twelve

Putting Style on Your Menu

The formal dining room is one of the easiest rooms in the house to decorate, because it serves only one very definite purpose — dining. You need to consider only the style or *look* you prefer. If you decide that your formal dining room will also function as a library or study, that complicates matters a bit because you must plan for multiple functions.

A foolproof approach is to stick with your living room's style. Extending the mood from room to room will make your dining room seem more serene. (To create some excitement, change styles and mood.) Color is one of the easiest ways to create unity. If your living room, for example, is tasteful beige with tangerine accents, reverse the color scheme in the dining room. Tangerine walls with a touch of beige will relate strongly — and dramatically — to your living room.

Think about how formal or informal you want the room to be before you begin to make decorating choices — floor covering, upholstery and drapery fabrics, and more. Many people whose houses lean toward the casual maintain a very formal dining room, but they never have a formal occasion to use it. If you do want a formal room for those few and far between special occasions, go ahead and decorate with fragile fabrics and materials. If you and your family use the room more frequently — perhaps even daily for dinner — consider sturdier materials that will hold up to wear and tear.

After you determine the mood and usage of your dining room, take a look at the following suggestions for decorating:

✔ **Formal:** If you have a formal dining room, you have several options:

• You can relax a little but still keep your dining room dressy, like the sophisticated dining room in Figure 23-1. In this mood, mix furnishings from various periods, mix and match patterns, and warm up your walls with lively wallpaper.

• You can be a purist and keep your furniture, walls, tableware, and linens all the same style (see Figure 23-2).

- You can go Contemporary with glass and chrome furniture, a light background, and plenty of dazzle. Keep all the dining furniture and furnishings modern, too.

- You can be eclectic and mix some Traditional and Contemporary elements, but keep them all equally fine, fancy, and formal.

✔ **Informal:** An informal dining room may seem like a contradiction in terms. Following are some options if you want an informal look.

- **Casual Friday charm: Give a room all the appeal of a weekend at your favorite resort.** An old but charming wood table with drawers for handy storage of flatware and napkins can set a note of relaxed elegance. Finely handwoven placemats, hand-painted dinnerware, handblown glassware, and interesting flatware (knives, forks, and spoons) all add up to a rich but welcoming atmosphere. Think polo, not rodeo, for this look.

- **Dressed-up country:** American Country and European Provence and Tuscany styles make room for individuality and informality. Dress up a round Country-style table with a to-the-floor tablecloth. Give period chairs a more relaxed look by painting them white or a light color and covering them in a cotton toile fabric. Light up the room with an extravagant rustic chandelier that adds to the festive mood.

- **Relaxed Contemporary elegance:** Dressy dining rooms needn't be formal. This is true especially if they visually flow into the great room, family room, or kitchen — as they do in many Contemporary open plans. Go ahead: Use fancy furniture and accessories. (Don't restrict dressy dining to eating at a table — an island or peninsula can offer an offbeat yet elegant eating experience.)

Figure 23-1:
Dining
formally
today
may mean
dressy, with
a certain
relaxed
elegance.

Photography courtesy Brewster Wallcoverings

Figure 23-2:
Formal dining conjures images of Traditional dining room furniture, but it need not be stuffy.

Photography courtesy Brewster Wallcoverings

Creating the Formal Dining Room

Formal dining rooms make even ordinary menus seem extraordinary. Even a fancy dining room can double as an elegant library or study (and with a hide-away armoire for the PC, perhaps a home office) between dining occasions. Whether or not your formal dining room does double-duty, decorate it with comfort, movement, color, texture, pattern, furniture, china and glassware, linens, and storage in mind. The following sections show you each piece of the puzzle.

Comfort

In many people's minds, formality translates to discomfort. But you and your family *can* be comfortable. Think about what makes you comfortable, and incorporate those things into your design. Take a look at the following suggestions for comfort:

- ✔ **Control the room's sound.** The noise level should be neither deathly quiet nor too loud. Fabrics (including rugs, tablecloths, and draperies) absorb sound. If your dining room is wired for music, so much the better, because soft music is a delightful sound for guests to hear as they enter the room.

- ✔ **Find the right lighting level.** Make lighting bright enough that diners can see what they're eating, but keep light levels low enough for a relaxed mood. For a lighting level that's just right, control overhead lights with a dimmer switch or use indirect lighting. (For lighting ideas, see Chapter 17.)

Keep candles above or below, but never directly at, eye level and surround them with hurricane globes to prevent wild flickering.

✔ **Opt for comfortable seating.** Padded chair seats fill the bill. A fully upholstered (seat and back) chair is most expensive. Upholstered slip seats, which unscrew for quick and easy recovering, are less costly. A thick, tie-on cushion is least expensive. For peace of mind, select a stainproof, wipe-clean fabric or material for chair covers. (Fabrics can be treated with stainguards by your retailer or with a home-use stain repellent.) Removable cushion covers that can be laundered or sent to the cleaners are also a great idea, even in a formal room.

Movement

Your family and guests need to be able to move in and out of their chairs without asking permission, bumping into each other, or knocking over their water glass and pulling the tablecloth with them (only magicians can pull that one off!). So leave 1½ to 2 feet between chairs, and add casters to the bottoms of chairs for easier movement.

Traffic should flow around the table and seated guests, so leave at least 2 feet for passage of one person and up to 3 or 4 feet for people who are serving from heavy trays. If your dining room is small and leaves little or no room for a china cabinet or additional furniture, face up to it. Position those items in a hallway or living room.

Color, texture, and pattern

Have you ever noticed that fast-food restaurants use red and orange in their decorating schemes, while fancier uptown restaurants tend toward soothing neutrals — off-white, beige, and taupe? Color affects mood and behavior. Warm colors stimulate people, and cool colors calm them. So if you want to people to eat excitedly, use a warm color, up to and including red, on the walls. Your own strategy can call for striking a balance — a cool background spiked with warm (and hot!) accent colors, or vice versa. (For more information on color, see Chapter 5.)

Heighten stimulating effects with more sheen in paint (with high gloss), wallpapers (with metallics), and fabrics (with silks, metallics, or light-reflecting glazed surfaces), or with mirrors. Tone down and slow down the emotional climate with matte (dull) finished surfaces.

The finer and shinier the texture, the dressier the room; the duller, rougher, and coarser the texture, the more rustic, informal, and casual the room.

Pattern also affects formality. Tiny floral and geometric patterns tend to be folksy and informal; whereas larger, more graceful, and symmetrically balanced patterns are more formal. Choose the patterns for your dining room based on the degree of formality you want to achieve. Realize that complex patterns offer the viewer plenty to see and think about, so they're very entertaining, which may be important when meals are long and your company isn't all that exciting!

Furniture

For the most part, the furniture you need in a dining room is basic — a table and chairs. Your first obligation is to make sure your guests have adequate room. After your guests are comfortable, you can consider adding a china cabinet, which is an impressive element in a dining room but can be housed nearby if necessary. A china cabinet with a lighted, mirrored back and glass shelves adds a sense of depth, sparkle, and glamour — and it also provides practical storage. Buffets and servers add much-need surface for stacking plates and foods to be served in courses.

If your dining room also serves as your library, handsome tall bookcases should also have decoratively arranged and accented (accessorized) shelves. If you have a desk in a handsome rich wood that matches the other furniture, a clean top can serve as another staging area for china, crystal, and dessert.

Don't crowd a formal dining room. If your dining room is too small for a china cabinet, table and chairs, and adequate room to walk around the room, you can compensate beautifully with a narrow, wall-hung shelf (which doubles as a buffet) with a large mirror above.

Take a look at the following furniture strategies for small dining rooms:

- **Build in your buffet.** Custom furniture can be smaller than readymade pieces, so it can conserve space in a smaller room.

- **Place your china cabinet in a nearby space accessible from the dining room.** Most furniture is designed for flexibility, so it works in more than one room. Putting the cabinet in a hallway or living room nearby where ample room is available can prevent you from having to crowd a small space.

- **Select chairs with see-through backs.** These chairs seem to take up less space than chairs with solid backs.

✔ **Substitute smaller pieces for a standard china cabinet.** A 10-x-48-inch glass shelf on gold or silver standards above a narrow buffet, a serving piece, or a 30-inch-high bookcase all work wonders. Store and display china at the same time by using small easels on glass shelves.

✔ **Use no high furniture; stick to pieces with a low profile.** The lower the furniture is, the more open the view and the more airy and spacious the room will look.

China and glassware

Tradition used to dictate that all your china, glassware, and silverware match. (Life around the formal dining table wasn't very creative.) But today, we're enamored of mixing and matching china patterns and glassware to create settings that never repeat themselves.

Take a look at the following suggestions for setting an exciting, mixed-up, but far from crazy dining room table:

✔ **Choose highly contrasting silverware.** Contrast plain and ornate handles, or silver-handled knives and forks with black-handled spoons. Use gold-tone dessert spoons if the rest of your silverware is silver. (If you use gold-tone spoons, use some china or glassware with gold trim.)

✔ **Look to creative centerpieces to underscore a particular mood for each meal.** Make sure your guests can see over and around them. See Chapter 27 for quick and easy ideas.

✔ **Match solid-color accent pieces to a color in your china pattern.** If you use solid white accent pieces, pick a china pattern with a white (not beige or ivory) background.

✔ **Mix a geometric china pattern with a floral pattern in the same colors.** The contrast of forms looks very of-the-moment.

✔ **Mix a large-scale floral pattern with a tiny, all-over china pattern.** The interplay of big and small looks dynamic.

✔ **Mix glassware — contrasting colors, clear and frosted, plain and fancy stems, and decorated and plain glassware.** When you add colored glassware to the setting, choose a color that matches or relates to a color in your china, or add a centerpiece of the same color as your glassware for a sense of unity.

✔ **Vary your table coverings whenever possible.** Your family and friends will have a sense of newness and surprise when they dine.

Linens

Linen is what we call all tablecloths, runners, place mats, and napkins — even though they may be made of cotton, wool, or some synthetic fiber. Old or antique linens were actually made of linen, which required a great deal of care. These true linens fell out of style, but they're now considered collectibles.

Linen tablecloths are still available and are very elegant. But save labor (especially if it's your own) by choosing crease-resistant, wash-and-wear types. Cotton lace is also an easy-care cloth for a formal table. Embroidered and cutwork tablecloths (in which patterns are created by cutting away some of the fabric and finishing cut edges with embroidery) are also good choices for formal tables.

Monograms add a sense of elegance to the formal table. Usually, the tablecloth isn't monogrammed, but the napkins are. (And, if your chairs wear slipcovers, consider monogramming the slipcover backs!)

A tablecloth for a formal dinner should drop 12 to 15 inches on each side of the table (to cover the apron and add a sense of grace). Using a protective underpad (available wherever you buy tablecloths) saves the tabletop from damage from heat and spills and makes the tablecloth hang better.

Wide runners and place mats are considered acceptable alternatives to tablecloths for all but the most strictly formal occasions. They're especially appropriate when the tabletop itself is particularly beautiful. Runners and place mats may be quilted for extra protection. Use them with heavier, chunky crystal, because delicate and fragile crystal may not be so steady on this uneven surface.

Storage

To store dining items efficiently, put them near the place of food preparation or near the table itself. Older houses have pantries for storing china, crystal, silverware, and linens. In modern houses that have no pantries and kitchens with minimal storage cabinets, these items are usually stored in a china cabinet, buffet, or small dresser in the dining room. If necessary, consider commandeering a nearby closet and fitting it with shelves for storing dining room items. Line the shelves in felt and keep a stack of felt or other plate dividers to prevent chips.

Don't crowd crystal, especially stemware. Assuming that your butler is on permanent leave, polish silver hollowware, and then wrap it in plastic wrap to prevent tarnish. Store the silver out of sight (otherwise, this tack looks tacky). Wash and dry sterling silver flatware by hand and handle it with care so you don't bang, dent, or scratch it. We hang ironed tablecloths on padded hangers, which keeps them from wrinkling as they do when piled in drawers. Cloth napkins get ironed and stacked on a closet shelf in matching groups.

Dining 'Round

Americans have new eating habits, according to trend watchers. Builders are accommodating this trend by creating multiple dining areas throughout the house. Consider these eat-in areas standard for new homes:

- ✔ Two casual eating places in the kitchen — a breakfast or snack bar and a table for four or more
- ✔ A full and formal dining room
- ✔ A butler's pantry for preparing and serving food, wine, and beverages
- ✔ A place for serving cocktails in the living room
- ✔ A full bar and kitchnette for the den
- ✔ A minibar and table for two in the master bedroom
- ✔ A California kitchen (full grilling and chilling facilities) on decks, patios, and poolside
- ✔ A minikitchen and bistro table and chairs for the guestroom

As for your house, the trick is knowing what makes you and your family happy and then planning for it. The following sections provide suggestions.

In the living room

What makes dining in a living room work? A wipe-clean tabletop, well-padded chairs, and a rolling cart. The cart transports everything you need to set the table (place mats, napkins, silverware, glassware, and dinnerware). It stays handily in place until its return with all the paraphernalia — in one easy and efficient trip — to the kitchen for cleaning and storing. Plug in a lamp with up-lighting on either side of the table for a pleasant, well-lighted setting. Keep tapers and matches in a handy end table drawer.

In a wide hallway

Some homes have kitchens too small to eat in, but they may have a wide hallway area just outside the kitchen. Maybe a glass door offers a spectacular outdoor view and lets in radiant light. In this situation, place a narrow table — with drop leaves that can be pulled out at mealtime and lowered during high traffic times — against the wall. As for seating, flank the table with chairs that can be pulled into place at mealtime, use folding chairs that can be stored out of the way in a nearby closet, or tuck stools beneath the tabletop. If you need extra light, plug one or more wall-hung lights or a skinny table lamp into a nearby wall socket. (Soft up-light is pleasant for dining. For more lighting tips, see Chapter 17.)

In the kitchen

Eating in the kitchen is a good idea because it's the place closest to the food and dishwasher (see Figure 23-3). Adding a few graceful elements — nice place mats and napkins, a bouquet of flowers, and soft lighting — makes dining in the kitchen very pleasant. Countertops (islands, peninsulas, or bars) are the handiest of eating spots, if you don't have room for a small dining table. The most comfortable have a 12- to 15-inch overhang so that when you pull a stool or chair close, you have knee room. For greater comfort, lower the countertop to standard dining table height and add upholstered chairs. Make sure that overhead lighting has a dimmer switch, and keep a few candles ready.

In a media room

Eating in front of the TV set is so popular that certain furniture manufacturers have created high-low tables that can be raised for dining and let down again to coffee table height. Sitting on most sofas (which are low) and dining at a coffee table forces you to bend over, straining your back. If you plan to eat on the sofa, you're better off choosing a higher sofa and substituting a tea table for a coffee table. Large individual trays (that allow each person to carry his or her laden plate to the table) are a must at our house. They double as place mats. Don't forget TV trays. Find them in all price ranges and styles, complete with holding racks.

In other rooms

If you eat in other rooms of the house, such as the bedroom, garden room, or screened-in porch, and have no permanent table there, keep collapsible TV trays and folding chairs handy. Store them near where you most often use them. Also, in the kitchen, keep a rolling cart stocked with napkins, salt and pepper shakers, and other items necessary for meals. Then you can add serving plates, glassware, and foodstuffs to the cart and roll it where they're needed. If you have no electric lighting in the space (for example, on a porch or deck), use candles with protective hurricane shades. Store those, and matches, on your rolling cart.

Figure 23-3:
A corner
of the
kitchen is
the ideal
dining
place.

Photograph courtesy Blonder Wallcoverings, French Accent Collection

Creating Instant Dining Magic

Planning a meal for a dozen guests and you don't have a big enough tablecloth? Don't even have a table that *seats* 12? Don't panic! Consider the following suggestions:

✔ **Bring into play a couple of sawhorses and a 4-x-6-foot sheet of sturdy ¾-inch plywood as a table for 10 or more guests.** Pad the plywood with a thick blanket and cover it with a cloth (king-sized sheets work well) to hide the legs. Add a generous centerpiece (Chapter 27), and you and the table are all set.

✔ **Try a wash-and-wear flat sheet as an impromptu tablecloth.** Usually even an expensive sheet is much less expensive than a similarly sized tablecloth, so we buy designer sheets at discount stores for this very purpose. (Does it matter that they're often irregulars? Not a bit.) And napkins can be in coordinating solids, which makes buying them on sale easier.

✔ **Find charming, patterned, standard pillowcases to make instant slipcovers for ladder-back or folding side chairs.** Gather the top corners and tie each corner with a grosgrain ribbon. Fold hems inside and scrunch under the bottom of the pillowcase where it bunches at the seat.

✔ **Knot a big tablecloth's corners for a casual meal at a smaller table.** For a fancy table, tie a beautiful ribbon around each corner, gathering them up until the cloth fits.

✔ **Use one or more round, glass-topped, or mesh outdoor tables for indoor dining.** Disguise them by padding the top with a blanket or quilt and adding a round tablecloth that drops to the floor. Use a king-sized sheet and tuck the corners underneath so that the cloth looks round, if you don't have time or want to cut and hem it. The tablecoverings don't have to be identical. Make each quite different from the other and then offer guests their choice. It's fun for everyone.

✔ **Create a candelabra by grouping your candlesticks (mix and match 'em) on top of a raised cake stand.** If you're placing the candlesticks on untempered glass, protect the glass from the candle heat with a coaster or other heat-absorbing surface.

A friend of ours collects colored candlesticks. Used together, and with different colored candles for each, this candle grouping is a favorite lighting and centerpiece solution.

Favorite traditional dining chair styles

If you're not sure about what chair style to select for your dining room, consider these classic styles that promise to endure forever. Check out Chapter 9 for more information.

✓ **Queen Anne.** The gentle curves and moderate scale of this style furniture make it neither too masculine nor too feminine. Depending on the wood, finish, and upholstery fabrics, this style adapts with equal ease to very formal, casual dressy, or comfortable Country moods. It's a perennial favorite because it's suitably scaled for most homes.

✓ **Chippendale.** This 18th Century or Traditional style with its squared-off shoulders, heavier scale, and usually dark finish is both masculine and formal. It, too, is an enduring classic and a favorite style for generously scaled but not overly large rooms.

✓ **Duncan Phyfe.** The distinctive saber leg, delicate scale, refined embellishment, and discreet wood finish make the Duncan Phyfe a welcome addition to fine dining rooms and especially to small-scale rooms.

✓ **Empire (called *Biedermier* in Germany).** This style of furniture is heavy, dark, deeply carved, lavishly decorated, and certain to bring out the emperor in would-be Napoleons. If your dining room is large and impressive, this furniture style is designed to reign.

✓ **Louis XV.** This gracious French style is seen in all the best places — in many guises, ranging from gilt-edged formality to antique painted finishes that seem just short of frivolous. In fruitwood finishes and relaxed fabrics, this style is casual enough for a den or even a breakfast room.

✓ **Louis XVI.** More slender, delicate, and refined, the Louis XVI style is more feminine than the other Louis and more formal — which isn't to say that you can't paint it a passionate purple, cover it in a wild and crazy Gucci print, and have tons of fun. This style promises to live forever, especially because you can always refinish that purple!

✓ **Victorian.** Once scorned by purists, Victorian furniture has proven its popularity with those who love its slightly exaggerated curves and feminine wiles. Often covered in gorgeous velvets, Victorian chairs also look wonderful in beautiful floral chintzes and ornate gimps and other fanciful trims. Most often seen in wood finishes, Victorian chairs take very kindly to faux and other painted finishes.

Chapter 24

Transforming Bonus Areas

· ·

In This Chapter

▶ Making bonus areas livable and workable

▶ Decorating attics, basements, and more

· ·

*I*n the race for space, turning your underused attics, basements, porches, patios, and laundries into usable rooms is smart. Perhaps your basement walls are unfinished, your attic has no flooring, and your porch, patio, or laundry room desperately needs some finishing touches.

In this chapter, we show you that transforming attics, basements, patios, and porches into real live-in spaces requires relatively little time, energy, and money. We also tell you how to give your laundry room new uses, including turning it into a game room (which is happening in more and more households these days). Whether you're remodeling or tackling a finishing project, this chapter helps you prepare and decorate your bonus spaces.

Annexing Attics

Early Americans often used attics as bedrooms, but we usually use them just for storage. Because the structure (walls, floor, ceiling) exists, they are relatively inexpensive to claim for living space.

You usually need to remodel an unfinished attic before you can begin decorating. Check out *Home Remodeling For Dummies* by James and Morris Carey (Wiley Publishing, Inc.) and read up on how to run the utilities (heat, electricity, and plumbing) that you'll need. After you've done this step, let the decorating begin! Follow these guidelines:

✔ **Keep it light.** Unless you add dormers and/or skylights, attics are dark spaces. Add ample artificial lighting, preferably set-in-ceiling, *high hat type* fixtures, which don't encroach on headroom. Use light, bright, cheerful colors for walls and furnishings, such as sunny lemon or banana yellow, apricot, or peach.

✔ **Consider the angles.** Attics are full of interesting (and confusing) angles. Create unity to cut the confusion by keeping walls and floors nearly the same light color. If you're using a patterned wallcovering for its old-fashioned charm, keep the background light and the pattern small to medium in scale and relatively open — like a trellis. A trellis creates a three-dimensional effect that makes any room seem spacious.

✔ **Raise those low ceilings.** Attics look smaller than they are because about 50 percent of the space has less than 7½ feet of headroom. To compensate, stick to a light color scheme for floors and walls. Use a wallcovering in a vertical stripe with a light background for the *knee wall* area (the short wall between the floor and a peaked ceiling; see Figure 24-1). Use a coordinating, small, open-ground geometric or floral pattern wallcovering for the ceiling.

✔ **Make the most of among-the-trees views.** Leave attic windows, which are usually small, uncovered. If you need the privacy, install a simple blind, but avoid draperies (they take up visual space). If you feel the need for the softness draperies create, keep the contrast between the drapery and walls minimal, to retain a sense of spaciousness.

✔ **Let flooring do double duty.** Let the flooring act as a sound absorber. A thick low-pile carpet with a generously thick pad does the trick and makes the attic seem more plush. Pass up noisy, hard-surface floorings, and avoid space-eating, deep-pile shaggy rugs.

✔ **Choose furniture that makes the space seem bigger.** No big, bulky furniture for attics. Keep all furniture low and horizontal, so that it seems to blend into the low knee wall and not encroach on the ceiling height (see Figure 24-2). If you plan to use your attic as a bedroom, consider dispensing with the bed frame and just placing the box springs directly on the floor. Or if the bedroom is for children or young guests, use a futon or camp cot as a bed.

Figure 24-1:
A vertical stripe with a light background works well in the area between the floor and the peaked ceiling of an attic.

Figure 24-2:
Low
furniture
makes an
attic space
seem
bigger.

Beautifying Basements

Basements are often the first areas that most homeowners consider using for additional living space — especially if ceilings are a comfortable 8 feet high. Check out *Home Remodeling For Dummies* for instructions on how to add heat, wiring, and plumbing, and how to finish walls, ceilings, and floors.

Before you begin remodeling, consider the function or functions your basement will perform. If you want it to serve as a home office, you need wiring for lights, computers, and phones (see Chapter 20). If a playroom for the kids is the goal, you want warm, comfortable, easily cleaned flooring. If you and your family pursue arts and crafts, you'll require a slop sink, shelves, worktable, and stools. Other possibilities include a laundry room (wiring and plumbing are critical), a guest bedroom (convenience and comfort are crucial), or a bedroom for a teenager (consider privacy needs).

After you decide how to use your basement, and you tackle the heavy labor of remodeling, you can then have fun decorating. Consider these basics:

- ✔ **Create overhead beauty:** Make the ceiling disappear by keeping it light (but not necessarily a strong-contrast white). Consider using a pale tint of your wall color. If you must use white, try an off-white that has a tinge of color. Avoid busy patterns on ceiling tiles or other ceiling materials. The simpler, the better — and the higher the ceiling appears.

- ✔ **Color it sunny:** Counteract basement gloom by selecting light, sunny colors from the warm side of the color wheel. If color seems too noisy for this naturally quiet space, select light, rich neutrals. And yes, if you've covered walls in inexpensive dark wood paneling as an expediency, you can paint it. Ask your paint dealer for the right primer.

✔ **Select the right flooring:** Ceramic tile is a good choice for basement floors and may or may not be expensive, depending on your choice of tiles. Synthetic tile flooring is a popular, relatively inexpensive choice because small amounts of moisture won't harm the material. If your floor is moisture-proof and you provide an appropriate subfloor, you may want carpet. Choose a synthetic fiber that can withstand moisture.

Real wood flooring won't work in basements because of the excess moisture. For the look without the problems, consider an engineered hardwood (for more information, go to www.hardwoodinfo.com) or wood-look laminate flooring. Ask your floor-covering dealer whether the material you're installing will perform under damp conditions.

Painting a cement basement floor is an inexpensive option. Check with your paint dealer about the right primer and paint. Some drawbacks are that painted cement doesn't wear as well as other surfaces, absorbs no sound, doesn't cushion your legs and feet, won't offer any visual softening, and will have to be repainted from time to time. Our advice: Paint only little-used basement floor areas.

Use the same flooring throughout your basement, even if there are different rooms. The continuity increases the apparent size of the space.

A dehumidifier takes out the dampness that is characteristic of many basements. You'll have less mold and mildew.

✔ **Furnish it your way:** With proper ventilation and humidity control, upholstery is right at home. If you're not using synthetic tile on the floor (which allows wicking away of moisture), you may want to use moisture-protection pads for furniture as a precaution. Otherwise, anything goes. Choose a style, period, or look that suits you.

✔ **Light your world:** Provide ample ceiling lighting, and install warm rather than cool bulbs (see Chapter 17), because warm bulbs tend to make the space more appealing. Your lighting also eliminates the need for table and floor lamps that eat up space physically and visually. If you want extra lighting, choose wall sconces or pendant lamps.

Mirrors bounce light back and tend to make spaces seem both brighter and bigger, so use them as wall coverings or accessories in basements.

✔ **Choose wall materials:** Before you finish basement walls, make sure that they're moisture-proof. Then, you may finish them with popular and inexpensive wooden paneling or wallboard. Paneling requires a one-step installation, so you can apply it quickly. Wallboard needs spackling and either painting or wallcovering, so this process is more time-consuming and a little more expensive than paneling. Paneling's vertical lines tend to make ceilings seem higher, but wallboard is more versatile because it can be either painted or papered.

✔ **Treat your windows:** Basement windows need privacy. Thin-slat *inside mount* blinds that fit inside the window frame (or *reveal*) look tidy, as opposed to *outside mount* blinds suspended awkwardly on a long wall. Long draperies for short, small basement windows can look awkward. If you want the softening effect of fabric, consider swags. They may sound old-fashioned, but they look smart in up-to-date fabrics.

Perking Up Porches and Patios

Make your porch and patio into a second living room. You may maintain continuity by decorating these areas in the same style as the interior, especially if a porch or patio is visible from the living room or family room. On the other hand, you may create a completely different mood — making your secluded porch or patio an exotic retreat. (We encouraged our East Hampton client, Michelle Janson, to do this — to transform her back porch into an exotic Oriental tent!) Either way, there will be some decorating differences because these areas are not completely protected from weather. Patios, which have no protection, need weatherproof furnishings.

Weather drastically and rapidly affects your porch and patio furnishings, so buy outdoor furniture. Outdoor summertime furniture can withstand moisture and extremes of temperature. Don't use indoor furniture — it rusts, rots, and fades if left outside. Most wood furniture needs protection (teak is a well-known exception). Wicker needs the protection of a porch roof in summer and must be stored indoors in winter. Metal furniture can withstand light summer rains but needs protection from winter weather in most areas. If in doubt, ask your furniture salesman.

Always check with your community and homeowner's associations to find out if ordinances or bylaws restrict or prohibit porch and patio decorations. Secure your furniture (if possible) to prevent loss to theft or storms.

When decorating your porch or patio, keep these tips in mind:

✔ **Accessories:** Potted plants — especially those that bloom — are a natural outdoor accessory. Pile a bunch into a child's red wagon (see Figure 24-3), antique wicker pram, or old wooden boxes. Hang lanterns (they look like paper but are made of weather-resistant plastic) surrounding electric light bulbs or votive candles. Painted wooden fruit and vegetables, dried or painted gourds, and marble fruits and vegetables are also festive for this outdoor environment.

Other fun and even practical ideas include gaily-painted watering cans, wooden duck decoys, equipment for outdoors games (such as croquet or badminton), and colorful plastic children's toys in brightly colored plastic crates. Just about anything that says "outdoors" and looks pretty goes well on your porch or patio.

✔ **Flooring:** Stone floors are a natural for the outdoors and usually need only an occasional hosing down to look great. Slate is a popular patio and porch choice, laid with grout or with moss or grass. Wooden floors on porches benefit from a good coat of paint (and perhaps a couple of coats of polyurethane). Choose a color that's compatible with the color of your house's exterior walls — maybe a color that matches the existing shutters; black or forest or hunter green may be dramatic in New England or the Midwest. In Southern climes, turquoise, navy, cobalt, aqua, Bristol, or some other terrific blue adds pizzazz. Use rag rugs for special events on patios, but bring them in when the party's over. Consider adding a sisal (fiber) rug, a washable cotton area rug, or a painted floor cloth on protected porches. Area rugs create an unexpected but desirable indoor ambiance for outdoor areas.

Don't expect a wool area rug to stand up to outdoor use. It will mold and stain, and moths will eat it. Instead, use tough, rubber-backed synthetics that look like Traditional rug designs.

✔ **Furniture for seating:** Some communities have ordinances against uphol-stered "indoor" type sofas on front porches. But then, you don't want to put indoor upholstery on the porch anyway, because sun, rain, and dust would damage it. Instead, use wicker (see Figure 24-4), teak, aluminum, wrought iron, or any material that can stand up to the elements. For comfort, choose cushions covered in special outdoor fabric. It's washable and stuffed with fiberfill designed to stand up to the weather. The new versions of outdoor cushions are plush and comfy, adding a certain luxe look to porch, patio, terrace, or balcony.

Arrange seating just as you would indoors, in close conversational prox-imity. Add tables for snacks, beverages, and books and magazines. If your children play here, provide a toy box for storage. Consider a hammock for extra seating and a great place for a nap.

If your porch or patio is large enough, provide groups of furniture for various functions, such as conversation, games, and dining.

✔ **Lighting:** Porches have protective roofs and come equipped with overhead lights or wall sconces for evening use. Make sure your porch and/or patio is adequately wired. You'll need to plug in floor and table lamps (choose those engineered for outdoor use, with heavy-gauge cords, shatterproof bulbs, and shades made of outdoor fabrics). White (or colored) patio lights add festivity. Don't forget additional lighting for patios that have outdoor wall lights and are surrounded with landscaping lights. Glass-globed hurricane lanterns fitted with candles and citronella torches serve as temporary lighting sources (and a great way to keep skeeters away).

✔ **Shelter:** On porches, treat openings between porch posts with hangings that block sun and rain. Consider installing louvered shutters, painted to match the walls or other shutters on the house. Custom awnings are another option (but they can be a bit expensive). Or substitute wash-and-wear sheets for awnings. We did this very simply (and inexpensively) by sewing curtain rod pockets into the narrow bottom hem of king-sized sheets and shearing the curtains on spring-tension shower rods between the porch posts. (Find nondirectional patterns for the sheets you use. But if your sheet does have a directional pattern, use the wide top hem for the rod pocket.) You can add cotton tiebacks, held by cup hooks, which secure the curtains when you don't need privacy or shelter from mild breezes. When it rains, you can undo the tiebacks and let the sheets blow dry.

Shelter for open patios and terraces may come in the form of umbrella-covered tables, awnings, or freestanding tents to shield the area from sunshine or showers. A friend stretched a large flat panel of *duck fabric* (sometimes called *canvas* and commonly used for sails, casual upholstery, and hammocks), which was tied at the corners with lightweight rope, between trees and above the patio to shelter it and her picnic table from the sun.

✔ **Walls:** Porch and patio walls are usually the same color as your house's exterior walls to keep continuity. But you can decorate them with hanging planters, ceramic tiles or plates, painted wooden plaques, a collection of decorative bird houses, and other appropriate items that neither sunshine nor rain will damage.

Figure 24-3:
Potted plants in a child's wagon are a great accessory for a porch or patio.

Figure 24-4:
Wicker
furniture is
especially
well suited
for sheltered
outdoor
seating.

Enlivening the Laundry

The new trend for busy people who want to spend more time with their families is to put the washer and dryer in a brand new room, which Whirlpool (www.whirlpool.com) calls the *Family Studio*. The family studio is a multifunction space where several people can work together or separately to accomplish one or more tasks, beginning with the laundry. The larger the family studio, the more activities can take place there. But even a smaller laundry space — especially one fitted with sinks — can do double duty as a craft center, potting room, hobby space, or exercise room.

No matter the size, every laundry room is a more cheerful work environment if you decorate it to suit your personal style. Following are some tips for decorating your laundry, first for its starring role as a fabric care center and then (if you have enough room) as a craft center, game room, and more:

✔ **Planning for action.** When laying out your laundry room, decide what functions will take place there — laundry, arts and crafts, plant potting, and so on. List the equipment you need for each, such as:

- Washer(s) and dryer(s) — front- or top-loading
- Sink for hand washing
- Bins for sorting dirty clothes
- Table for folding dried clothing
- Chair(s) or stool(s)

- Drying cabinet that allows you to hang-dry wash-and-wear items

- Clothes vitalizing system that removes wrinkles and odors in 30 minutes (see Whirlpool's Family Studio collection, `www.family-studio.com`)

- Storage for soaps, stain-treatment sprays, and other fabric-cleaning supplies

- Ironing board and iron

After you've made your list, draw your floor plan, noting openings such as windows and doorways. Take a good look at existing wiring and plumbing. Do you need more outlets and in different locations? Do you need a dedicated circuit for the washer and dryer? Is there an electrical outlet for other equipment, such as exercise machines and a radio and TV? Talk with an electrician about adding any wiring you need. What about plumbing? Is a waste line handy, or does a plumber need to create new hookups for your washer, dryer, and sink?

If your laundry is in the basement, consider hiring a carpenter to create a laundry chute. Perhaps you have room (through a closet floor, for example) for a dumb waiter, which can haul up clean clothing.

After you determine these basics, organize your space to provide activity areas for doing laundry functions (sorting the wash, folding clean clothes, and ironing), as well as potting plants, making arts and crafts, and so on. Don't have enough space for everything you want? Top-loading washers and dryers (as opposed to front-loading) are space savers, as are stacking units for storage. Perhaps storage cabinets that double as work surfaces are in order.

✔ **Installing floors.** Choose flooring that is impervious to water and that you can easily wipe clean. Ceramic tile may be a good solution — especially for the sink area. Hard rubber flooring works well, as well as vinyl flooring engineered to work in damp areas. If small children are to play in this space, a cushy area rug provides warmth and comfort. Make sure it's washable, so you can rid it of watercolors and other spillables.

Painting concrete is a decent choice, as long as the basement is dry. As a quick-fix, we painted the concrete floor in Liz Hart McMillan's East Hampton, New York house a bold tropical aqua — just the right antidote for long, cold, and very messy winters and a nice foil for sunny yellow beadboard walls. For comfort and to protect the floor, we placed thick washable bathmats in front of the washer and sink.

✔ **Choosing wall surfaces.** A laundry room's wall materials should be easy to clean, impervious to moisture, and sound absorbing. Ceramic tile is easy to clean but it's probably not a good choice because sound reverberates (no matter how quiet the laundry equipment). Wallpaper doesn't adhere very well in moist conditions.

Painted sheetrock or wallboard is a good, practical, and relatively inexpensive wall covering and can be wiped clean. Wood paneling works well, but if your room is below grade, you must make sure the walls are insulated against moisture and that the paneling is covered in washable paint. Our East Hampton client used beaded board paneling in her laundry because she liked its old-fashioned country character. We painted it a sunny banana yellow — washable, of course.

Color for your walls can be anything you like, but if your laundry room is in your basement, it will benefit from bright, cheerful colors. Consider watermelon red, coral, peach, or a yummy mango.

✔ **Accessories.** What about a wall-hung collection of wicker laundry baskets? Or a collection of old clothes pins on display — perhaps on clotheslines strung across the ceiling? Or photographs (especially black and white or sepia) of laundry drying on a clothesline in the great outdoors? You may choose to escape the laundry theme altogether and opt for some other theme that takes your mind off the chores at hand.

✔ **Seating.** Plan on placing some chairs, just as you would if this were your den. Rocking chairs with removable, washable pads work well. Wicker chairs with cushions are also a casual, comfortable choice.

✔ **Storage.** Whether you opt for armoires, bins, bookcases, cabinets, gym lockers, or open wire or wooden shelving, an assortment of storage is a must. An armoire or freestanding bookshelf is great for storing children's toys and arts and crafts supplies. Open wire shelves are good for holding stacked, freshly dried laundry. Open wood shelves can hold laundry supplies. Rolling bins that can be stashed beneath a large table used for clothes folding can hold just about anything you need.

Part VII
Embellishments: Accessorizing with Art and Other Stuff

The 5th Wave   By Rich Tennant

"I just can't figure out how we overshot our decorating budget by $8.4 million already. We haven't even bought the new dining set."

In this part . . .

Art and accessories, like icing on a marvelous cake, embellish to the *nth*. They're sometimes called the finishing touches. Truly, they are. Can you imagine a room without art, lamps, ceramic bric-a-brac, candles, press pillows, throws, and so on? What a dull room that would be! Here, we define art (or arts, since we call many things *art*). We treat art differently than accessories, a subject that gets its own chapter. So what's the difference between different kinds of art and accessories? Now that your interest is piqued, read on!

Chapter 25

Acquiring and Arranging Art

. . . .

. . . .

A rt adds something to your room's decor by furnishing otherwise boring or empty spaces. But finding the right art and knowing what to do with it can be tough. You have plenty to discover about art — the types of art you can own, where to buy it, how to hang it, and so much more!

In this chapter, we talk about fine, decorative, and fun art in a variety of media — textile art to hang on the wall, sculpture and soft sculpture, and more. You also discover where to place the art and how to tastefully mix art with other furnishings.

Affairs of the Art

You've probably heard the saying, "I don't know what's good, but I know what I like." Find out what's good as well as what you like. Take art appreciation courses and tour museums. You'll come to appreciate what you thought was hideous and to cherish what you already like.

One common way to accessorize is with framed art, which we usually think of as "pictures" that we hang on walls. Framed art can be divided into three categories:

✔ **Decorative art:** Pretty, but doesn't belong in an art museum

✔ **Fine art:** Investment quality art

✔ **Fun art:** What we call anything we (and you) find pleasing to the eye

For decorating purposes, we use the term *art* in the traditional sense — to refer to pictures (or other wall hangings) or sculpture (including figurines).

Artists create art to stir the intellect and delight the imagination — it has no functional purpose. In decorating, art functions as an accessory to complete the decorative scheme. Art should harmonize with a room's theme, color scheme, and mood.

Art as investment

Fine art is always interesting, but it's not necessarily beautiful. Expect to pay more for it because it is *original art* — the only one of its kind. Originals are investments that will increase in value over time. Following are a couple of important points to remember when considering fine art:

- ✔ **Buy from a reputable source.** Ensure that you get what you pay for by dealing with an established gallery. See the section "Fine art from fine sources" later in this chapter for some general tips.
- ✔ **Develop an eye for quality.** You can sharpen this skill by participating in museum tours, seminars, gallery visits, and art history and media classes, as well as by reading magazines and books.

You can achieve the same basic look from reproductions without breaking the bank! (See the section "Decorative reproductions," later in this chapter, for more information.)

Art for art's and decoration's sake

Decorative art doesn't do battle with your brain cells; it just brightens up your day! Certain original oils, acrylics, and watercolors fall into this category. So do reproductions (copies of originals) in oils, acrylics, and watercolors, as well as graphic media and some original photographs.

Don't buy decorative art as though it were an investment, because these pieces aren't expected to grow much in value. In other words, you're not going to make a killing when you put it in your garage sale or on eBay.

Decorative originals

Decorative original oils, acrylics, and watercolors may be the work of a trained artist who works alone, or be created by teams of artists, each of whom paints only a part of the total picture. (Interior designers facetiously call this "art by the yard.") Purely decorative art isn't intended to contribute to art history; it's meant to hang over your sofa and look nice.

More than one original?

Pieces of original graphic art — woodcuts, etchings, and lithographs — are called *multiple originals* because more than one exists. They're still considered originals because each one is created by the artist's hand.

The artist usually signs and numbers these multiples with sequential numbers to form a limited edition. The first number designates which one of the series it is, the second number (after the slash) indicates the total number of the edition. No one piece in an edition is considered more valuable than any other. Usually, a small edition with only a limited number of prints (say 100 total pieces) is more valuable than a large or unlimited edition of as many as 1,000 pieces.

Another exception to the "fine art is unique" rule is investment-quality photography — especially black and white photography — which has gained acceptance as fine and collectible art. Original photographs may or may not be released in signed and numbered limited editions. See the "Photography style" sidebar, also in this chapter.

Decorative reproductions

Reproductions are copies of original fine art that can look amazingly like the real thing — right down to the brush or knife stroke. Traditionally, they weren't considered in the best of taste and were labeled "fake." But tastes change. Today, fake is exalted as *faux,* and faux is the way to go.

We can think of several acceptable reasons for decorating with reproductions:

- ✔ **Availability:** Reproductions are readily available. You can't turn around in many home stores without bumping into reproduction art.

- ✔ **Cheap insurance:** Obviously, household insurance rates are much lower for reproductions than they are for the real thing.

- ✔ **Cost:** They're affordable.

- ✔ **Tasteful subject matter:** Oftentimes the subjects, like certain Beatles tunes or operatic arias, are old favorites. The Taste Police won't slap the cuffs on you for the subject matter!

Posters are a favorite form of decorative art and make great accessories because of their bold graphic design. Despite the fact that they're one of a multiple series, some even become collectibles. For example, we know a professor of Greek who is a talented amateur magician and prizes a poster of Thurston, a magician more talented, he says, than Houdini. The poster has become rare and the subject culturally significant. Naturally, this gift from his wife hangs prominently in their living room.

Photography style

Black-and-white photography, a fine art form, makes for striking displays, especially when framed simply and hung in groups. Work by certain photographers is considered to be original, collectible, and investment art. Some photographs, like works by Alfred Stieglitz and Man Ray, have sold at auction for hundreds of thousands of dollars. Works by some lesser-known artists from the same period (the 1920s and 1930s) are considered as good but sell for less.

Today, you can order work by noted artists from catalogs, such as Ballard Designs (www.Ballard Designs.com), Exposures (www.Exposures OnLine.com), Light Impressions (www.LightImpressionsDirect. com), Pottery Barn (www.PotteryBarn.com), and Spiegel (www.Spiegel.com). With photographs, beauty and value is in the eye of the beholder. Price is determined by the marketplace, which pays according to inherent beauty, rarity, and a host of other criteria. To learn more, visit a gallery that specializes in photography and quiz the owner, who will be delighted with your interest.

Art for fun

Fun art — which may not be art in the strictest definition of the word — is just about anything you want to hang on your walls. Fun photos by amateur photographers, including family members, make excellent decorations, and they have an added benefit: real sentiment that truly personalizes a room. You can also frame theater tickets, a child's first artwork, your old ballet shoes, the front door key to your first house, or rusty horseshoes. Framers love to rise to the challenge of showcasing these unusual objects. Often, the framing itself is artful!

Buying Do's and Don'ts

Buy what you love and can afford — regardless of the type of art. Don't hesitate to hang different types of art together. The only time you shouldn't mix fine, decorative, and fun art is when it doesn't look good together.

Following are some tried-and-true tips for selecting art:

- ✔ **Buy art that speaks to you.** Well, not literally, but something that makes you laugh, sing, feel nostalgic, or jump for joy.

- ✔ **Don't use art that bores you.** Art should evoke a mood, but boredom isn't the one you want!

> ✔ **Don't pit your art against your furniture.** Don't hang fabulous artwork over furniture if the art fights it. A great piece of art and your sofa both deserve the right setting.
>
> ✔ **Do buy artwork that you enjoy looking at, that boasts colors that look smashing with your furnishings, and that grabs your attention each time you see it.** With so much art available, all it takes is a little looking around until you find the right piece. So, what's the rush?

Finding Art

Art is anywhere and everywhere. For best results, bring along snapshots or sample boards and floor plans to help you decide whether a particular piece of artwork fits in with your room. And don't be afraid to let gallery owners, artists, and others know you're looking for art that works well with your room — they just might have the perfect piece in the storeroom.

Fine art from fine sources

Buy fine art from a reputable dealer who knows the artist whose work he represents and who sells pieces at fair prices. Visit galleries. Ask questions. If you're not sure about which gallery to deal with, talk with museum curators and art professors. Ask them to recommend galleries. Read art journals and magazines to find the names of excellent galleries, the names of the artists they represent, and the value of these artists' works. Visit artists' studios when you have an opportunity. Talk with artists at openings. Check their biographies, which tell the names of celebrity clients, museums where their work is hung, awards won, and so on.

Decorative art from many sources

In addition to galleries, artists' studios, and designer showrooms, retail art shops and furniture stores are the easiest places to find decorative art. You can sometimes find pieces in consignment shops, flea markets, and antique shops, and at auctions and estate sales. Personally, we've found some of our favorite pieces at thrift shops. As for knowing whether you're paying the right price for a particular piece, *you* have to be the judge. Don't forget your area's colleges, where students and teachers may sell their art.

Not every piece by a great artist is great art. You may like a lesser, purely decorative piece and get a kick out of owning something by a big-name artist!

Placing Art in the Right Relationship

Where should you hang that 24-x-48-inch oil painting of a herd of Holstein cows that your Uncle Willie left you? What objects look right together? Professional decorators use a long list of traditional criteria. You're free to accept or reject experts' opinions, but it never hurts to consider them.

Picking up on a picture's colors

When you hang a large, important picture, repeating some of the dominant colors in other accessories throughout the room is a good idea. Recently, a friend bought a painting with a lot of bright golden yellow and deep purples and pinks. We repeated the purple in a lounge chair across the room from the painting, and we added purple toss pillows to the off-white sofa beneath the painting. Relating the painting to other objects in the room is a kind of bonding that emphasizes unity.

Considering basic conventions

Some strong social conventions do exist. Following are a few no-nos:

- Don't hang nude paintings in your living room or dining room — it's inappropriate. Beauties *au naturel* are naughty-but-nice for bedrooms and bathrooms.

- Traditionally, fruit or vegetable still lifes are for dining rooms and kitchens — not bedrooms or living rooms.

- Don't hang family photos or too many wedding photos in the living room. Opt for portraits instead.

- Never hang religious art in the bathroom; save it for the bedroom or its own niche.

- Don't hang small landscape paintings near large still life fruits or vegetables. The disparate scales of the two paintings make both of them look ridiculous.

- Barnyard scenes are foul in a formal living room, but fair in the den.

- Don't hang blood-and-guts war scenes in the dining room.

Flowers, landscapes, and seascapes are welcome just about anywhere.

Pleasing the eye of the beholder

Floral subjects are usually considered feminine, boats and seascapes masculine, and whimsical themes childish. Feel free to take advantage of this traditional thinking to make quick, easy, and uncontroversial choices.

If you have an educated eye, you may want to go beyond traditional thinking. At least do some experimenting — most shops make that possible by permitting you to return and exchange art that didn't work out as you thought it would.

Discuss the possibility of exchanging your art at the time of purchase, keep your receipt, and return the art by the store's deadline in like-new condition.

Finding homes for your art

Look at how professionals — curators, interior designers, and others — hang various kinds of art. Visit museums, galleries, showcase houses, and furniture and department stores with room settings that include art. Browsing through decorating magazines is an inexpensive and timesaving alternative.

Back to the future

A good starting point when finding the proper setting for your art is to look at what's worked in the past. For example, each of the various graphic media — woodcuts, etchings, and lithographs — have characteristics that are compatible with certain decorating periods and styles:

- ✔ Woodcuts have a rustic, naive quality that fits with Renaissance, Gothic, and Early American décor (see Chapter 9). Some make a nice counterpoint to Contemporary furnishings (see Chapter 10).

- ✔ Etchings are composed of finely drawn lines that are elegant and get along well in dressy rooms.

- ✔ Lithographs are more painterly and colorful and take on a wide range of looks and styles, ranging from romantically Impressionistic to boldly Modern.

Up-to-the-minute looks

Black-and-white photographs look fabulous with just about any period or style of furniture. They breathe fresh air into period rooms and sing the same tune as Contemporary style. Depending on the subject matter (no nudes in the living room, please), black-and-white prints are at home in any room.

Eclectic mixes

Contemporary interiors stress individual approaches to very personal rooms where just about anything goes. Some eclectic ideas follow. (Note that the

first two approaches are the yin and yang of eclecticism. The third involves
an artful mix.)

- ✔ Create interest by contrasting a large, important, period-looking artwork
  with a crisp, modern background.
- ✔ Pit boldly colored, extremely geometric subjects against stark white
  walls in rooms furnished with wildly colored furniture.
- ✔ Create *art walls,* which mix a diverse group of works in interiors where
  all other furnishings are subdued and play second fiddle to the art.

None of these three techniques mixes a lot of disparate stuff together — that's
not a style but a hodgepodge. These personal statements require a great deal
of taste and a lot of confidence.

Artful Backgrounds

A little fresh paint can help give your art a boost. Notice that the '70s and '80s
trendy art gallery look, with light bleached floors and pure white walls, is giving
way to rooms with more Traditional color schemes. Some of the leading decorating magazines show a renewed interest in strongly colored walls, including
dark greens, deep rusts, intense corals, passionate reds, and sunflower yellows.

If you're painting a wall to show off your art collection, choose a color that
looks best with the dominant color in your collection. Test your choice by
painting a portion of a wall (or poster board) and propping several large
pieces against it.

For best results when you're hanging art against a busy background, choose
a substantial frame that contrasts strongly with the background. If your art has
a mat, be sure that it, too, contrasts with the wall. Also consider the subject:
Pink roses against pink rose wallpaper will disappear, whereas a landscape or
seascape provides contrast and maintains the romantic mood.

The Art of Art Placement

Hang art where the eye *expects* to see something (and feels a distinct sense of
something missing when nothing is there). The most obvious gaps often occur
on the wall area above a piece of furniture. Consider these guidelines:

- ✔ Art should be no wider than the furniture below. If the art is narrower, it
  should be at least half the length of the furniture.

✔ If a major piece of art is too narrow for the chosen spot, flank it with smaller pieces of framed or three-dimensional art that fill the space and satisfy the eye.

✔ The bottom of the art should be close enough to relate to the furniture, but allow for breathing space (generally about 8 to 10 inches).

If, for any reason, you need to leave as much as a foot between the furniture and bottom of the art, you can close the obvious gap with a floral arrangement or some other space-filling device.

Consider adding art to unexpected places, too. Art over a door or window pulls the eye up and makes the door or window look taller and more interesting. Art hung in the blank space between a windowsill and floor gets noticed. A tiny piece of art hung below the lampshade on a bedside table is a nice last thing to see as you turn off your light.

Rearrange and move your art, hanging it in different places around the house from time to time. You'll discover new things in each of the pieces after they're hung in a different light, at a different angle (higher or lower than before), and with different furnishings.

Relating Artwork in Groups

Grouping art is a great way to decorate walls against which no furniture is placed. Usually these walls are adjacent to a walkway, as in a hallway. You can adopt an "all-over" approach and hang groupings higher and lower than expected, in order to cover more wall area.

Do's and don'ts of group displays

What you hang reflects your point of view. Make sure that you effectively showcase whatever you decide to hang. Consider these tips for hanging groups of artwork:

✔ **Think of art as reflecting your passion for beauty.** Collections can give you great pleasure and satisfaction. To paraphrase Matisse, at the end of the day, you should be able to look at your paintings and be refreshed by their beauty.

✔ **Master the mix.** Frame a Contemporary piece in an ornate period-style frame. Hang similarly themed art from different periods together, as long as colors and scales relate.

✔ **Mix and match frame styles and art styles if you're hanging several small- and medium-sized pieces of art.** Having a wall of art looks energetic and artsy.

✔ **Remember that size counts.** Smaller items look best clustered in a group. Larger pieces look best when singled out. Place smaller artwork to the sides or above medium pieces.

✔ **Stair-step your paintings only in stairwells, not on the walls.** *Stair-stepping* refers to hanging one painting several inches lower than the other, and it makes sense only on a staircase. On any other wall, hang two paintings next to (and level with) each other or one directly above the other.

✔ **Think outside the box.** Groupings don't have to be symmetrical (look exactly alike on each side). For example, you can hang a grouping of art on one side of a shelf or tabletop and balance the other side with tall vases or sculptures.

Simple symmetry

Any grouping of art that can be halved down the middle and look the same on each side is symmetrical. *Absolute symmetry* occurs when exactly the same objects are used on each side of the room (see Figure 25-1). *Relative symmetry* also creates a mirrored effect, but the objects on one side of the room aren't identical to the ones on the other side of the room (see Figure 25-2),

Figure 25-1: Absolute symmetry, the most formal arrangement, creates mirror images using identical items on each side of a grouping.

Figure 25-2:
Relative symmetry strives to create a mirror image effect using objects that are similar but not identical.

An art grouping composed of similarly sized frames hung equidistantly from each other is an example of a symmetrical arrangement. Traditional room settings use this approach by hanging a dozen botanical prints in rows and columns. Do symmetrical groupings when all the pictures are framed and matted identically. The effect is formal, serene, and Traditional. Consider using this classic arrangement to add stability to a Contemporary setting.

Not-so-simple asymmetry

An art grouping of variously sized framed pieces hung in a straight line, in rectangles, in triangles, or in other similar patterns, but placed so that it creates an optically balanced arrangement, is *asymmetrical*. Asymmetrical arrangements achieve a sense of balance by carefully grouping items of unequal size, shape, and color (see Figure 25-3).

When you use numerous paintings of various sizes and shapes, composition is trickier to achieve. Usually, hanging the paintings to create similar-sized masses in close proximity makes them work like a mural. Plan your groupings to form a square or a rectangle by keeping tops (or bottoms) of frames level to create unity and order. Another option is to create a circular or oval arrangement. These groupings are dynamic, casual, and Contemporary, the exact opposite of Traditional compositions.

Figure 25-3:
In this asymmetrical arrangement, the dark rectangular mirror and the dark ball beneath it equal the impressive visual weight of a large dark pot.

The eye finds a grouping of an odd number of paintings (which provides no logical place to settle on and keeps the eye moving) more dynamic than a grouping of an even number of paintings, which the eye reads as a single entity (see Figure 25-4).

Great groupings

If you follow these steps, you can create a perfect grouping every time, without making frustrating mistakes:

1. **Measure the wall space that you want to fill.**

2. **Outline that exact size on your floor using masking tape.**

3. **Arrange the art on the floor within the given area.**

   Doing so enables you to move pieces around until you arrive at the optimum arrangement.

4. **After you're pleased with the grouping, measure and hang.**

Be prepared for some surprises. You may need to shift pieces from spot to spot, because unusual factors can affect the sense of balance that you're striving for:

✔ **Generally, heavier pieces should go below lighter pieces.** A large, delicate oil may seem lighter than a smaller, darker, more rustic woodcut. Size alone doesn't make a picture seem heavier — color does. Ultimately, you'll have to use your own judgment.

✔ **Leave several inches of breathing space around each piece.** Pieces hung too close together lose any sense of individuality; those hung too far apart don't look like a group.

Figure 25-4:
The grouping on the right is more dynamic than the grouping on the left.

Arrange groupings of art on the floor first. After you're satisfied with the arrangement, hang the first framed piece at eye level (not too high, not too low) and at the center of your wall area. Then hang a work on one side, and one on the other, checking as you go.

How to hang

Use the correct hooks designed to hold the weight of the art you're hanging. Using two hooks for larger works helps keep them hanging straight. And make sure that the hook you're using is the right one for your type of walls (plaster or plasterboard).

If you're nailing or screwing a hook into a plaster wall, put a crisscross of adhesive tape on the wall to keep the plaster in place and then drive the nail or screw through the tape. If you're hanging art on a slanted wall such as a *dormer* (slanted) ceiling, attach the artwork at the top and bottom of the frame. If you're creating a precise rectangular or square grouping, secure the pieces at the bottom, too, so that none become crooked.

For added excitement, add mirrors, sconces, and brackets with sculpture to your art grouping. Add textural interest with tapestries and quilted, woven, or embroidered wall hangings.

Displaying in Off-the-Wall Ways

You don't have to hang art to display it. The following list gives you our favorite alternatives:

- ✔ Intersperse paintings with books in a bookshelf.

- ✔ Lean your art on an easel. Easels, large and small, have never gone out of style.

- ✔ Place an array of artfully framed miniatures inside a glass-topped display table, coffee table, or end table, or atop a big round table.

- ✔ Set a large picture on the floor (unless you have small children or pets). Set a small picture on the mantel, place a bunch of pictures atop a bookshelf, or just lean them against the wall (see Figure 25-5).

- ✔ Prop up a plethora of small artwork, including black-and-white photographs, on wooden shelves. This allows for quick and easy changing of your display (see Figure 25-6).

Figure 25-5:
Art doesn't have to be hung on the wall but can be set on the floor or tabletop and leaned against the wall.

Figure 25-6:
An art shelf holds framed art that can easily be added to, rotated in and out, or regrouped without a nail hole in the wall.

Chapter 26

Accentuating Your Style

- -

In This Chapter

▶ Stretching your decorating budget

▶ Creating surprise with accessories

▶ Arranging accessories stylishly

▶ Discovering beauty in unexpected places

- -

Accessories are the small furnishings — pictures, toss pillows, sculptures, vases, and so on — that give a room a personal, lived-in look. Accessories may serve a useful function, but they don't have to.

This chapter shows how to accessorize to show off your personal style. We take a look at where to find the right pieces, how to breathe new life into items you already have, and how to imaginatively use tried-and-true secrets of professionals. Then we tackle several categories of accessories, giving you tips and tricks for making the most of your finishing touches.

Hunting for Accessories

Many confident decorators find beauty in unusual, surprising objects. We've seen collections of kitchen utensils, bits and pieces of rusty metals, and old toasters displayed as accessories. Accessories should look as though they belong, so they don't feel staged — crystal decanters and stemware looks out of place on a family room ottoman. If you have one of those oddball collections — metal shears, leather working tools, barbed wire, and so on — create a deliberately stylish display.

You'll be amazed at the number of items that work as accessories. Do you have baskets, birdcages, and birdhouses to set out on display? Try framing old lace, perhaps salvaged from a worn-out pillowcase or dresser scarf, and hanging it over a painted chest. Look around for the unusual and unexpected items — children's art, old greeting cards, and so on — to add a note of individual style.

Old family photographs placed in beautiful or interesting frames make great personal accessories. When redecorating offices for our clients Richard and Stephanie, we spied their daughter's stunning black and white photographs, as well as her fingerpaintings from kindergarten. We enlarged a dozen photographs, framed them in matching narrow black frames, and hung them throughout the office. A grouping of fingerpaintings became part of Richard's Contemporary art collection.

Allow yourself time to discover objects of desire. Attending weekly auctions may provide great accessories at terrific prices — and they're fun, too! Or perhaps you'll decide to craft your own accessories. Our friend Norma saw a mosaic mirror that she liked, enrolled in a short course, and figured out how to make her own. To her surprise, people who saw her mirrors wanted them. Now she's selling them at flea markets.

Updating Your Arrangements

Relocating your accessories gives them new impact. When we moved a hand-painted mirror from the entry of a condominium lobby and placed it over a chest with a small lamp, condo residents who had walked past it for years commented about how much they loved the "new" mirror!

So, what's the lesson? Don't rest on your decorating laurels. Consider changing your decorative arrangement seasonally, or in response to special occasions. If you gain fame among your friends as someone who reaccessorizes when the creative mood moves you, people will look forward to seeing what you do next.

You don't have to bring out a new group of accessories for a total makeover. Just move a few accessories to different spots in the room, or from one room to another, to give your rooms a fresh look. Things look different in different settings; this is the reason gallery owners and retailers change their displays, especially when an item has been in-store too long.

Finishing with Pizzazz

Accessories are like spices — they add zest to your decorating. A pinch of *this* and a dollop of *that* produces a total effect. A well-accessorized room seems finished. Try some of these tips from the pros:

✔ **Pick an accessory style — more or less.** Contemporary style calls for only a few key accessories, like in Figure 26-1, while Traditional calls for many more accessories Use a few accessories or a lot, depending on your personal style (see Chapter 11).

✔ **De-clutter.** If your style is *more is better* when it comes to accessories, avoid a cluttered look by grouping similar or related items together.

✔ **Dramatize.** If your style is *less is more,* be sure that accessories have dramatic shapes, exotic colors, heroic sizes, or provocative subjects.

✔ **Favor a material.** Group accessories by material (such as porcelain, leaded glass, or antique silver), color, or subject (for example, sculptures of animals). The stronger the relationship among the objects, the stronger the personal style statement.

✔ **Look through a lens.** Have you ever wanted your room to look like one in a magazine? Stand in each of the room's four corners and look through your camera. Is there a blank spot? Add a suitable accessory! Do a few accessories in a group look weak and unimportant? Add more. Is there too much clutter and confusion? Remove or reorganize until your new "camera eye" likes what it sees.

✔ **Pick a color.** If you're not sure, take a cue from the most important pattern in your room and use its most important color (or colors).

✔ **Unify.** Accessories provide contrast to your overall scheme. But you can unify accessories by choosing items in the same color or material. A dozen vases have more impact if they're all cobalt blue than if they're assorted colors.

Figure 26-1:
A few key accessories make a dramatic statement.

Accessorizing One by One

Just what accessories do you really need? Accessories that have a function have a competitive edge. For example, pillows can cushion as well as add color and pattern. An *ego wall* of your diplomas and awards in your home office lets your clients know how accomplished and professional you are.

Pillow talk

Toss pillows were originally intended to add comfort and support. Over the years, they've become a major decorating tool because they're an easy source of color and pattern. You can find them covered in every conceivable fabric, color, pattern, and shape, to suit any decor. The more decorative (and expensive) ones are treated with trim that may add a masculine note (with welting, moss, or deep fringe; see Figure 26-2) or a feminine note (with ribbons, fringe, ruffles, or lace). Some toss pillows are reversible — a solid color on one side and a pattern on the other, two different colors, or two different patterns (see Figure 26-3).

Figure 26-2: Decorative pillows with a masculine touch have hefty trims.

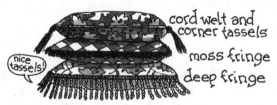

Figure 26-3: Patterned pillows contrast boldly with the white slipcover that dresses a wicker sofa for indoors.

For easy cleaning, look for readymade pillows with removable covers. Stuffing may be down feathers (which need plenty of plumping), cotton batting, or hypoallergenic synthetic fiberfill.

The current decorating strategy is to pile several pillows deep on sofas and beds. Just be sure to leave enough room for sitting! Do this by varying sizes and shapes. (Keep extra pillows handy in a basket.)

Alternating patterned and plain pillows of the same size and shape is one easy way to arrange them. Another way is to mix shapes such as triangles, circles, rectangles, and squares, and pick sizes ranging from jumbo to tiny. Experiment — stand rectangle pillows vertically or horizontally, as needed. Giving the top of a too-bulky pillow a quick whack with your hand creates a V-shaped groove that brings the pillow into scale and makes for a more interesting shape. (In the trade, we call this a *Donghia chop,* named for the late designer Angelo Donghia who originated it.)

To successfully mix pillows of various patterns and materials — such as chintz, needlepoint, suede, or embroidery — vary pattern sizes and scale and stick to a dominant unifying color.

Mirror magic

Mirrors are decorating magic. They serve as looking glasses, double the view they reflect, and add sparkle. Perhaps best of all, mirrors make spaces seem larger, a real bonus for the too-small room.

Place a mirror where you want to see your own reflection (an entry hall), reflect an interesting view (opposite a window), create a strong focal point (above a mantel), or light up a dark area (above a hall console or table in a corner). Regardless, make sure it reflects something interesting.

Frame-ups

Selecting framed mirrors that echo the shape of other furniture is always a safe bet. In a dining room with round- or shield-back chairs, for example, a round mirror above the mantel is a subtle unifying element. Mirror frames come in every conceivable furniture style and period, including such favorites as Chippendale, Federal, the Louises, and Contemporary, so matching mirror and furniture style is easy. (To find out what style is what, see Chapters 9 and 10.) But using a large Contemporary mirror to add an eclectic note to a Traditional scheme, for example, is perfectly acceptable.

For the non-traditionalist, you can find many fabulous ethnic, whimsical, and purely creative styles — or whip up your own. A friend of ours took two white birch branches, crossed them at the bottom (attaching them with glue and tiny nails), rounded them gently around a round mirror glued onto a plywood circle, then crossed them at the top (with some leaves attached) and secured them. The branches made a delightful frame for a mirror in her summer cottage's entry hall.

Frame finishes range from traditional woods and wood tones to gilded bright or antique golds to antique painted and decorated finishes. Match the frame's finish to the level of formality or informality of your furniture. Choose one that contrasts with the wall it's hung against: a dark frame to hang against a light wall or vice versa. Traditionally, you want the mirror frame to relate to the furniture below it in value (one shouldn't be too much lighter or darker than the other), if not in color. In Contemporary interiors, contrast is key, and eclecticism is perfectly okay.

Frame materials include finished wood, metal, bamboo, and stained glass. Newer, more eccentric designs may be ultra simple or heavily carved and embellished with natural-looking leaves and flowers as well as jewel stones, bits of marble, and colored glass. The plainer the wall, the more elaborate the frame may be. In an artsy room, the busier both are, the better.

Frame size is also important. Like a work of art, a mirror shouldn't be wider than the furniture below it nor less than two-thirds the width. If a mirror is too narrow to adequately fill the wall space, add paintings or sconces on either side. For more drama, hang a mirror vertically above a chest or console. Large mirrors — especially long, vertical mirrors — can hang alone, without furniture beneath them. Medium-sized mirrors look more important if you group them with framed art, porcelain plates, or figurines and hang them above a dresser, chest, or table. You can group a collection of tiny mirrors — especially those with inventive frames — as you would a collection of paintings (see Chapter 25). We did this in a small, dark hallway, and the mirrors added sparkle and a sense of fun.

Frameless fashion

Modern-style wall-hung mirrors may have no frame at all. Less expensive mirrors without frames, wall-to-wall mirrors, and do-it-yourself mirror tiles and panels can be found with plain or beveled edges. Beveled-edged mirrors are heavier, more substantial looking, and work well in Traditional interiors. Plain-edged mirrors look especially sleek in Contemporary settings. Against a dark wall, you don't notice the absence of a frame.

Clear and colored mirror glass

Clear glass is the norm for framed mirrors in Traditional styles. But more decorative glass includes mysterious, darkened, splotched, antique-looking glass. (The real effect occurs when the mirror backing begins to deteriorate.) A wide variety of colored glasses are available, ranging from steel gray to various metallic colors, including copper and bronze. Another unusual glass is amber, a jewel-stone color. Factor mirror glass color into your scheme.

Clear glass reflects only what's put in front of it, so it's acceptable in almost any setting. Antique glass is a natural with antique or Traditional frames and furniture and can be a striking eclectic accent in a Contemporary room. Colored glass — especially metallic copper and brass, as well as the various grays — requires a greater understanding of color relationships and a deft hand, but it's generally at home in Contemporary situations. Copper glass in an antique copper frame can also take on a Western or Lodge look, while grays framed in driftwood (also gray) can take on a Country or beach house look.

Colored glassware

Colored glassware, popular in Victorian times, adds a great deal of excitement to table settings that use colored goblets and serving pieces. Venetian or Murano glass, blown in exciting color combinations and extraordinary shapes, looks beautiful in Traditional and Contemporary decor. Little wonder that it's more popular than ever — not just for use at the table.

Sandwich glass, made in Sandwich, Massachusetts in the 1800s, is a collectible, as is the iridescent glass developed by Louis Comfort Tiffany in the late 19th century. Distinctive 20th-century green glassware by Anchor Hocking is a recent collectible. Swedish Modern glass is distinctively bold and beautifully colored. If colored glass has always held a fascination for you, now is the time to indulge your passion.

Stained glass

Old stained glass windows have been favorite decorative accessories for years. If they're in good shape, these old windows can easily be hung from hooks inside an existing window. An architect we know installed one as an interior window between an entry hall and an adjoining family room. Another way to display a stained glass window is to put it inside a custom-made back-lit frame. You can then hang it in any room or space where everyone can admire it.

If the glass in an old window is loose and rattles in the frame, or if the lead channels sag so that there's space between the channel and the glass, take the window to a restoration shop for repair before hanging. Hang more than one stained glass window together, if you like.

Ceramics

Ceramics is a general-category name for fired clay decorative objects (such as vases and ashtrays) and functional objects (including dinnerware). Ceramic dinnerware is made from a variety of ceramic or fired-clay materials. Because of distinctive differences in quality and price, it's good to know the names of specific kinds of ceramic materials used for dinnerware (and some decorative objects).

China is a word broadly given to all ceramic dinnerware (such as plates and bowls used for dining). This is because of the fine dinnerware made in China of pure, white kaolin clay known as *porcelain,* which found its way to Europe. Kaolin clay is rare, so Europeans sought and created more readily available and less expensive substitutes. Today, the three major types of ceramic dinnerware are all made from clay but may be described more accurately as:

- ✔ *Bone china,* which adds bone ash to the clay (not kaolin) mixture. Fine bone china dinnerware (originally made in England), while beautiful, is not as hard as porcelain dinnerware manufactured in Limoges, France (where many factories are located). As a result, it chips more easily. Bone china, while considered fine and suitable for formal tables, also is not as white, translucent, or thin as porcelain dinnerware (which is increasingly referred to as *limoges porcelain*).

- ✔ *Earthenware,* sometimes called *pottery,* is made from red clay. It's quite porous and absorbs stains. The finishing glaze that gives it color and pattern is vulnerable to chipping. Earthenware is both inexpensive and popular. It's also rustic and right for Country-style rooms.

- ✔ *Porcelain,* the most expensive ceramic for dinnerware and fine art objects, is made from a particularly fine, pure white, kaolin clay that becomes glass-like when fired in the kiln. Because it is *vitreous* (as glass is), porcelain is extremely hard and durable and doesn't absorb stains. Most of the finest porcelain — for decorative and functional objects — comes from Limoges, France. Porcelain is extremely delicate looking (but most durable) and elegant, and is at home in the most beautifully decorated interiors. One great way to display a collection of pretty porcelain (or other ceramic) plates is by hanging them in a decorative arch, such as the one shown in Figure 26-4.

Items made of these ceramic materials, along with colored and decorative glassware, are abundant for decorating. If you compiled a complete list of items made of china, you'd be writing for a long, long time. Just a few of the possibilities include vases, ashtrays, small boxes, candy dishes, bowls, plates, sculptures, figurines, umbrella stands, and photograph frames.

Texture is an important part of your decision about which ceramic materials to choose when buying decorative accessories or dinnerware.

Figure 26-4:
Fine porcelain plates hung in a decorative arch add width and importance to a floral painting and create an arresting grouping.

When you buy functional ceramic items — especially glazed and painted pottery and glass — check to see whether they're safe to use for eating and drinking and that you can clean them in your dishwasher.

Ceramic tiles

Decorated ceramic tiles are becoming popular as wall decor. Some tiles come self-framed; others are framed in wooden moldings. Subjects are often framed murals of rural scenes, floral bouquets, and Renaissance images made up of several tiles, with and without grout lines showing. Crackled glazes add an aged look. You can also display individual tiles on a small easel, group them for tabletop display, or use them as coasters. (Add felt circles to the bottoms of ceramic tile coasters so they don't scratch your table.)

Blooming beauty

Nothing is more decorative than flowers — fresh, of course, when they're available and advisable. The English way with flowers — straight from the garden and plopped into a big vase — is informal and fun. So is the idea of sticking a few stems into an old teapot, an interesting goblet, or a quaint tin can.

We once picked up a rusty, used paint pail from a rubbish heap, filled it with branches of green leaves and roadside tiger lilies, and placed it on a picnic table as a centerpiece for a photo shoot for a national remodeling magazine. "Whoa . . . pretty sophisticated," the photographer yelled. Actually, the rusted can with gray-blue and deep coral paint drips down its sides, filled with green leaves and orange tiger lilies, was pretty stunning. It was also handy (we were 25 miles from the nearest nursery) and cheap!

Professional arrangements

Arrangements by florists don't have to look contrived and formal. Just tell your florist what you're looking for. You may want to bring your vessel in so they can arrange your flowers just so. Tell the florist where the arrangement will be placed; describe the furniture, the painting or mirror that will hang above it, and the color of your walls. The more information, the better.

Silk flowers

At one time, silk or any kind of artificial flower was frowned on. Not anymore. Silk flowers not only look real, but they're also beautiful in their own right. Mixed with corkscrew vines and branches, they make dramatic focal points. They're the perfect solution if you travel a lot or want to stay within budget (you won't have to buy fresh flowers weekly!). And, when it's time to seasonally change, just put them on a shelf, and they'll wait patiently for their next turn. (Put a dust cloth over silk flowers to store them.)

Save on silk flower arrangements by selecting individual stems and creating your own arrangement. You don't have to follow a convention; use your own judgment. You can change the look by just exchanging a few blossoms.

Dried plants

Dried flowers and plants have also come into their own now that folks have discovered how to appreciate their soft, faded beauty. You can air-dry plants by hanging them in bunches upside down in a dry, dark room that's well ventilated; air-drying takes about three weeks. Silica gel products are available in craft shops, and easy-to-follow directions for gathering, drying, and preserving make creating your own dried arrangements and wreaths of wild and cultivated flowers, weeds, and foliage an enjoyable pursuit. This process absorbs the moisture from the plant quickly so that it retains its form and bright color. (Check out craft shops for instruction books and supplies.)

Show off both silk and dried flowers in season. A bouquet of jonquils doesn't look nearly as convincing in December as it does in the springtime. Mix only flowers that bloom during the same season (no spring irises with fall mums, for example), and keep color schemes synchronized to both reality and your decorating scheme. Nature knows best!

Also consider geography when creating your arrangements. Mums in Florida — in or out of season — just don't seem credible. And Birds of Paradise may not work in Cape Cod. Savor your place. Don't rush to imitate what "they" are doing somewhere else after reading a decorating magazine.

Trees and shrubs

Don't forget trees and shrubbery as indoor decoration. Fake is fine, but don't use fake potted plants in illogical places. Trees, like flowers, need light, so place them by a window or door. Everyone may know that your tree is a fake, but you'll suspend disbelief if you put it in a natural spot. Placing even a fake tree in a dark, unlighted hallway seems silly.

Collections

Collectors eager to show off their spoils have led the way in using collections of all sorts as decorations. Old toys, rusted iron farm objects, baskets, pottery, sculpture, thimbles, dolls, doll houses, miniature furniture, quilts, samplers, matchbooks, fans, antique evening purses, gelatin or chocolate molds — the list of possibilities is endless.

Despite the number of china and curio cabinets and glass-topped display tables available, finding a way to adequately protect your collection while you show it off can present a challenge. Here's where you need ingenuity and perhaps the advice of professionals. Drapery shops can help you solve the problem of how to hang textiles best. Cabinetmakers can help you create a piece of furniture for displaying three-dimensional objects that are a challenge. Frame shops and catalogs are also excellent sources of ideas for displaying collectibles on the wall. Magazines now run feature articles on displaying collections; watch for and clip these sources of inspiration.

Quilts

Collectible textiles in the form of quilts, tapestries, and handcrafted area rugs make impressive wall hangings. They're especially good for use in rooms with cathedral ceilings and in stairwells where large pieces are needed to fill two-story wall spaces. These wall hangings need special consideration. First, carefully mount them so that the fibers aren't strained. Secondly, avoid hanging them in direct sunlight, which fades and weakens the fibers. Trade them out: Switch one for another, to give each a chance to rest. Being an accessory can be a hard job.

Throws

Throws, afghans, and giant shawls, kept handy as cover-ups during a quick snooze on the sofa or to snuggle in while you watch TV, are now decorative mainstays. Fortunately, throws and afghans are readily available in a growing variety of fabrics, including wool, synthetics, and woven cotton. Afghans typically are knitted or crocheted, but woven throws come in every conceivable color and pattern and in fabrics as plain as washable cotton and as fancy as cashmere. Shawls are readily available in department stores in challis wool (a very soft, finely woven wool) and synthetic fabrics. Antique silk and satin shawls and throws with rich, exotic trims may be more difficult to find, but they're worth the search. Of course, you can make your own silk or satin shawl, complete with fancy fringe.

Throws are instant decorating at its best. Don't limit the many decorating roles of throws (see Figure 26-5); instead, help yourself to these ideas that make the most of these textile treasures:

Figure 26-5:
Cozy throws
add a
layer of
interesting
softness.

✔ **Be handy.** Stack several colorful throws in a handsome basket and set it beside the hearth or near a favorite easy chair.

✔ **Coordinate**. If your sofa is dull and colorless, drape a beautifully colored or patterned throw across one end. At the other end, add toss pillows in the same colors.

✔ **Cover up.** Cover a round table or fling a large fringed shawl over your grand piano to give it glam, just like in old movies.

✔ **Disguise.** Hide the wear and tear on your footstool or ottoman by folding a throw and laying it across the top.

✔ **Drape it.** Create an instant valance by draping a throw over the top of the window. Secure it with high style holdbacks found in drapery shops.

✔ **Hang it.** Brighten a boring wall by hanging a colorful throw on a low wooden curtain pole and brackets.

✔ **Reduce.** Lessen the impact of a big, boring recliner by draping a throw across one side.

✔ **Slipcover.** Re-do a small chair the easy way: Toss an eye-catching throw over it and tuck the throw around the pillows. Secure the throw around the chair base with a rope or ribbon.

✔ **Spread cheer.** In the bedroom, cover a rectangular table with a throw to serve as a dressing table or desk, or drape one across the end of your bed as a minispread.

Screen tests

Movable screens have been around for about 3,000 years, and designers haven't tired of them yet! They were probably invented for practical reasons — to conceal things, shield a door, serve as a dressing screen, create a wall, or block an unattractive view — but they're also very decorative. A screen makes a romantic frame for a sofa, introduces a sense of architecture (height and depth), holds pinned-up snapshots, and provides gorgeous color, texture, and pattern that can be a room's focal point.

Carved screens only partially conceal light. Screens with *transoms* (see-through tops) provide privacy but look lighter than solid screens. Small, decorative, Oriental screens are often mounted on the wall, like art, above a sofa, a chest, or the headboard in a bedroom.

Select a screen that is compatible with your furniture style and the mood of your room. An undulating screen with a sculptural Contemporary look, for example, doesn't mix well with Traditional furniture.

Screens intended for practical use are usually at least 6 feet high and have no fewer than three 2-foot wide panels. A screen that's 8 feet high is more dramatic but can be intimidating. A screen of four or more panels provides better coverage if you're using it as a dressing screen. Keep screens light enough to be easily moved, preferably by one person.

Check the hinges; they should be heavy-duty and double-action to allow the screen to bend in two directions for greatest flexibility. If your favorite screen style has feet, they should be sturdy and stable.

Why not make your own screen? Follow these suggestions, and feel free to send us photos of your completed masterpieces:

- Using two-way hinges, connect three or more doors — old, new, solid wood, or hollow core. Paint, stain, or faux finish the doors to suit your decorating needs.

- Hinge together shutters, whether old and paint-chipped or new and ready to finish. Choose tall ones for tall-standing screens that provide privacy, and shorter ones when privacy isn't the goal.

- Join framed mirrors to work as screens. Finish off the unfinished side with paint, paper, or fabric. Double your pleasure by facing the mirror toward the scene you want to reflect.

- Connect (old or new) iron gates for a see-through screen that provides a beautiful pattern.

What are some unorthodox ways in which you can use a decorative screen? Try these suggestions to get your own creative juices going:

- **Add architectural interest.** Transform a plain square room into an octagon by placing standing screens in the four corners. The screens direct the eye to the center of the room — hang an interesting chandelier to create a focal point. Neither screens nor the chandelier need be expensive — it's the idea that counts.

- **Create a privacy wall.** Do guests camp out on your sofa? Give this area privacy by using a series of standing screens. They're quick and easy to put in place or to move aside.

- **Make a headboard.** A raised- or recessed-panel or single plane solid wood door, or an inexpensive hollow-core door, can be transformed into a screen/headboard that makes a statement. Stained in a dark color, a paneled door seems more masculine. Painted in a beautiful jewel or pastel color, your paneled screen/headboard seems more feminine. Paint a single plane, undecorated door a rich neutral for a modern headboard. Stencil any type door for a screen/headboard with a Country look. Add decorative moldings to give your creation French style.

Hardware

Add a smashing bit of style with decorative hardware. Metals — wrought iron, antique and hammered bronze, brass, gold, silver, pewter, and aluminum — all have distinct character that lend themselves to designs of particular styles and periods. Select the ones that add to your plan.

If you haven't looked at hardware recently, take a trip to a home improvement store. The number of artistic knobs and pulls will astound you. Consider creating a few of your own! Experiment with these ideas:

- **Attach wooden shapes to your cabinet doors.** Some children's toys or toy parts, such as small wagon wheels or ABC blocks, are good for this. Paint them a contrasting color, or stain them to match wood door and drawer fronts.

- **Glue on gorgeous big glass marbles, interesting (not too big or rough) pebbles, or chunky beads.** You can find all the fixings at craft stores or discount retailers, or you can pick up marbles at a toy store.

- **Paint plain ceramic knobs.** Choose the right paint from your local craft shop and paint away.

Found objects

Countless times, we've said to clients and friends, "What you need on this coffee table is a big, round, bowl. Do you have one?" More times than not, the answer is "Yes." Usually it's stashed away in some dark closet — when it should be on display. Check your cabinets and closets for potential decorative objects.

Think outside the box; consider new ways to use old things. For example, check your attics for old suitcases that you can stack and use as tables (see Figure 26-6), as well as for trunks that can double as coffee tables. Drums — no longer in use as musical instruments — may strike just the right note as end tables in the den. Children's wooden toys — outgrown and cast aside — may be perfect for the mantel in the den or great room. A California client of ours collected unusual musical instruments from around the world. We arranged them on the corkboard wall behind her TV, where they created a fascinating design, and our client could easily remove them for playing!

And don't forget the barn. Handsome leather saddles that linger after the horse has gone can do double-duty as footstools. Of course, old yard and farm tools make unique accessories in Country-style rooms. One client hung a chunky old floor-length chain from a ceiling hook in one corner of her kitchen. With small S-hooks, she hung baskets up and down its length. The chain and baskets not only looked great in the formerly empty corner but were also very useful when it came time to pick vegetables from her garden.

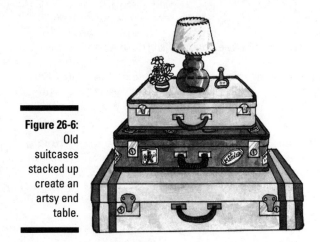

Figure 26-6:
Old
suitcases
stacked up
create an
artsy end
table.

Beaches and backyards are good sources for interesting objects that cost nothing. Rocks and shells, washed and piled up on a beautiful plastic, glass, or silver tray, can be captivating and fill up a blank spot on that table by the window. Driftwood makes great sculpture. So do birds' nests (without the birds!). Tree branches and bamboo poles are even showing up in homes as curtain rods. We all discovered these treasures as children. Adulthood is a good time to recall and use them with the same unadulterated pleasure.

Part VIII
The Part of Tens

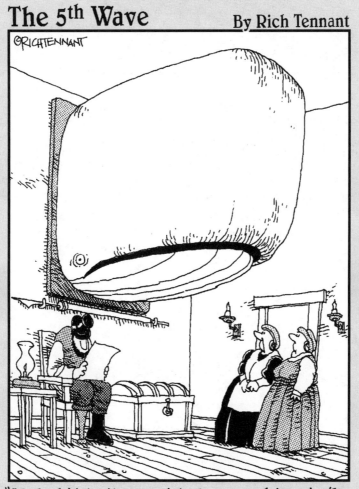

The 5th Wave   By Rich Tennant

"We had it in the guest bedroom, and then in the hallway, but for now we're leaving it in here until we figure out which room it seems to want to be in."

In this part . . .

*A*part of every *For Dummies* book, The Part of Tens provides quick, handy information. Here, we pass along hands-on ideas and know-how that will send you scurrying to your tools of choice — paintbrushes, sewing machine, glue gun, and so on. Had our editor not called "Halt," we would have written ten Part of Tens chapters. We love them! We hope you find them helpful. E-mail us at McMillanUS@aol.com or KKMcMillan@aol.com and let us know.

Chapter 27

Ten Quick and Easy Centerpieces

Is company coming — unexpectedly? What to do? First, take a deep breath. Then, while you're whipping up a gourmet meal, think about a quick and easy centerpiece that you can whip up with on-hand ingredients. You can come up with an enviable centerpiece that will add a little spark to your imaginative meal. Does your creativity need a nudge? Consider these ideas — some of which we've actually demonstrated on live Miami and Palm Beach TV programs. The host and the weather forecaster loved them!

Centerpieces should be low enough so that your dinner guests can see and converse with each other!

Indulging in Child's Play

If your company includes a youngster, consider using a child's wooden train as a centerpiece. The open coal car can hold a spray of dried plants that seem just right with rustic pottery and nubby woven placemats. Give it a boost by placing it on a wooden tray or even a wooden cutting board.

Adding an Artistic Touch

A piece of sculpture can serve as a great centerpiece in the dining room, especially if you have one of those busts of a great composer (such as Beethoven or Mozart) or conquering hero (such as Caesar or Washington).

Whether made from real or faux white marble, this is the right choice when you're using fine, formal dinnerware. With informal dinnerware — perhaps pottery, tin, enamelware, pewter, wood, or even paper plates — use a clay figure, such as a child or an angel. Or you may choose a painted ceramic (china, glass, or clay) clown, bird, or floral bouquet.

Pluck your sculpture from its place and plop it down in the center of your table. For ballast, surround the base with fresh evergreen twigs from a holly bush. Any of these sculptures will work best if they're truly compatible with your dinnerware.

Bejeweling Your Holiday Table

For a Christmas holiday table, we once piled golden glass Christmas tree ornaments on a footed glass cake plate, then dribbled gold beads (rope for the Christmas tree) over the top. The whole thing took about five minutes to create and was smashingly beautiful. Later, we did a variation, using colored glass ornaments and red and green beaded rope, which was just as beautiful and just as quick.

Creating a Colorful Collection

What could be more beautiful for Easter lunch than a bowlful of dyed Easter eggs? But why save the effect for just one day a year? At other times, you can create a centerpiece using a collection of beautifully colored eggs in marble, onyx, or quartz; wooden eggs, carved from olive trees; and eggs decorated with exciting African motifs. We keep ours in a dark mahogany wooden salad bowl that we rescued from a trashcan on the street.

Flying Your Flags

An exciting and simple centerpiece for a Fourth of July table is a cluster of small flags flying from the center of your table. Hold these small flags (which come attached to long, slender round wooden dowels) in place with *oasis,* the stuff that florists stick flower stems into for secure arrangements. You'll need a simple vase. In a pinch, transform a tin can into a vase by covering it with red, white, or blue paper.

Using Your Marbles

Glass marbles are beautiful. And they're useful for tons of things, including holding plant stems in place, decorating the aquarium, and filling a glass jar to set on your windowsill. Press these wonderful objects into centerpiece service by filling a footed glass compote bowl with them. Add candles in glass candlesticks, and you and your table are all set.

Thinking Fresh

Fresh fruit is a tried-and-true, straight-from-the-counter centerpiece that never fails. It's also handy for dessert. Remember those TV chefs' advice: Presentation is everything! Take an extra minute to arrange the bowl or platter with as much artistry as you can muster, alternating a banana and orange, or editing your arrangement by using just one kind of fruit (such as a bowl of Granny Smith apples, a cluster of deep purple grapes, or a long skinny platter of perfectly aligned lemons).

Sharing the Bounty

If you've just come from the bakery with loaves of beautifully baked bread, serve them as a centerpiece. Arrange the loaves in an interesting basket, metal bowl, or chunky pottery bowl, or on a nice tray. If you arrange your bread on a tray, consider serving some interesting flavored butters in small bowls on the side.

Lighting Up the Table

A clutch of candlesticks not only flanks a centerpiece but also becomes the centerpiece. Our favorite trick is to place a group of candlesticks — five or more — around a small pot of philodendron on a small tray. Trail the philodendron in and out among the candlesticks. If the candlesticks match, we often add a variety of colored candles. If candlesticks don't match, we use a single color candle for unity.

Bowling Them Over

Consider the fact that a beautiful bowl doesn't necessarily need anything in it to be a fascinating and successful centerpiece. A decorative pottery, etched crystal, or hand-painted porcelain bowl may speak clearly that less really is more.

Chapter 28

Ten Tips for Leftover Wallpaper

In This Chapter

▶ Creating shades of glory

▶ Bringing new life to books, shelves, and more

Saving some leftover wallpaper is a good idea, just in case you need to mend a spot. But if you have several rolls left over, you can use that lovely wallpaper pattern in a clever and decorative way. The ideas in this chapter whet your appetite for crafty projects that make the most of resources at hand. We're always thinking of people who did that with great style (and sometimes overwhelming results). Grandma Moses comes to mind. So do patchwork quilters. The idea of "waste not, want not" is a great motivation and the inspiration for some truly wonderful work.

Slipcovering Your Lampshade

A quick way to give your old lamp a new look is to top it with a new shade. And an easy way to make one is the same way you made those pleated fans in grammar school. To make a lampshade, trim your paper to the same height as your existing shade. Use a strip two to three times the circumference of your old lampshade so that you'll have plenty of paper to press into narrow pleats.

When the pleating is done, use a hole punch to create a small round hole in each pleat about one inch from both the top and bottom. Run a cord or ribbon through each row of holes. With one hand, hold onto both ends of the top cord as you place the pleated wallpaper shade over your old shade. With the other hand, gather the pleats along the cord, tightening as you evenly distribute the pleats around the circumference of the shade. When it's a fit, tie the cord. Repeat the process at the bottom.

Adding Flower Power to a Paper Shade

Tired of your plain white paper lampshade? Match it to new bedroom wallpaper by cutting out floral motifs from the paper and gluing them onto the shade. Give your design — random or rigid — a dry run before applying glue. For a finishing touch, add a row of gimp trim in the color of your wallpaper motif along the bottom of the shade.

Refreshing a Wastebasket

We didn't say that all our ideas are original. *Au contraire.* Some of the best ideas are the oldest — like covering a beat-up wastebasket with a lovely wallpaper. If the wastebasket isn't roughly handled, the paper can be paper, not vinyl. If it's the kitchen or home office wastebasket, you may want to cover it with a washable vinyl. For paper, use white school glue (Elmer's works just fine). You may need to use vinyl glue with vinyl wall coverings.

The procedure is as simple as cutting paper to fit and gluing it on. If in doubt, cut out a paper pattern — we use newspaper. If your newly covered wastebasket is for a bedroom, you may want to add ribbon trim to the top and bottom for a finishing touch. Grosgrain easily glues onto surfaces.

Dressing Your Books in New Jackets

Designers often use pretty papers to cover rows of books with tattered covers. Wallpaper — patterned or textured — may be just the ticket for your favorites. Cut jackets to size, tucking a generous flap inside both back and front covers. Label your books, if you want to tell these identically covered volumes apart.

Wallpapering a Backsplash

The backsplash area behind a pedestal sink is seldom protected. Perhaps the one in a child's bath or a small powder room would benefit from a lovely wallpaper backsplash (vinyl, of course). Just cut to size (and shape, as you see fit, perhaps cutting around and silhouetting a flower or leaf) and glue into place. Of course, you can go a step further by cutting out floral motifs from your backsplash leftovers and gluing them around the mirror hanging above the sink. (And the wastebasket can match!)

Lining a Shelf

Use your leftover paper to line bedroom and bathroom closet shelves and kitchen cabinet shelves. Don't forget to use leftover bedroom wallpaper to line shelves in a hall closet.

Decoupaging Your Lamp Base

We've already suggested that you cut out floral motifs from a roll of wallpaper and glue them onto a plain lampshade. You can also decoupage them onto a plain china or wooden lamp base, which is charming for a Country Cottage style and a pretty effect for a feminine Victorian bedroom. And if you choose the right motif, this technique is also an effective way to decorate a lamp for a little boy's room.

Transforming a Box

Collectors' hatboxes are always covered in a lovely wallpaper. Cover any simple box with paper to create your own special container. It's as easy as gift wrapping! Just have your scissors and glue handy, and exercise necessary patience. Neatness counts!

Covering a Notebook or Journal

Transform your office-looking journal into a work of art and a joy in which to write by covering it in a pretty wallpaper. Give journal covers a finished look by covering the inside and outside of back and front covers. If you have plenty of paper, you may want to cover several — a year's supply — at one sitting.

Decorating Kitchen Canisters

If your kitchen wallpaper has a motif that you love — a plump yellow lemon, cheery red cherry, or cocky chicken — why not cut out enough to decorate plain ceramic or wood canisters? Glue the cutouts into place and spray with a fixative that also protects the surface. (Check at your arts and crafts store for the right stuff.)

Chapter 29

Ten Favorite Sources

In This Chapter

▶ Reading magazines, newspapers, and catalogs we love

▶ Going online

▶ Checking out trade associations and organizations

Knowing everything and storing it efficiently and readily available in our busy little gray cells is quite difficult. Once in a while, we all need to go to the source. In this chapter, we introduce you to our ten favorite categories of sources of information and inspiration. Use our "favorites" list as a basis for building your own expanded list. You may want to add key manufacturers, retailers, and designers. You can find many listed in the sources pages of most decorating and remodeling magazines. And, while you're reading the editorial features and departments, check out the advertisements — they're a great source of information and inspiration.

Subscribing to Magazines

Magazines are truly amazing. For pennies, these incredible sources bring us invaluable information from ordinary and extraordinary people. We enjoy our magazines until the last tattered page is but a wisp. We find it impossible to rank our favorite magazines, because we've never met a magazine we didn't like. However, the following (listed in alphabetical order) are outstanding:

- *Architectural Digest* (www.condenast.com), for superb quality and diversity

- *Better Homes & Gardens* (www.bhg.com), for richly helpful information

- *Elle Decor* (www.elledecor.com), for the glimpse of Continental style

- *House Beautiful* (www.housebeautiful.com), which stays in touch with American style

- *House & Garden* (www.condenast.com), for its keen know-how and high-level how-to

- *Metropolitan Home* (www.methome.com), which touts Modern style

- *Old House Interiors* (www.oldhouseinteriors.com), because of its special focus

- *Southern Accents* (www.southernaccents.com), because it speaks our language

- *This Old House* (www.thisoldhouse.com), which combines sound remodeling and practical redecorating

- *Veranda* (www.veranda.com), for its lush coverage of gracious, home-defining Southern style

Sighting Online Sites

After you've read this book, as well as *Home Remodeling For Dummies,* by James and Morris Carey, and *Kitchen Remodeling For Dummies,* by Donald Prestly, visions of re-doing a room or your whole house may be dancing in your head. *Home Improvement For Dummies*, by Gene and Katie Hamilton, has tips on how to paint, paper, and repair your home yourself. (All three books are published by Wiley Publishing, Inc.)

The next good place to go for more information is a Web site. If you're thinking of kitchens, see www.kitchens.com. This site is chock-full of information about new products and appropriate kitchen designs for architectural styles, and it has a virtual design guide that can help you organize your project. And try *Better Homes & Gardens'* www.bhg.com (where you can arrange a room online), www.homeportfolio.com (which features thousands of products), and www.home-xpress.com (which offers product information and Web site links).

Cataloging Catalogs

Catalogs are ideal for those of us who prefer shopping in our own good time, at our own pace. Of course, we stack ours alphabetically, for those rare quick-action ordering occasions.

A favorite source for traditional furniture is *Storehouse*, which, as Company President Caroline Hipple says, prides itself on being your specialty resource that makes good design accessible. Contact 888-STOREHOUSE or www.storehouse.com. (If you really want to get dressed and go out, you can shop in one of 61 Storehouse retail stores.) For modern and contemporary furniture, see *Design Within Reach* (www.dwr.com). Other terrific catalogs include *Horchow Home Catalog* (www.horchow.com), *Spiegel* (1-800-345-4500), and *Smith+Noble* for window dressings (www.smithnoble.com). Also try *Sundance* (www.sundancecatalog.com) — we thrill to its Western flavor.

Buying Books

Books are information and experience at your fingertips. In addition to this book and others we've written (such as *Sun Country Style* and *Sun Country Elegance*), available online at www.barnesandnoble.com and www.amazon.com, consider adding these favorites to your library:

- ✔ *Color Palettes: Atmospheric Interiors Using the Donald Kaufman Color Collection* by Suzanne Butterfield, Donald Kaufman, and Jacqueline Goewey (Clarkson N. Potter)

- ✔ *The Decoration of Houses* by Alexandra Stoddard (Avon)

- ✔ *Flea Market Style: Decorating with a Creative Edge* by Emelie Tolley and Chris Mead (Clarkson N. Potter)

- ✔ *Hamptons Style: Houses, Gardens, Artists* by John Esten, Rose Bennett Gilbert, and Susan Wood (Little, Brown & Company)

- ✔ *Interior Design and Decoration, 5th Edition* by Sherrill Whiton, Stanley Abercrombie, and Augustus Sherrill Whiton (Prentice Hall)

If your bookstore shelves only new books, look for our favorite older books at our favorite online used books site, www.allbookstores.com.

Watching TV

We often lock onto and stay tuned to HGTV (Home and Garden Television) and the Discovery Channel. Consider HGTV's *Homes Across America, Remodeling America,* and anything hosted by Joe Ruggerio a joy to watch. Chris Casson Madden's *Design by Style* on HGTV is a "must see." *Home Matters* on the Discovery Channel really does. And who doesn't think that Discovery Channel's Christopher Lowell is a "must watch"? Only envy and downright smallness would prevent our pointing out that some of Martha Stewart's HGTV shows are both informative and dream invoking. Of course, when we're guests on the Discovery Channel *(Home Matters),* HGTV *(Decorating with Style),* or our local Miami and Palm Beach stations, we never fail to watch.

Talking on the Radio

Talk radio doesn't get quite the attention that TV does, but several shows are very informative and provide listeners with an opportunity to ask an expert. One of your authors, Kaye McMillan, is a regular on "Ask The Handyman," Joe Gagnon, Team 1270AM, Detroit. Your other author, Pat, is a guest on various talk radio shows in the United States and Canada. Write us about decorating talk radio shows in your area. And call in — your comment may prove the most thought provoking!

Asking Associations and Institutions

Trade and professional associations often have consumer educational outreach programs. We rely on the following:

- American Lighting Association (800-BRIGHTIDEAS; www.american lightingassoc.com)
- American Society of Interior Designers (202-546-3480; www.asid.org)
- Hardwood Information Center (800-373-9663; www.hardwoodinfo.com)
- International Furnishings and Design Association (e-mail: info@ifda.com; Web site: www.ifda.com), whose members are professionals from all facets of the furnishings and design industry
- National Association of the Remodeling Industry (800-611-6274; www.remodeltoday.com)
- National Kitchen & Bath Association (877-NKBA-PRO; www.nkba.org), which certifies kitchen and bath design specialists
- Pat's alma mater, the New York School of Interior Design (212-472-1500; www.nysid.edu)

Dropping by Designer Showcase Houses

Showcase houses aren't just rooms with nifty ideas. They're rich sources of information and design direction. Topping the list — and worth a trip from anywhere — is The Kips Bay Designer Showcase House, an annual spring event in New York City. Some other favorites include Mansions in May (www.wammh.com) in New Jersey and the Red Cross Designer Showcase House annually in the spring in West Palm Beach, Florida. Watch local news media for showcase houses in your area and mark your calendar for design a la carte.

Scoping Out the Dailies

Thanks to smart, aggressive editors, special home and garden pages in America's big city dailies are invariably the first with the latest national and regional home furnishings news. Read them and you'll be in the know about people, places, and things.

Our favorite, which just happens to be our home paper, is the Ft. Lauderdale, Florida-based *Sun-Sentinel* (www.sunsentinel.com). Under editor Charlyne Varkonyi Schaub's eagle eye, this paper never misses a beat. In addition to the Thursday *New York Times* (www.nytimes.com) Home and Garden section, which is an absolute *must* with us, other papers we enjoy perusing include the following:

- ✔ *The Atlanta Journal-Constitution* (www.ajc.com)
- ✔ *Buffalo News* (www.buffalonews.com)
- ✔ *Detroit Free Press* (www.freep.com)
- ✔ *Houston Chronicle* (www.chron.com)
- ✔ *Orange County Register* (www.ocregister.com)
- ✔ *Philadelphia Inquirer* (www.philly.com)
- ✔ *San Francisco Chronicle* (www.sfgate.com)
- ✔ *USA Today* (www.usatoday.com)
- ✔ *Wall Street Journal* (www.wsj.com)

These newspapers are top-notch, featuring on-their-toes, original, and relevant reporting. These and other papers carry syndicated columns by such gifted writer-reporters as Rose Bennett Gilbert (Copley), Elaine Markoutsas (Universal), and Mitchell Owens. Even if you have to find them in the "out-of-town" newspapers section, you'll be rewarded far beyond the purchase price of the paper.

Checking Out the Library

Naturally, you've already added your own public library to your list of sources; but if you're even remotely interested in furniture and you live in the United States, you need to visit the Bernice Bienenstock Furniture Library (www.furniturelibrary.com), 1009 N. Main St., High Point, North Carolina. Plan to spend considerable time there. Brushing elbows with leading furniture and interior designers, convening via the written word with histories' design legends, and chatting with ever-helpful director Carl Voncannon, you'll be in the very best of design and decorating company.

Index

• C •

• *G* •

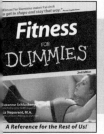

FOR DUMMIES®

A world of resources to help you grow

TRAVEL

0-7645-5453-0

0-7645-5438-7

0-7645-5444-1

Also available:

America's National Parks For Dummies
(0-7645-6204-5)

Caribbean For Dummies
(0-7645-5445-X)

Cruise Vacations For Dummies 2003
(0-7645-5459-X)

Europe For Dummies
(0-7645-5456-5)

Ireland For Dummies
(0-7645-6199-5)

France For Dummies
(0-7645-6292-4)

Las Vegas For Dummies
(0-7645-5448-4)

London For Dummies
(0-7645-5416-6)

Mexico's Beach Resorts For Dummies
(0-7645-6262-2)

Paris For Dummies
(0-7645-5494-8)

RV Vacations For Dummies
(0-7645-5443-3)

EDUCATION & TEST PREPARATION

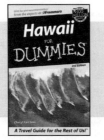

0-7645-5194-9

0-7645-5325-9

0-7645-5249-X

Also available:

The ACT For Dummies
(0-7645-5210-4)

Chemistry For Dummies
(0-7645-5430-1)

English Grammar For Dummies
(0-7645-5322-4)

French For Dummies
(0-7645-5193-0)

GMAT For Dummies
(0-7645-5251-1)

Inglés Para Dummies
(0-7645-5427-1)

Italian For Dummies
(0-7645-5196-5)

Research Papers For Dummies
(0-7645-5426-3)

SAT I For Dummies
(0-7645-5472-7)

U.S. History For Dummies
(0-7645-5249-X)

World History For Dummies
(0-7645-5242-2)

HEALTH, SELF-HELP & SPIRITUALITY

0-7645-5154-X

0-7645-5302-X

0-7645-5418-2

Also available:

The Bible For Dummies
(0-7645-5296-1)

Controlling Cholesterol For Dummies
(0-7645-5440-9)

Dating For Dummies
(0-7645-5072-1)

Dieting For Dummies
(0-7645-5126-4)

High Blood Pressure For Dummies
(0-7645-5424-7)

Judaism For Dummies
(0-7645-5299-6)

Menopause For Dummies
(0-7645-5458-1)

Nutrition For Dummies
(0-7645-5180-9)

Potty Training For Dummies
(0-7645-5417-4)

Pregnancy For Dummies
(0-7645-5074-8)

Rekindling Romance For Dummies
(0-7645-5303-8)

Religion For Dummies
(0-7645-5264-3)

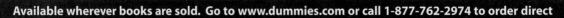